The Craft of Teaching

Kenneth E. Eble

The Craft of Teaching

A Guide to Mastering
the Professor's Art

SECOND EDITION

Jossey-Bass Publishers · San Francisco

Published by

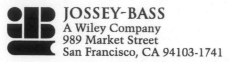

JOSSEY-BASS
A Wiley Company
989 Market Street
San Francisco, CA 94103-1741

www.josseybass.com

Jossey-Bass books and products are available through most bookstores. To contact Jossey-
Bass directly, call (888) 378-2537, fax to (800) 605-2665, or visit our website at
www.josseybass.com.

Substantial discounts on bulk quantities of Jossey-Bass books are available to corporations,
professional associations, and other organizations. For details and discount information,
contact the special sales department at Jossey-Bass.

We at Jossey-Bass strive to use the most environmentally sensitive paper stocks available to us.
Our publications are printed on acid-free recycled stock whenever possible, and our paper always
meets or exceeds minimum GPO and EPA requirements.

Jossey-Bass also publishes its books in a variety of electronic formats. Some content that appears
in print may not be available in electronic books.

Library of Congress Cataloging-in-Publication Data
Eble, Kenneth Eugene
    The craft of teaching

    (The Jossey-Bass higher education series)
    Bibliography: p.
    Includes index.
    1. College teaching—United States. 2. Teaching.
I. Title. II. Series.
LB2331.E328   1988   378'.125'0973   87-46351
ISBN 1-55542-088-5
ISBN 1-55542-664-6 (paperback)

SECOND EDITION
HB Printing   10
PB Printing   10 9 8 7 6 5

The Jossey-Bass
Higher Education Series

Contents

Preface to
the Second Edition

Since 1972, I have probably visited more colleges and universities, and talked with more faculty members and administrators (though with fewer students), than during my two years of full-time commitment to the Project to Improve College Teaching from 1969 to 1971. Much of this visiting was a consequence of renewed interest in faculty development which continues to the present time. Some was a result of the publication of the first edition of this book. During that period, I continued to teach full time in a variety of courses, from freshman to graduate level. In any span of time a teacher cannot help but pick up new ideas, gain new perspectives, and refine and modify what has already been learned about teaching. This new edition of *The Craft of Teaching* puts many of these into print.

Like the first edition, this one keeps the focus on teaching itself. The first chapter sets forth my views about teaching. They have not changed greatly in ten years, but some substance has been added about the perspective teachers gain with experience. One new chapter has been added to Part One, a chapter on what is currently called "critical thinking." My own interest is broader than that, for a basic concern of all education is to teach students to think, however we label it. Two new myths have been added to Chapter Two, "The Mythology of Teaching," but without any claim to having revealed all the many loose assumptions teachers and the public make about teaching. In this chapter, as elsewhere, I have given more attention than in the first edition to the relationship of college teaching to teaching in the public schools.

In Part Two, I have added current citations about the various skills of teaching. Literature on these topics has increased as much as that in any other field, and what I have drawn upon directly represents only a small part of the whole. A lengthy addition to Chapter Five describes in some detail William G. Perry's and others' work about how students learn. As teachers can develop effective teaching styles, so should they be aware of how students change and vary in responding to instruction. An additional section on mentoring has been added to the original Chapter Eight. More has also been added to the chapter "Outside the Classroom," now called "Teaching Without Teachers," to reflect the impact of the computer on teaching and learning.

In Part Three, I have added a chapter on motivating both students and faculty. Tests and grades, the subjects of two preceding chapters, may be for many teachers the chief sources of motivating students. But motivating students involves much more than giving tests and assigning grades, the negative aspects of both set aside. Faculty need motivating too, so the chapter addresses itself to the necessities most college and university teachers face in carrying out with continuing enthusiasm the multiple expectations placed upon them.

In extensively revising the last part of the book on how men and women become college professors, I experienced some disappointment in how little has changed with respect to better preparing college teachers. Repeated recommendations to graduate schools to improve the preparation of future college teachers have been largely ignored. In the research universities an increasing load of undergraduate instruction has been assigned to graduate assistants. The faculty development movement, touched upon in the last chapter, may be a counter effort, an attempt to expand opportunities for faculty to develop as teachers and to provide support for many aspects of instruction.

Teaching in colleges and universities is marked by paradox. Teaching is what almost every professor does, but it may suffer from that very commonness. It takes up the greatest amount of most professors' time, but it does not often gain the highest level of commitment or competence. Though surveys find a majority of professors identifying teaching as their greatest source of satisfaction, that satisfaction doesn't keep them from wanting to teach less. Under the domination of the research universities, research is about as compatible with undergraduate teaching as lions are with lambs. Only by one devouring the other are they likely to lie down comfortably side by side.

Still I think there is some room to demonstrate excellence in teaching, to gain great satisfaction from it, and to reconcile it with scholarship, if that expansion of one's learning is not defined narrowly. If I remain optimistic about college teaching, it is because what underlies teaching is the unquenchable human desire to learn. Responding to that desire, wherever and whatever one teaches, is reason enough for working at one's craft.

Salt Lake City Kenneth E. Eble
February 1988

Preface to
the First Edition

This is unashamedly a book about teaching and teachers. If I did not think both important, and important in themselves, I would not have bothered to write this book. At the same time, if I did not think that most learning takes place quite apart from teachers and formal teaching situations, I would have despaired about what teachers can do.

If I did not think that teaching and learning are unavoidable aspects of human growth and inseparable from the personal, I might have written about teaching machines, instructional technology, and learning conglomerates. And if I did not think that teaching is one of the most natural and primary of human acts, I would not be committed to being a teacher nor still be trying to master my craft.

Most of what I know about teaching comes from observing, working with, and learning from students and other teachers. At some periods, I have subjected my own teaching practices to close examination. At other times, I have suspended scrutiny and have taught pretty much as past experience and present opportunities inclined me. At most times, I have found teaching exacting and rewarding work. In this book, then, I have attempted to look at the acts of teaching carefully, to analyze teaching without rendering it lifeless, and to see teaching in relation to all the resources highly skilled teachers use to develop their craft.

Like others who find teaching and learning fascinating, I have through the years read much material that promised insight into the mysteries of the craft. But my curiosity about teaching has caused me to poke around outside my own discipline of English into fields besides the humanities and beyond my own experience with college and university students into primary, junior-high, and high-school classes. My experience was further widened by my work from 1969 to 1971 as director of the Project to Improve College Teaching of the American Association of University Professors and the Association of American Colleges, which gave me the unusual opportunity to observe teaching in many kinds of college and university classrooms across the country.

In my report on that project, *Professors as Teachers* (Eble, 1972a), I examined college teaching within its institutional and professional frameworks. Professors in American colleges and universities find many impediments to teaching well, ranging from the inattention given teaching in graduate programs to a general slighting of teaching within the reward structure. Thus, while my report did not set teaching aside, it focused on such matters as evaluating and recognizing teaching, improving institutional support for teaching, and enhancing the teaching environment. An important aspect of that book was its emphasis upon career development of effective college teachers, an important institutional responsibility only now beginning to be given proper support.

The present book focuses on teaching itself. The first part of the book provides a short overview of teaching, looking particularly at the assumptions teachers make and at the attitudes and skills they do well to develop. The second part deals with teaching inside and outside the classroom, detailing both common and not-so-common modes of instruction. The third part is concerned with the practical problems and predictable crises of day-to-day teaching. The fourth and final part discusses better ways of preparing teachers in graduate school and stresses the importance of the attitudes and commitments new teachers bring to teaching.

My purpose throughout is to help teachers improve their teaching practices and to urge them beyond the conventional, where they might perceive afresh how best to serve learning. Teaching is a craft, and as with any craft, one's performance can be bettered by careful attention to detail. Choosing textbooks, assigning papers, preparing for class, testing, grading, learning to improvise despite the best-laid preparations—these are all important skills well worth continuing attention. Yet the vitality of teaching depends upon more than methodology. The center of all teaching and learning is the interaction between the teacher and the learner. The personal cannot and should not be set aside. Information and skills become important as they serve individual and social ends, ends inextricably bound up with our values and our perceptions.

In spirit, this book is not unlike Gilbert Highet's *The Art of Teaching*, which defined teaching for many professors in the fifties against the background of the classic English and European university. Much has happened in the twenty-five years since Highet's book, and the tone of this volume, I think, reflects these happenings. The elite universities with their highly selected faculty and students are not where my attention is centered, though the need for great teaching in such universities is a pressing need. Although I am neither hostile to art nor opposed to perceiving the teacher as artist (Joseph Axelrod's recent book bears that title), my aims are less lofty. They are closer to those of the practical and useful book *Teaching Tips*, through which Wilbert McKeachie has guided many young teachers. I would hope, however, that this book will speak to both beginning and established teachers, address itself to the particulars of daily practice as well as to those aspiring parts of soul and mind that commit worthy teachers to their calling.

Salt Lake City   Kenneth E. Eble
August 1976

The Author

Kenneth E. Eble was professor of English and University Professor at the University of Utah, Salt Lake City. He received his B.A. and M.A. degrees from the University of Iowa (1948, 1949) and his Ph.D. degree in English from Columbia University (1956).

Eble began teaching at Upper Iowa University in 1949 and also taught at the Columbia School of General Studies (1951–54) and Drake University (1954–55) before joining the faculty at the University of Utah in 1955. He served as visiting professor in American studies at Carleton College (1967), directed seminars in college teaching for the Colombian Ministry of Education (1975) and the Kansas City Regional Council for Higher Education (1976), and was Visiting Robinson Professor at George Mason University (1986).

From 1964 to 1969, he was chairman of the English department at the University of Utah, taking leave from 1969 to 1971 to direct the Project to Improve College Teaching, co-sponsored by the American Association of University Professors (AAUP) and the Association of American Colleges (AAC) and funded by the Carnegie Corporation. In 1973, he was awarded an honorary Doctor of Humane Letters from Saint Francis College (Biddeford, Maine) and was Distinguished Visiting Scholar for the Educational Testing Service in 1973–74.

For more than twenty years, Eble was a guest speaker and consultant on teaching and faculty development at more than 200 colleges and universities in the United States and Canada.

He served in many official positions within the AAUP, the Modern Language Association, the National Council of Teachers of English, and Phi Beta Kappa. He served on the Board of Directors of the American Association for Higher Education from 1983 to 1986, and was named to the Advisory Board of the National Center for Research to Improve Postsecondary Teaching and Learning in 1986. He was one of ten finalists for the Council for the Advancement and Support of Education's Professor of the Year in 1985.

Eble's writing embraced not only education but American literature, the humanities, history of ideas, and popular culture as well. In addition to *Professors as Teachers* (1972), *The Aims of College Teaching* (1983), *The Art of Administration* (1978), and *Improving Undergraduate Education Through Faculty Development* (with Wilbert McKeachie, 1986), Eble's books include *William Dean Howells* (1982), *F. Scott Fitzgerald* (rev. ed. 1976), *The Profane Comedy* (1962), *A Perfect Education* (1966), *Old Clemens and W.D.H.* (1986), and, as editor, *Howells: A Century of Criticism* (1962) and *The Intellectual Tradition of the West* (1967). He was a field editor for the Twayne United States Author Series and edited the Jossey-Bass sourcebook *New Directions for Teaching and Learning* from 1980 to 1988.

The Craft of Teaching

PART ONE

Teaching and Learning

1

The Author's Stance

Let me begin by asking the reader to take a fresh look at teaching and learning, to free one's mind of cant. I will state my philosophic biases at the outset. First, I share one of the oldest of opinions about learning—that learning is essentially pleasurable. To me, that opinion puts great weight upon preserving a sense of play in teaching. It leads me to believe that teaching is an improviser's art. It also makes me back away from another established attitude that views teaching—metaphorically in these enlightened days—as the systematic beating of learning into dumb objects. My stance does not deny that pleasure and pain, rewards and punishments, are powerful human motivations. But as a learner, a teacher, and a teacher counseling teachers, I take my stand on the side of pleasure.

In one sense, we human beings may never really learn anything except through the skin. That is, as in Kafka's "In the Penal Colony," vital lessons have to be stitched into the skin, engraved by needles on the flesh. Perhaps that is the only way to take into ourselves the human compassion that might save us all. Yet, since we live short of salvation, there is much to be learned that can come easier even as it will depart easier. In this sense, I think, we tend very much to learn what we want to. When we endure the drudgery of some kinds of learning—playing the piano, acquiring a foreign language, mastering mathematics—it is either because an affinity for such learning masks the drudgery or because the pleasure anticipated makes the drudgery worthwhile.

3

The enemy of learning is primarily other learning. The same student who will not, seemingly cannot, do problem sets in algebra will learn to ski or surf or shoot pool or play a guitar, facing the drudgery of learning—repetition and mistakes, failure and frustration. Whitehead may have best defined the terms of the conflict I have raised. Freedom and discipline, he says, are the essential conditions for teaching and learning. The developing individual passes through stages in which freedom dominates at one time, discipline at another. At no point is the learner completely free of either. Thus, the unresolved arguments about the easy teacher and the tough teacher, the permissive instructor versus the disciplinarian, the one who leads against the one who drives. The teacher's task, simply put, is to determine the most profitable blend of freedom and discipline for each student in a group. Ultimately, both merge in arousing the pleasure of learning.

By no means do all college and university teachers accept what I have avowed. There is some heightening of pride in teaching at the higher levels, some lingering effect of prolonged formal education, that inclines college teachers to discipline. They themselves work in disciplines, professional fields of study that emphasize standards, order, rules, and rigor. Once they become teachers, disciplinary scholars tend to worry about standards and rigor and to make sure that they don't let their students get away with anything. I admit to these feelings, too, but age and inclination have tempered them, and I now leave fierceness to new teachers fresh from graduate school. If there is no place for pleasure in teaching, surely our learning has failed us altogether.

My broader philosophic bias is that I am a pluralist: I cannot conceive of any *one* way of teaching that will excel all others. Nor am I inclined toward insisting on those few things that must be taught as opposed to all those things that humans want to learn. Moreover, I see formal education as a means of respecting, drawing upon, passing along human diversity. But as firm as I am about this preference, I do not deny the appeal of the unifying idea as a way of ordering a world of diverse particulars. However, the importance of diversity over unity is what makes teaching different from writing or research. In teaching, thoughts flow more freely, find their way into temporary categories, stop short of conclusions, proceed tentatively toward some future synthesis. Unless one is foolishly mesmerized by his or her own words, the provisional nature of what one does as a teacher is clearly apparent. It is nonetheless important, important precisely as it remains pluralistic, leaving students free to resolve issues and problems in their own ways.

A third bias that will declare itself in the pages of this book is that teaching skill can be acquired. More bluntly, teaching can be taught. This is why I choose to think of teaching as a craft, even though my ego would have it recognized as an art and myself an artist. I had good reasons, though I was not aware of all of them at the time, for calling this book *The Craft of Teaching*. But I did not anticipate how many readers would be curious about that choice of title and how that would open up discussions about teaching. *Craft* has many shades of meaning and application. In thinking of a teacher as "crafty as a fox," of fashioning some useful object that works, of a craft not taking on some of the pretensions associated with art, of an honest craft—in all these and other ways I was endorsing a belief that in anything we do well we are both born and made. More made, generally, I think than we allow. As Whitman, a fitfully successful journalist until the age of thirty, posted above his desk before beginning *Leaves of Grass*, "Make the works."

I differ from many of my colleagues, I think, in the interest I have maintained over the years in the particulars of teaching. The act of teaching constantly engages me, pleases me because of the endless variety of ways that substance and teacher and student appear before one another. Teachers who grow stale, who find the same classes boring, may suffer from an inattention to detail or from a want of the details that would enliven their teaching. For myself, teaching varies with every class, every hour, every new group of students.

Diversity does not mean that there is no common set of good practices, no common characteristics that identify the good teacher. (See Chickering and Gamson, 1987; Marques, Lane, and Dorfman, 1979.) Since I believe strongly in the place of the person in teaching, I am mindful of the idiosyncratic in teaching. The great teacher, even the consistently effective one, may have a combination of personal qualities and behaviors that seem to defy analysis. If one does not demand that analysis identify the good teacher's precise molecular weight, however, one can find a firm set of attributes, intentions, principles which underly diverse practices. Pleasure in learning and in teaching is the common ground necessary to sustain great teaching. But even the ways pleasure manifests itself are as varied as other expressions of nature. There are some professors who growl to express pleasure just as there are plants, like the prickly pear, which are deadly to bare feet and unattractive at most times, but which flower and produce fruit of a sweet and sustaining kind.

Most of this book is taken up with looking at and stimulating thought about the particulars of teaching, for it is attention to particulars that brings any craft or art to a high degree of development. Although the focus here is on college and university teaching, there are great similarities among teachers and teaching at all levels and subjects. Teachers at the higher levels have much to learn from teachers in the lower schools, just as teachers of academic subjects can learn much from those who are chiefly concerned with vocational and occupational skills. Wherever they work, teachers can improve their own practices by going out to see teaching elsewhere.

I have had, off and on, a small amount of teaching in high schools, less in junior highs, and very little experience in elementary schools. What I learned there recently is still fresh in mind. First, elementary students—these were second graders—use up material at a terrifying rate. The exercises I had prepared for composing poetry were used up in half the time I'd expected. Second, these twenty-five or so children were not classroom-trained as college students, often unfortunately, are. They moved around, vied with one another for attention, tried to take *my* chalk and *my* eraser. Third, I learned once again that all teachers have specific tricks of the trade. At the point when I needed to be rescued, the young woman who had invited me said quietly, "I think we should try desk-work." And lo, she had them sitting at their desks busily drawing pictures to match the poems, and I had five minutes to think of something to do next. Fourth, children are enormously receptive and responsive. How can I repay them for the drawings and poems they sent me thanking me for my visit?

Such experiences should not be denied college teachers. A first-rate in-service training for college teachers might consist of nothing more than teaching in the public schools. Perhaps more opportunities will become available in the current movement (Daly, 1985; Gaudiani and Burnett, 1985/86; Gross, 1988; Maeroff, 1983) toward school/college collaboration. For, in addition to sharpening skills, college teachers benefit specifically from exposure to teaching in the public schools by keeping up-to-date on what has been happening to their students before they reach college.

Some differences do set college and university teaching off from teaching in the public schools. In the lower grades, teachers may experience more freshness, responsiveness, and vitality than is evident in college students, particularly as they pass into graduate school. However, although all teachers are concerned with discipline in the larger sense, the college and university teacher need not spend the time a public school teacher must enforcing order in the classroom. Also, college and university teachers generally have better working conditions than do public school teachers. Professors teach fewer students for fewer hours, receive more pay, are accorded more status, have more opportunities for leaves, and are freer to teach as they please. Such differences may divide teachers in higher education from those in the public schools and, at the worst, incline university teachers to condemn "educationists" and to reject their own role as "educators."

The differences in teaching various subjects are less important, I think, than those that mark off college teaching from public school teaching. Some college teachers, however, make much of these differences. One professor I encountered argued vehemently that physics—it was his subject—was the hardest of the liberal arts to teach, and he had ranked all the other liberal arts in terms of their difficulty. I was not convinced by his arguments, nor do I think the subject worth much more than coffee-table conversation. Recognizing the difficulties in teaching any subject is worth pondering; trying to prove that one subject is more difficult to teach than another is not. The differences I consider important in comparing the teaching of particular subjects fall into two categories. One comprises a number of commonplace practices; the other relates to specific objectives and the ways of achieving them.

The commonplace differences are, for example, those which make teaching a skill somewhat different from teaching information. A ski instructor does not get his or her students heavily engaged in the history of skiing, the makeup of snow crystals, or the inner dynamics of woods, epoxies, and glass resins. A teacher of studio art has different teaching practices from those of the art historian. The teacher of basic French employs different classroom and out-of-classroom activities than does the teacher of the French Revolution and its consequences. These differences, however, are not necessarily absolute or immutable. The possibilities of effective teaching grow as teachers realize how practices commonplace in one area can be usefully adapted to others.

The other differences arise from an assessment of objectives and ways of reaching them. The lecturer in physics, as one example, adapts his practice to the fact that classroom work accompanies laboratory work. The marginally defensible use of the large lecture for conveying information is even less defensible for teaching skills. "Behavioral objectives," as one more of the panaceas which will transform teaching, fail to recognize that not all teaching aims at *behavior* in any precise or commonsensical use of the word. In some kinds of teaching, such as studio courses aimed at developing skills, behavioral objectives offer a reasonably accurate, if clumsy, description of what is to be accomplished. In other kinds of teaching, such as literature or history or philosophy, changing behavior is a distant objective at best.

"Teaching," Carl Rogers writes, "in my estimation, is a vastly overrated function" (1969, p. 103). Even as I address myself to developing a craft of teaching, I hear Rogers' remark that "we should do away with teaching, do away with examinations, do away with grades and credits, do away with degrees as a measure of competence" (p. 154). I share much of his distrust of teachers and of formal methods, yet teachers and teaching have enjoyed too long an existence and too great an investment to be cast aside casually. The shift of attention away from teaching toward learning is healthy, not as it moves to a technological, human-less learning but as it makes teachers more human by making them more responsive to their students' needs.

Attention to the particulars of teaching does not slight the primary importance of learning. Rather, it recognizes the practical fact that teaching will continue in most of the common modes as well as in new ways that shift the emphasis to self-learning. Within these modes, teaching and learning practices do make a difference, not only in terms of a defined subject matter but of the larger personal development of the individuals involved. The teacher's prime responsibility may well be to reduce his or her importance to help learners arrive at their own freedom to learn. But the teacher does not exercise that responsibility by merely withdrawing nor by denying the many ways in which humans can interact to affect one another's learning.

I sympathize with those who question the omnipotence of teachers, but I am uneasy about practicing teachers who diminish the importance of teaching in raising the importance of learning. A woodworker does not get into quarrels with his hands because it is a sharp chisel that does the work. He develops skill of hand, keeps his tools sharp, and his thumb out of the way. Learning and teaching are constantly interchanging activities. One learns by teaching; one cannot teach except by constantly learning. A person properly concerned about education will come to grips with the practical realities of both teaching and learning.

What I have just said does not diminish the high respect I have for teachers and teaching, and as much for those at the lower levels as at the higher. Or maybe more. For the public school teachers maintain an awareness that they are dealing with more than the students as he or she appears in a single class. They remain in touch with education in a way that many col-

lege and university teachers do not. It pains me to have college
teachers ask, "But you're an English professor. What are you
doing getting involved in education?" I am inclined to answer
somewhat as Thoreau answered Emerson when Emerson asked
him why he was in jail: "Why are you *not* involved? Why are
you *not* an educator?"

I make these points at some length here because I believe
that teaching is a presence of mind and person and body in relation to another mind and person and body, a complex array of
mental, spiritual, and physical acts affecting others. Moments of
direct interaction expand into the lives of both students and
teachers, keeping alive the desire to learn and the will to make
learning count. Any one part of teaching—conducting classes,
making assignments, testing and grading, directing work, counseling and advising, writing books and preparing means for independent learning—is but a small part of the forces that affect a
student's learning. Before that fact, teachers must necessarily be
humble. But humility should not stop one from recognizing
that teaching does matter and that developing teaching skills is
a good way of furthering learning.

2

The Mythology of Teaching

No group is more full of myths about teaching, more reluctant to admit that there are good teachers and bad teachers, and more resistant to the notion that teaching skills can be acquired than teachers themselves. This mythology is often grounded in dubious assumptions about the nature of teaching and learning and about the characteristics of teachers and students. Maintained by many teachers over many years, these assumptions are too seldom confronted by close reasoning, precise observation, or experience. Clearing away these assumptions, or at the least casting doubt on their validity, is a necessary first step toward developing a craft of teaching.

   At the outset, then, I propose to examine twelve common assumptions that help create a mythology of teaching:

1. That teaching is not doing.
2. That teaching is not a performing art.
3. That teaching should exclude the personality.
4. That students' "worst" teachers now will become their "best" teachers later.
5. That the popular teacher is a bad teacher.
6. That teachers are born and not made.
7. That good and bad teaching cannot be identified.
8. That research is complementary to teaching.
9. That teaching a subject matter requires only that one know it.

11

10. That college teaching is not a profession.
11. That teaching is better at the higher levels than at the lower.
12. That teaching is both less and more mysterious than it is.

First, *the belief that teaching is not doing.* George Bernard Shaw formulated this common suspicion about teachers: "He who can, does; he who cannot, teaches." Whatever the marginal truth of this gibe, its falsity lies in the assumption that teaching is not, in itself, "doing" of a very important kind. The "doing" in teaching consists of many acts, from the unseen work of preparation for a class to the activities during and after. If teachers would develop a respect for their craft, they must begin by acknowledging that what a teacher "does" matters and proceed by developing skill in the many things teachers do.

Despite the obvious fact that teaching requires specific skills, the second of our assumptions still persists: *that teaching is not a performing art.* Of course, it is not only a performing art, but to deny the importance of performance is to countenance teaching that employs the professor but little engages the student. The suspicion against teachers as performers is an ancient one. In any age, it is difficult to distinguish false teachers from true, to tell show from substance. Socrates criticized the Sophists in ancient Greece for being concerned chiefly with the appearance of truth, the means of persuasion to a truth, the practical uses to which knowledge could be put. Socrates himself was singled out by Aristophanes as a kind of Sophist who could make the worse case appear the better. All of these old passions of true scholars and teachers are aroused in the present age, in which *media* is another word for sophistry and in which public performers can hardly escape being pitchmen of one kind or another. Within such a climate, it is hard to argue against the scholar-teacher's suspicion against teaching as a performing art.

Nevertheless, that claim must be made, and strenuously, for the very reason that, like it or not, professors are in competition with others who lay claim to their students' attention. Professors do not need to court media popularity, but they can learn from the performing arts. No professor should be blind to the intelligence and knowledge that goes into an effective teaching performance, nor to the strengths and weaknesses of teaching practices that try to grapple with, and make visible, any part of truth.

The young teacher with a high aptitude for teaching will make efforts to develop a speaking voice that has range, force, and direction; a presence that uses the dynamics of physical movement to lend conviction to inner strengths of mind and imagination; and the dramatic abilities that can fashion scenes, build climaxes, manage stage props and business (Civikly, 1986a; Lowman, 1984, pp. 75-93). Hamming it up, faking it, putting on, showing off—we have plenty of terms to warn teachers against taking this advice. College teachers can be phony, hokey, flashy, trashy, thin, unsound, shallow, deceptive, and false. But in my observations of teachers on many campuses over the past decade, I have seen fewer charlatans than mediocrities and been less appalled by flashy deception than by undisguised dullness. And I have never encountered any evidence that a dull and stodgy presentation necessarily carries with it an extra measure of truth and virtue.

Not all teaching, of course, draws upon the performer's skills. There is a strong current trend to remove the teacher from the stage and to put the main attention upon the student's learning. But whether teachers themselves perform or concentrate upon getting students to perform, both are engaged in devising ways of translating passive acts of teaching and learning into performance. Some teachers may minimize the teacher's role, stress facilitating learning, as current jargon has it, over traditional teaching. Other teachers may argue that the plain truth of a subject is what matters and that efforts to enhance it increase the chance of deceiving students, just as making no impact at all on students is the surest safeguard against affecting them adversely. As I will argue at length in this book, effective teaching and learning can go on in many ways; the teacher's performance remains essential to most teaching and learning.

A third common assumption is *that teaching should exclude the teacher's personality.* Reservations about the prominence of the teacher's ego may have helped shift current atten-

tion away from teachers and teaching to focus upon learners
and learning. In my own discipline, English, George Lyman
Kittredge displayed an overpowering personality during his
forty-eight years (1888–1936) at Harvard. Rollo Walter Brown
describes one of many instances of Kittredge's personal teaching
style (1948, p. 72):

> Some professor of economics had great charts
> and maps on rollers all over the front of the room,
> and there were two or three long, gracefully sloping
> pointers at hand. "Kitty" picked up one of these
> and used it as a stafflike cane as he paced back and
> forth and commented. He was magnificent. He was
> an Anglo-Saxon king speaking to his people.
>
> Once in his march as he socked the royal
> staff down, it came in two where there was a knot
> in the wood, and he made a somewhat unkingly
> lurch. A few students snickered very cautiously.
>
> He glowered upon them. "You have a fine
> sense of humor!" Then without taking his eyes off
> the humbled faces, he drew his arm back as if he
> were hurling a javelin, and drove the long remnant
> of the pointer into the corner of the room. "Now
> laugh!" he dared them.

At the other extreme are the many teachers, certainly a
majority, whose teaching does not possess this personal power.
Some teachers are simply lacking in notable personality traits;
others deliberately refrain from letting the personal enter into
their teaching. In looking through reminiscences about memorable teachers, I am struck by the unobtrusive, yet distinctly personal impression so many make. Guy Stanton Ford had the
good fortune to study under three eminent historians, but one
of his most memorable teachers was "an indifferent scholar
[who] inspired his students to become scholars," a teacher, he
admits, who "did not have a magnetic personality" (1955, pp.
482–483), but whose influence on students was fully as strong
as that of the more eminent scholars.

Within the common practices of ordinary teachers, personality surely has an important place. Without intending to make a potential teacher self-conscious about developing a teaching personality, one still advises new teachers not to deny their personalities. A conscious attempt to be impersonal, dispassionate, and totally objective is likely to work more harm than good. Human beings interest other human beings. Once, as I was teaching a junior-high class, I noticed that the students seemed unusually attentive. The material didn't seem to be that interesting (though my mastery of it may have been compelling), and I found out before long that it was neither the material nor my teaching skill. What animated them was that I was wearing a sweater. "How come you're wearing a sweater?" they said. "Teachers don't wear sweaters." "Where do you get your hair cut?" "How many children do you have?" This eruption of personal questions marked my establishing of rapport with the students. Questioning me as a person was the beginning of accepting me as a human being. Recognizing our common humanity opened all of us to further learning.

Beginning teachers concerned with the proper role of the personality in teaching may have to overcome some of their graduate school conditioning. The insistence upon objectivity in most scholarly pursuits seems to rule out personal opinion and expression, and graduate study may have a way of subduing personality itself. Arguing that a teacher can have opinions and convictions but denying them a place in the classroom robs both students and teacher of a valuable means of fostering learning. Few subjects are value-free, and honesty about where one stands, illumination about how one has arrived there, and respect for the beliefs of others form a better basis for teaching than does a resolute, ultimately dogmatic posture of impersonal objectivity.

There are other ways in which one person's interest in another can be useful to teaching. The personal anecdote that illuminates an idea or clarifies a concept is neither ego-indulgence nor mere wandering from truth. The personal is a way of gaining the kind of interest absolutely necessary to learning. Moreover, an anecdotal account of how some aspect of the subject

matter itself came to have value for the teacher exerts a powerful force upon the student to grant that subject matter personal
worth. And it is surely among the simplest truths of public
speaking that the audience's interest picks up when the discourse turns personal. Thus, a deliberate introduction of the
personal is a teaching technique as vital as the use of illustrations and examples, which themselves gain in interest as they
are drawn from the teacher's personal experience.

Somewhere in the mythology of teaching exists an image
of the bounder who awaits each day's class period as the chance
to enlarge his ego by laying his personality on the students to
the exclusion of everything else. His gripes at the world, quarrels with his wife, triumphs over his colleagues, and tearful confrontations with harsh fate are all out front. Doubtless, the
myth is grounded somewhere in reality, but the presence of
such egocentrics serves as a useful check on our own more tem-
perate ego-tripping. Denying the place of personality in teaching
exposes us to a contrary danger of forgetting that *human* learning is the aim of teaching.

Many of the strong assumptions that underlie teaching
practices are embodied in archetypal forms, mythologic teacher
figures who embrace some supposed truth about teaching. These
mythic figures embody both the desires and shortcomings of
real teachers. One key mythological figure is the dimly remembered persecutor: *"the worst teacher I ever had who really
turned out to be the best."* The same figure appears in reminiscences about teachers who did everything wrong but were
superb and about the ones who were detested by students then
but are revered now. "I hated old Dworp's guts," a professor
will say, "but I really learned from him."

If it were not for our altogether inadequate grasp of
teaching, these stories would have been long recognized for
what they are. Clearly, they are the common reversals of expected outcomes by which we keep human hopes alive. The
bad-teacher-become-good is one with the ninety-eight-pound
weakling who whips the biggest kid in the block, the prize fight-
er who reads poetry, the minister's son who is the biggest hell-
raiser in town. The examples are legion, and most embody partial

truths: Weak kids under stress may show surprising strength or may on occasion meet a big guy with a glass chin. All such examples speak to a human desire to escape the norm—to accept the patterns of our lives but to keep alive the possibilities that defy them.

Let's examine briefly that mythic worst teacher who turned out to be the best. There is an internal paradox in the making of this claim, for it invariably comes forth as evidence against presuming to identify good or bad teaching. Obviously, though, the claimant has a firm set of standards for determining the worst and the best in teaching. The defender of this myth may be badgered into setting forth particulars of this worst teacher's performance. "Well, I mean, he mumbled and read from old notes, and he was badly organized, and he gave low grades." Some such particulars are bound to come out. If not mumbling, then a quavering or squeaking or irritating voice; if not old notes, then reading from the textbook or forgetting his or her place or lecturing to the air; if not badly organized, then repetitious to a maddening degree or caught up in trivia or overburdened with defining and classifying; if not low grades, then slashing remarks on papers or withering responses to questions.

Almost all the examples of this kind that I have heard come down to the teacher's having a marked distinctiveness in one way or another: "Professor X was a son of a bitch, but a real son of a bitch." The lesson is not that being a conspicuously "bad" teacher now will make you a "good" teacher then. It is, rather, that a teacher who thinks being a son of a bitch or a nit-picker or a bore is a means to truly good teaching should aspire to be a real son of a bitch, a consummate nit-picker, a colossal bore.

A reviewer of the first edition of this book felt that I too much emphasized the pleasures of learning and slighted the grim hard work. She cited the fact that her mother, a sixth-grade teacher known as "Battle-Ax ———," still got letters from former pupils grateful for her "driving and teaching them discipline." I do not challenge the story, and I do recognize that a good deal of learning is not immediately pleasurable. But I think her anecdote reveals but a variant of the myth being dis-

cussed: that of the relentless taskmaster or -mistress who is
feared, even hated at the time, but who in retrospect is one who
really made the students learn. Jack the Ripper certainly established his efficiency among those who survived; we do not hear
from his victims.

Ford Maddox Ford's reputation at Olivet College ampli-
fies the myth of the bad but good teacher. Considering Ford's
achievements at the time he began teaching there—he had published eighty books—and the rarity of such an eminent man of
letters at an obscure school, Ford could hardly have found a way
of not making a lasting impression on students. He is remembered by one Olivet student, himself now a professor, as "eccentric, inaudible, but nonetheless instructive" (Hungiville, 1974,
p. 9):

> As he lectured, he stumped up and down
> across the front of the classroom, leaning heavily
> on the cane, intoning his views on the classics. As
> he ran short of breath, his voice got higher and
> thinner, until, as he reached the far side of the
> room, he turned suddenly, drew a large breath,
> which renewed his voice, and he would shout out
> "LITERATURE" or "DON QUIXOTE," or what-
> ever word he happened to be coming to at the mo-
> ment. The result was that what the class learned
> about world literature was every fiftieth word that
> Mr. Ford uttered, plus a very intimate and heart-
> warming recollection of him as a person.

This myth runs all through Hungiville's account of Ford's
distinctions as a college teacher. "The special effectiveness of
the artist would not necessarily make for elite scores on the
computerized trivia of instructor-evaluation forms," Ford's former student writes. Nor would Ford's manner make for an
effective teacher who lacked the man's past accomplishments
and personal presence. One might like to become a "great" English teacher by that route—publishing eighty books and becoming an eminent person of letters—but it is extremely difficult. For

meretricious—

the great majority of teachers, it is a less practical route than taking some modest set of gifts and working at the craft of teaching. I am not discouraging uncommon efforts, eccentric behavior, or even positive rottenness, but if one chooses that path to teaching fame make sure that other things are in evidence: a towering reputation, a vast bibliography, plus-fours, and a Hupmobile.

This brings me to a related assumption, the fifth on our list, *that the popular teacher is a bad teacher.* Popular teachers, as this assumption would have it, win popularity by meretricious display to the neglect of scholarship. Such teachers are not sound, or they are personality types, easy graders, soft touches, bullshit artists. This myth even has a reverse twist: the conspicuously unpopular teacher who must, by reason of his or her unpopularity, be good.

Like the earlier assumptions, this one also arouses my impatience. Those who believe in it are not likely to perceive of learning as pleasure. The most valuable lessons, they believe, are hard and unpopular, a belief that casts doubt on almost all learning attractive to large numbers of people. Even if they grant that learning can afford some kind of pleasure, they are sure that there are higher pleasures beyond the range of popular teachers and their students. I cannot do much to win over these types; in a way, they are the teaching profession's sadists and masochists.

The well-known "Dr. Fox" experiment is worth commenting on here (Naftulin, Ware, and Donnelly, 1973). "Dr. Fox" was a professional actor who supposedly by his rhetorical skills fooled an academic audience into accepting a nonsensical lecture as authentic. That experiment was loosely accepted as evidence that student evaluations of teaching were distorted by the impact of a lecturer's style regardless of substance.

In the actual initial experiment, however, the audience was not primarily students or the setting a classroom. Those taken in were chiefly faculty within the context of a professional meeting. One certain but neglected implication is that the bogus performer might succeed once in a favorable setting but is not likely to escape being labeled a "bullshit artist" by students who hear him day after day. When other studies (Meier and Feldhusen, 1979; Perry, Abrami, and Leventhal, 1979; Williams and Ware, 1977) replicated the experiment with students and under more carefully controlled conditions, the results tended to show that students "both learned more and rated instructors higher in sections with more content and in sections in which the instructor was more expressive" (McKeachie, 1986, p. 277).

Graduate school education often tends to foster arrogance about one's little learning rather than humility toward one's greater ignorance. How many students one can scare out of class the first day, how many flunk out at the end, and how many drop out during the quarter become marks of distinction, supports for a false and vicious pride that undercuts the very essence of teaching as giving and sharing and understanding. The specialization that brings professional acclaim is at the opposite pole from that which appeals to the populace. Belief in the vulgarity of the world outside and in the priority of the pursuit of truth within the academy further supports elitist postures.

Moreover, within the ordinary college and university, popular teachers get little enough reward. Large numbers of students may bolster one's ego, but they do not build professional reputations or necessarily gain the respect of colleagues. Assumptions about what makes classes popular contain a fair amount of self-deception and hypocrisy. In the humanities, for example, the early historical periods of any subject are assumed to be unattractive to students—"They won't pay attention to anything that happened more than ten years ago"—even though some teachers in many different kinds of schools attract large numbers to subjects presumed "dead" on other campuses. The nearer truth is that gifted teachers can make subject matters attractive and interesting no matter what they are.

Most of the assumptions discussed thus far come together in the common folk belief *that teachers are born and not made.* "He or she is a born teacher," is said of too many teachers who don't find teaching drudgery by those who do. And some good teachers fortify the belief by an "Aw shucks" pose: "I guess I'm a good teacher. Students seem to like what I do, but I can't figure out how I do it."

The marginal truth in this belief applies no more to teaching than it does to any occupation, profession, or skill. Hence, there are born actors, born salespeople, born politicians, born comedians, born athletes, and maybe born doctors, dentists, engineers, seamstresses, and certified public accountants. Athletes come closest to being born-anythings; a seven-foot male with good hands, fast reflexes, and sharp peripheral vision can hardly escape being a born basketball player. Yet even natural athletes spend an unnatural amount of time conditioning their bodies, acquiring skills, and practicing amidst conditions of intense competition. Potentially great teachers become great teachers by the same route: through conditioning mind and spirit and body, acquiring skills, and practicing in respectful competition with great teachers living and dead.

The more I have looked at teachers, the more I come back to an old truth of human existence: We are both born and made. At most, some teachers may have certain natural advantages: high intelligence, verbal fluency, patience, a capacity for service, good looks, a pleasant speaking voice, charm, a mind for detail, a good memory, a head for generalizations. Most of these skills are as likely to be acquired as inborn, and, when examined closely, all lose the aura of mysterious capabilities that some people have and others haven't or that some can develop and others can't.

The next assumption on our list is *that good and bad teaching cannot be identified.* Faculty opposition to ratings by students and to other means of evaluating teachers is rooted in part in the unwillingness of professors to accept the idea that characteristics of effective teaching exist. Research studies dating from early in the century to the present have arrived at reasonably consistent findings about the earmarks of good teaching (Ryans, 1960; Costin, Greenough, and Menges, 1971; Eble, 1972b; Ericksen, 1984). Most studies stress knowledge and organization of subject matter, skills in instruction, and personal qualities and attitudes useful to working with students. If personal characteristics are emphasized in a particular study, good teachers will be singled out as those who are enthusiastic, energetic, approachable, open, concerned, imaginative, and possessed of a sense of humor. If characteristics of mastering a subject matter and possessing teaching skills are emphasized, good teachers will be those who are masters of a subject, can organize and emphasize, can clarify ideas and point out relationships, can motivate students, can pose and elicit useful questions and examples, and are reasonable, imaginative, and fair in managing the details of learning. Such characteristics as stupidity, arrogance, narrowness, torpor, cynicism, dullness, and insensitivity are commonly associated with bad teaching, as are shortcomings in command of subject matter or in teaching skills.

Both common sense and research support these findings. No one argues that they include everything important or that they are precisely formulated. But they are useful rules of thumb in guiding developing teachers, and certainly they better serve the profession than does an insistence that no basis for judgment exists. Recent books which discuss these matters and cite many specific studies are Lowman (1984), chap. 1; Ericksen (1984), chap. 1; and McKeachie (1986), chap. 30.

Assumptions 8, 9, and 10 are closely related: No. 8, *that teaching and research are complementary activities;* No. 9, *that teaching a subject matter requires only that one know it;* and No. 10, *that teaching is not a profession.*

Attempts to correlate effective teaching with effective research have arrived at little correlation (Milton, 1976). Duplication of the studies that have already been made promises little more than a display of possible variations: Some good researchers are good teachers; some good researchers are poor teachers; some poor researchers are good teachers; some poor researchers are poor teachers; the majority of both researchers and teachers are mediocre but in different combinations and ways. That present empirical evidence agrees with common sense should be no surprise.

Teaching and research may be usefully compared with writing and reading. Teachers draw upon ideas and information that come from research as writers draw upon their reading, but both teachers and writers use other resources as well. Research may stand in the way of teaching as reading may keep a writer from writing. Any writer knows how insidious an enemy reading can be. Professors are less willing to recognize that research can be the foe as well as the friend of teaching. Like teachers who do little formal research, writers may not be voracious readers or may read at their own discretion and pace. Lacking an inquiring mind, however, neither the teacher nor the writer will achieve very much.

Research as practiced within the American college and university is often only indirectly related to the teaching of undergraduates. I have discussed at length the relationship between teaching and research in *The Aims of College Teaching* (1983). It is a subject much complained about but little subject to change from within. Recently, Jacques Barzun (1984, 1987) has attacked the flood of research and the triviality of much of it, writing, appropriately in this context, "To suppose that every owner of a Ph.D. can carry on valuable research while also teaching, and find time to write it up in publishable form, is contrary to fact" (1987, p. 20). Page Smith, an equally eminent scholar/teacher, concludes flatly: "Indeed, it can never be stated too often or too emphatically: *the great majority of modern academic research is not complementary to the teaching function; it is antithetical to it*" (1987, p. 55).

A close but limited study of what influences tenure and merit pay at a research university arrives at the not-surprising conclusion that the effects of teaching and service are "moderate in comparison to the effect of research and somewhat idiosyncratic" (Kasten, 1984, p. 513). Specific research activities are likely to be hostile to specific teaching responsibilities in a number of ways. The specialized character of the bulk of research does not match the level and generality of the subject matter in most undergraduate courses. Time devoted to research comes out of the same number of free hours one can allot to teaching; college teachers commonly complain that there is never enough time for either. The psychological set, the satisfactions, even the physical postures for research—the researcher must isolate him- or herself; the teacher cannot—are not the same as for teaching.

Despite the obvious diversity of individuals attracted to college and university teaching, two distinct and somewhat opposing types can be distinguished. The one likes to work alone, responds poorly to outside distractions and pressure, is more at ease with the stuff of ideas, facts, and materials of a discipline than with students and learning. The other seeks out company, can handle pressures and distractions, and prefers interacting with students to manipulating materials or ideas. The scholar-teacher who combines both types is a recognizable figure as well as an anomalous one. Considering the great numbers of college and university teachers, it is not surprising that a large number would not be particularly successful teachers, chiefly because they are not strongly attracted to teaching or because they may accept teaching as a condition of enabling them to pursue the research aspects of the scholar's life.

The ninth assumption is *that teaching a subject matter requires only that one know it.* Colleges, and particularly universities, tend to stress the production of knowledge over its dissemination. Emphasis is placed upon defining, accumulating, analyzing, and storing information and upon refining the methodologies that govern these acts. The dissemination of knowledge, in which teaching plays such a large part, is regarded as a lesser activity that often infringes on the higher one. Stimulating and developing skills, sympathies, and attitudes that do not involve the production of knowledge, even though such qualities are vital to teaching, are secondary considerations.

The belief that subject matter competence is primary and all else secondary underlies the conflict between subject-oriented teaching and student-centered learning. College teachers bristle at their public-school colleagues' claim, "We teach students, not subjects," but they are no more right in their demand of utter fidelity to the subject matter. No good teacher can afford to believe strictly in either side of the argument. If we are learners and teachers, we master both subject matter and the skills that go into teaching it.

Pushed to an extreme, the belief in the primacy of subject matter may lead to a related assumption: *that college teaching is not a profession.* Rather, the specialized pursuits of knowledge that engage professors of physics or history or economics comprise the true professional categories. There is a surprising amount of self-delusion in this claim, for there is no question that only millions of students seeking basic college instruction support the many specialized scholars who make up higher education faculties. The vast number of these professionals are, in fact, teachers. It is somewhat surprising that although there are so few independent professional historians, for example, many historians supported by teaching would deny their classroom work professional standing. But the denial is implicit in the tendency of college professors to seek recognition within professional, disciplinary associations and to repudiate professional identification for the teaching role. A corollary of this denial is the possibility that college professors, as Cross (1986) has suggested, do not take teaching seriously.

The eleventh myth is *that teaching is better at the higher levels than at the lower.* This myth is rooted in one of the most entrenched of human beliefs, that higher is better. Thus it is not likely to come about that elementary school teachers will be paid more, given more respect in society, than college professors.

Yet there are good arguments to be made for just that position. College teachers are distressingly blind to the fact that what may most affect their students' learning has already happened before the student arrives in college. Recent research (Hirsch, 1987, pp. 26-28, 33-70) indicates that the most basic of college-level skills, reading, may get effectively established by the third or fourth grade. Few college teachers' complaints about why students can't read or write or figure go beyond general condemning of the public schools. Few efforts are made to extend university expertise or even understanding to public schools outside the formal relationships maintained by colleges of education.

As to college teaching being better, insofar as college teachers have little acquaintance with what is known about how human beings learn, little chance for supervised practice, and a surrounding context of teaching indulgent of bad habits and ill-informed practices, it could be surmised that it is worse. Only the fact of vastly better conditions for teaching than public school teachers enjoy—fewer classes, fewer students, greater access to subject matter resources, better facilities, higher pay, more room for advancement, and students with greater skills for learning—may restore some balance in this comparison.

But the point is not to compare; rather it is to get college teachers to perceive education as a seamless web and to perceive education to be as much their business as the public school teachers'.

The last myth is *that teaching is both less and more mysterious than it is.* That it is regarded as less mysterious reveals itself in the panaceas that periodically sweep through public school education. Often these have less impact on college teachers, perhaps because of the sturdy ignorance much of the professoriate maintains toward pedagogical ideas of any kind. But to cite only two movements of recent times, both *behavioral objectives* and *performance-based learning* have gained strong adherents among college teachers. *Writing across the curriculum* was college-created, and it and *critical thinking,* which I will address at length in the next chapter, are affecting both public schools and colleges and often in a simplistic way.

It is not that these myths are wrong—few myths are—but that they contain a partial or buried truth that must be examined to be made most useful. Clearly placing objectives before students and helping them carry them out, and trying to establish learning so well that it can be demonstrated, and getting students to write and think in every class, are important to teaching. But adhered to too strictly, seized upon to the neglect of other equally important matters, adopted as a simple means to simple ends, such methods and programs belittle teaching by reducing its complex and often mysterious nature.

On the other hand, John Granrose (1980, pp. 28-30) has usefully called attention to teaching's "greater mysteries," deliberately borrowing that term from theology. What he refers to lie beyond "the marks of competence and craftsmanship in one's profession." They are not so much advanced skills as marks of character and engagement and love. As Granrose observes, they receive little attention because "they are difficult, sometimes embarrassing to talk about." Still, teaching would be a less satisfying, less demanding profession were it not for the fact that every committed teacher works within the possibility that a student will say, "You changed my life." To teach without some awareness of that possibility is to sell short the "greater mysteries." "To wake our students up, we ourselves must be awake," Granrose writes; "to inspire them, we ourselves must be inspired; to love them, we must be loved ourselves."

A mythology as rich as teaching's embraces more assumptions than can be listed here. Teachers who accept these assumptions may not necessarily be impossible, nor are those who question them guaranteed excellence. All teachers employed by formal institutions of education fall prey to what may be the largest myth of all: that learning is best served within the formal structures the past has provided. Despite what we know about the vast amount of learning taking place in informal ways, within those primary groups like family and peers, higher education has removed itself from these useful contexts. Colleges and universities have, to be sure, modified the rigidities of structure in some ways, but they have moved slowly in developing new modes of noncampus learning. Moreover, though the idea of collegiality of the campus, as a place where teaching and learning benefit from interaction, is well established, that idea makes little headway against the divisions of subject matters, the creation of departments, the division into administrators and faculty, and the classification of undergraduate and graduate students. If there is little wholeness in teaching and learning, part of the blame must fall upon formal education within which have arisen myths not only about teaching but about the indispensability of formal education itself.

3

Getting Students to Think

If there is one common aim for most college teaching, it is to get students to think. From time to time, some thinkers, probably soft-headed ones or artists admitted into university respectability, point out that thinking is not everything. Shakespeare said it best when he had Lear remarking to the recently blinded Gloucester, "Yet you see how this world goes." And Gloucester replies, "I see it feelingly."

Still, most college and university teachers have in mind that in some way they must help their students think. Within the past decade "critical thinking" has become as fashionable a word in education as "creative thinking" was in the past. Very recently, but in the line of *Why Johnny Can't Read* (Flesch, 1955), E. D. Hirsch's *Cultural Literacy* (1987) has attacked how schools, following Rousseau and Dewey, have subverted the goal of thinking by a misplaced emphasis on developing skills rather than learning things. Alan Bloom's *Closing of the American Mind* (1987) follows a similar line, identifying some of the same cultural villains and posing a reengagement with the true and the good as higher education's proper course. Neither book does justice to the basic complexities that bother both educational theorists and practicing teachers: getting people to think, having something to think with, having something to think about, and thinking to some purpose.

Teachers are likely to get better guidance from the many sources which, through the years, have tried to shed light on thinking. Rubinstein and Firstenberg (1987, p. 23), for example, speak for the common-sense notion that thinking involves both process and stuff. Their succinct definition is a reasonable starting point for thinking about the nature of thought: "Thinking constitutes the performance skills that we use in order to apply our intelligence to a knowledge base derived from the totality of our experience."

Put simply, getting people to think, however thinking is defined, is an enduring goal not just for teachers, but for human beings in general. Long before formal education emerged, parents must have been saying to children, "Think about it," or more likely, "Why didn't you think about it?" or to themselves, "I should have thought about it."

"If we could just get our students to think ... " we say, letting the sentence end in wondrous accomplishments of every imagining. This wistfulness does not arise for lack of thinking about thinking or even of thinking about how to teach people to think. The long list of books in this century alone gives any classroom teacher an abundance of resources and also suggests how thinking was viewed decade by decade: John Dewey's *How We Think* (1910); Dimmet's *The Art of Thinking* (1925); Clarke's *The Art of Straight Thinking* (1929); Jastrow's *Effective Thinking* (1931); Burtt's *Right Thinking* (1946); Jepson's *Clear Thinking* (1956); Wertheimer's *Productive Thinking* (1959); Hultfish's *Reflective Thinking* (1961); Buzan's *Use Both Sides of Your Brain* (1976); Savary's *Mindwarp* (1979); Perkins' *The Mind's Best Work* (1981); Sternberg's *Intelligence Applied* (1986); Meyers's *Teaching Students to Think Critically* (1986); and Brookfield's *Developing Critical Thinkers* (1987).

Long before any of these, Socrates, as we have him in the Platonic dialogues, was exemplifying a way of thinking, the dialectic method, and at the same time forcing his listeners to think about fundamental questions. I have some suspicions about the term *critical thinking,* as not so much sharpening a teacher's conception of thinking as maybe narrowing it to the kind of thinking the teacher wants. At best, the term calls the thinker away from imprecise, unfocused, unexamined thought, and thus is a guard against prejudice, superstition, and authority.

At worst, critical thinking is tied to various paranoid strains in modern scholarship which reject all ways of thinking other than those of the critic and all conclusions to which someone else's thinking may have brought them.

"The importance of critical thinking can best be evaluated by the undesirable attitudes and beliefs it would eliminate," an author of a book on critical thinking writes (D'Angelo, 1971, p. 1), oblivious to how much is wrapped up in "undesirable attitudes and beliefs." "The development of critical thinking," he goes on, "will provide the means of carefully examining moral, social, and religious points of view." This last illustrates what I mean by narrowing one's attitude toward thinking, for though "moral, social, and religious" cover a wide territory, they are but a small part of what exists within the vast domain of thought.

John Dewey (1910, p. 2) observed that "In its loosest sense, thinking signifies everything that, as we say, is 'in our heads' or that 'goes through our minds.' He who offers 'a penny for your thoughts' does not expect to drive any great bargain." A later psychologist (Thomson, 1959, p. 16) writes: "Even confining thinking to 'the sense of reasoning,' 'reflecting,' or 'pondering' has its difficulty." He concludes that "if one wants to study what a man does who is described as thinking . . . it is necessary to sort out typical cases and select some of these for special scrutiny." David Perkins' *The Mind's Best Work* is a valuable book in this respect, for it offers a variety of "personal experiments" which usually "couple a task with some sort of introspection into the workings of the mind" (1981, p. 7). Though Perkins' book is about "creative" thought, it has a larger purpose of wanting to show "how creating in the arts and sciences is a natural comprehensible extension and orchestration of ordinary everyday abilities of perception, understanding, memory, and so on" (p. 4).

It is within these frameworks that this chapter is written. It begins with a brief introspection into my own thinking which led to an interest in Galileo's thought which provides the basis for observations about thinking and their practical application to teaching.

If my thinking about this chapter has a true beginning, it goes very far back. It may well have had its originating point in a demonstration about the nature of motion in an undergraduate physics class in 1943. Facing an auditorium full of students, the professor demonstrated something of the immutable character of basic laws of motion and his professional confidence in that immutability. He took a heavy iron ball attached to a long cable suspended from the high ceiling of the auditorium, walked to the side of the room with the ball, held it a moment exactly at his eyebrows' level, and let it swing back and forth. We students watched in macabre fascination (for he was a likable as well as effective teacher), but not altogether appalled at the prospect of having his brains dashed out before our eyes. It did not happen, however, and within that context, I think, I first heard about Galileo.

Galileo surely rates among the world's great thinkers. His writings give much direct and indirect evidence about how he went about thinking, and therefore are useful to teachers interested in getting their students to think. Every discipline furnishes similar models that can give interest and tangibility to the elusiveness of trying to foster thought. Problems and puzzles, brain-teasers and conundrums are time-honored ways of stimulating thinking.

For me, Galileo's work added a context, the actuality of problems he wrestled with and his own successful and unsuccessful solutions. These, in simple form, are four problems I set before my students:

1. According to Aristotle, if the earth actually did rotate, objects would be spun off into space. In one of Galileo's writings, Salviati uses the example of a rock in a sling to convince Simplicius that Aristotle must be wrong. Can you reconstruct Galileo's argument?

2. The telescope opened up great opportunities for ships to keep track of their exact position at sea. What was required for that instrument to be used effectively on board a ship and in what ways did Galileo attempt to make its use possible?

3. Among other inquiries Galileo made was that of trying to determine the speed of light. How might someone in Galileo's time have tried to measure the speed of light? Why would it likely have failed?

4. Why does ice float? Observation might tell us that it is

because when water on a pond freezes, the ice is a thin, flat shape, something like a leaf, and it is this shape that causes it to float. Galileo challenged this idea, but his opponent brought pieces of ebony, cut them in various shapes, and demonstrated that the thin flat pieces did float while the squares and cylinders and triangles sank. Galileo devised a counter experiment, not using ice. What might it have been? What important conclusion could this lead to about the nature of physical substances?

Before revealing the answers (which are probably not the most important part of this exercise), let me state some of my speculations about Galileo's way of thinking and about our own thinking.

First, there was a randomness in Galileo's thinking, as there probably is in all thought. He did not always go directly to an idea; our own ideas may proceed from what we call idle as well as purposeful curiosity.

Second, that randomness was not altogether random, wholly disconnected, or fitful. Those like Galileo who are notable for the quality of their thought are also notable for its quantity. Thinkers think a lot. One thinks of things because one is always thinking.

Third, there was often a purpose connected with Galileo's thought—even in the seeming casualness of challenging established ideas about how objects fall in space by proposing simple demonstrations.

Fourth, there was almost always a rejection of conventional thought, a contrariness to what others had thought, which stimulated Galileo's own act of thinking.

Fifth, there was a movement of thought to an operational level and at many points a connection with the world of tangible things and acts. Thus, what might be called a complete and satisfying segment of thought was fused into action.

I do not claim that these five characteristics describe Galileo's thinking accurately, much less identify everything important about thinking, but they do have important implications for teachers trying to teach or stimulate thinking.

First, acknowledging that randomness plays a great part in thinking is important for teachers and students in a number of ways. It may break down some of the student's frustration in trying to think straight or reduce some of the friction occasioned by having to think the way the teacher seems to want. It may also restore the spirit of play that seems to disappear the higher and more formal education becomes. It may remove some guilt from woolgathering, and sanction idle thought as having more utility than is commonly allowed.

On the teacher's part, it may encourage developing exercises that stimulate thinking by entertaining and encouraging this randomness. *Brainstorming* is by now an accepted formal technique conferring academic dignity on the vast amount of engaging the mind that has always gone on in dormitories and coffee shops. *Free writing,* as it has developed in teaching composition, can be incorporated into many classes. The college classroom should be a place where vagrant thoughts have a chance of becoming speculative propositions. The Hewlett-Packard corporation, after all, has built an entire advertising campaign around bright young men and women emerging from some unlikely place, rushing to the phone, saying, "What if . . . ?"

Who does not recognize the flow of unrelated thought that may precede and follow arriving at an important idea? Who does not recognize that ideas do pop into one's head? Much of human thinking is composed of idle thought, random thoughts going in and out of our heads. The sixties, whatever else they brought, expanded our conceptions of the mind's workings. And even as scholars can propose a list of things that schools should teach as a means toward "cultural literacy," one has to observe that the game of Trivial Pursuit anticipated this scholarly idea by a decade.

One need for recognizing randomness of thought is as a counter to the inhibitions to thinking that arise from formalizing education. I am not talking about the distractions to thinking that college campuses so mindlessly promote, but about such pressures as "I could never be a thinker like that" and "there must be something wrong with me that I can't think better" and "why think about it when you can look it up?" Melville is surely right when he says, "There are some enterprises in which a careful disorderliness is a true method."

The second point is that to think well, one must think a lot, just as writers write a lot, composers compose a lot, painters paint a lot. Their sheer bulk of thought counts for much, and why should it not. For thinking, like writing, is not easy if we think of it as being other than the nonthinking thinking that none of us can escape. Thinking must often be forced, and forced on the college campus in face of the many excuses and alternatives provided to keep students from thinking.

It is part of my own thinking, I think, to resist setting down for myself or for others a set of principles about how more thinking might be done. The splendid multiplicity and diversity of both experience and thought deserves better than its being reduced to a digest of particulars, a schema or outline. Still, I respect attempts to do just this, such as Edward de Bono's various highly systematic "courses" in thinking (1983), the many attempts to identify problem-solving techniques (Bransford and Stein, 1984; Stice, 1987), and a recent textbook, *Thinking About Thinking* (McKowen, 1986), which goes about it in quite another way.

What is most important, however, is getting students to spend more time thinking. Those who think a lot—and college teachers vary in this respect as widely as any other group—might pass on to students the usefulness of thinking at almost any time and place. Much can be done in one's head when the body is otherwise engaged. Galileo's life furnishes a classic example in his working through the particulars of pendulum motion while sitting in the cathedral in Pisa. Writing and figuring and conceptualizing can be done walking to and from class, while waiting for a bus or parking space.

Third, teachers can do more than encourage students to make use of the fact that the brain keeps functioning even as the person may be doing quite unrelated things. Providing reasons for thinking is a fundamental teaching responsibility. Thought arises and persists from need. "Having something on your mind" is a vague but important way of emphasizing how thought is connected with purpose, with a task to be performed, a need to be satisfied. Often this is not a blessing; it keeps one awake at night and it probably creates dreams which disturb our sleep. In extreme cases, thought becomes both an enemy of sleep and an enemy of purposeful actions.

The success of such simple classroom techniques as the one-minute quiz, the after-class half-page summary of most important ideas, the overnight problem assignment attests to success in getting students to think. There are an infinite number of questions in any discipline that have a puzzle quality about them that is almost certain to stimulate student thought. Why does coal burn? Why is goose down warm? Why does a wet finger feel cool? Why does the New Year begin in January? Why do we shake hands instead of rub noses? Why do dogs bark and cats meow? And do dogs and cats bark or meow differently in German or French or Spanish? There is no great purpose embodied in any of these, but they have the purpose of satisfying a curiosity and they lie within the range of thinking by which most students might satisfy that purpose.

Purpose may well be connected with a contrariness in thought, marked in Galileo's life and work. Pondering the motion of a pendulum while sitting in church is a mild contrariness familiar to any young person urged to listen carefully to what the preacher, or teacher, is saying. Moreover, wondering how an object swings, giving that question any importance, is also being contrary to simply letting the *what is* stay there *as is*.

An element of contrariness, from either confronting ourselves or being challenged by someone else, may be necessary to force us out of the pattern of nonthinking by which we human beings can very well get by, or often, "get by better." Students know there is an obvious risk in disturbing a teacher's accustomed patterns of thought, and teachers, therefore, must find ways of breaking down the authority of their position if not their presence.

Discussion techniques are worth developing for this reason alone. A good discussion draws in students because the teacher creates an atmosphere in which students are not punished for thinking, and in fact are rewarded—rewarded by the dynamics of the discussion—for thinking in contrary ways.

Discussion is not an economical method if measured by how information might be organized and transferred. Thinking is probably similarly uneconomic; it is quicker and safer to send students to the library. But students are not likely to question what they find in the library. In discussion among peers and with a wise teacher both entering in and staying out, supporting and playing devil's advocate when necessary, students can not only gain a firmer command of whatever topic is under discussion but gain some insight into ways and ends of thinking.

Finally, the teacher's duty, with respect to much teaching, is to provide catch-points where the student's own web of thought can take hold. Thought must have some embodiment, some connection with the tangible, to realize and reinforce itself. Galileo's thought is rich because it often begins in the observation of a physical phenomenon and ends in demonstrating other phenomena.

Teachers need to find ways appropriate to whatever they are teaching to make thought tangible. One of the great attractions of the computer is how it can render so many abstract things tangible. Scientific thinkers often work with physical models, visualize if not that, and at an extreme of abstracting, still require the tangibility of chalk and blackboard. Thoreau wrote: "The necessity of labor and conversation with many men and things, to the scholar is rarely well remembered; steady labor with the hands, which engrosses the attention also, is unquestionably the best method of removing palaver and sentimentality out of one's style. . . . The scholar may be sure that he writes the tougher truth for the calluses in his palms" ([1849] 1980, pp. 106–107). Writing itself has a tangibility beyond both spoken and unspoken thought. It is not only that our thoughts can be preserved, frozen in print, it is the physical activity of writing which also connects thought with thought, thought coming down the shoulder past the elbow into the forearm through the fingers out on the page by way of the pen.

In teaching all subjects, dramatizing, exemplifying, getting students physically involved are justified with respect to furthering thought as for other reasons.

Having sketched some of the ways in which an analysis of Galileo's thought can be applied to teaching or stimulating thinking, let me turn back to the specific problems confronting Galileo and my students.

The first problem is part of Galileo's probing of the nature of motion. His most stunning act of thought turned our perceived world topsy-turvy. Our stable world is not as we perceive it to be but is in constant, restless, if orderly motion. In this problem, common sense says that the rock will fly from the sling; and hence, that if the earth is really spinning, we will fly from it. But a further extension of thought and observation reveals that such a rock does not fly off indefinitely. That in turn led Galileo to seek further explanations. His manner is engagingly revealed in an anecdote about the idea that the Babylonians were able to cook eggs by whirling them in a sling at high speed. "Since," he wrote, "we do not lack eggs, or slings, or sturdy fellows to whirl them, and still they do not cook, the answer must lie in getting a Babylonian to whirl them." Galileo's discussion of this and related problems is in *Dialogue Concerning the Two Chief World Systems—Ptolemaic and Copernican* (Galilei, [1632] 1953, p. 214).

The second problem is described in Colin Ronan's *Galileo* (1974, pp. 170-171). The aspect of this problem that interests me is how to provide for a stationary observation on a pitching ship. Galileo designed a helmet to anchor a binocular telescope to the observer's head and had a kind of floating seat devised for the observer. These two experiments did not work, but the best of thinking is often frustrated when measured by the end toward which it strives.

The third problem is described in Galileo's *Dialogues Concerning Two New Sciences* (Galilei, [1638] 1914, pp. 41-44). The method of trying to determine the speed of light—and it didn't work either—was to set two lanterns on two peaks across a wide valley. By having the operator expose the light at point A and the operator on the other peak expose his light as soon as he saw the first, a measure of light traveling twice the distance between the peaks could be made. The speed of light was too great to produce a measurement. However, Galileo retained his belief that light was not instantaneous.

The fourth problem is more complex than it appears. According to the Aristotelian doctrine that cold condenses, ice should sink. That it does not, Galileo argued, is because ice does not condense but somehow becomes lighter. His opponents shifted their ground to say that it was the shape of an object that accounted for its floating or sinking. Neither knew that water does condense as it cools, but only to 4 degrees centigrade, at which point it begins to expand, forming a crystalline structure lighter than water itself. Galileo's counter demonstration using wax is not as important as his refusing, once again, to accept received opinion about the nature of physical phenomena. Stillman Drake, in *Galileo Studies: Personality, Tradition, and Revolution* (1970), has a chapter discussing this dispute in great detail.

Much of the success of these exercises resides in the fact that they are done in the spirit of fun. They are not graded, but students do conscientiously and overnight write out their solutions. Some spend time in trying to look them up, for it is a very useful aspect of this exercise that Galileo's confrontations with these problems are all in his works. I have never told them that they are very hard to find, leaving it to their frustrations to teach indirectly that thinking about something may be easier than looking it up.

Some extra dividends which may be expected from using such practical exercises in thinking are these:

For what may be a rare occurrence in a student's life, he or she may find it fun to be wrong as well as right. The student who said the telescope would be useful because you could see the land ahead recognized the rightness and yet the absurdity of what he was saying. In these exercises, Galileo was almost as much wrong in some respects as right. Giving students encouragement to make mistakes in an atmosphere where going down the tube is an ever-present threat surely is a first step in encouraging thought.

The sharing of responses to an actual "thought" problem can reveal many specific and useful aspects of how we think. Contexts, for example, are vital. The question about using a telescope on a ship would undoubtedly get more sophisticated answers from students who lived with some acquaintance with ships and the sea. Good answers among any group disclose that other things than being "smart" may be involved in thinking, another incentive to students who may think they have little power of thought.

Something of the specific findings about learning can emerge in these exercises. How we learn "chunks" of material and how we develop "schemata" can be understandably intruded into discussions.

It is not negligible that while this exercise is one about thinking, it also conveys at the same time something about Galileo and about the time in which he lived and something about physics and religion and science and the dialogue form; science can pay its respects to the great thinkers of its past as surely as the humanities or the behavioral sciences, and without loss to science.

Finally, and without apology, such exercises can be designed, should be designed, for fun. If we would have students think, get ourselves to think, we must get some fun out of it. Thinking *is* hard, but the popularity of quiz games, conundrums, puzzles also argues that it is fun. If it does not appear so to the student, then the teacher's job is to make it so. Being able to play with serious ideas, to recognize the comic within the deadly serious, to live with the incongruity of the world are indications of a person's capacity to think.

The incongruity that is at the basis of most humor is basic also to thought. With visual humor—the overdressed man slipping on the banana peel—the one who laughs must be able to juxtapose in the mind the expected experience with the actual one. With verbal humor, the one who would laugh must respond as well to the language in which the experience is expressed. Inseparable from "getting it" are fundamental acts of thinking— remembering, imagining, relating. When we say a person is lacking wit, we are talking about an aspect of mind, thinking in as sure a sense as that purposive thought which arrives at profound answers to serious things.

I think we may best approach "teaching students to think" not by relegating it to a course but by stimulating and providing assistance to thought in every course. As we value the arts and the soft sciences and literature as having ways of their own, we need to be wary of acting as if "thinking" were all of one kind. Hence, those classes which actually demonstrate how thinking has been involved and what its nature may be in relation to specific subject matters—or more precisely, specific achievements—seem more inclined to enlarge a person's thinking in ways that are important to that person. Pondering with students, thinking at that point closest to pinning it down, may be the best way of proceeding.

Many teachers do something like this. A common defense of the lecture method is that, done well, and particularly done not by reading from notes but by thinking as one goes along, a lecture can be a powerful way of demonstrating processes of thought. A well-conducted discussion session accomplishes a similar end and with the added advantage of actively involving students in their own processes of thought. Problem sets at the desk or at the blackboard are commonplace but often badly carried out ways of stimulating thinking. Best of all are opportunities for teacher and student to sit down together over writing or computations or objects and, with some shrewd and non-threatening questioning, lead a student to think and to recognize patterns of thought. Large classes are, in general, detrimental to thought, except perhaps the teacher's thinking about what a spellbinder he or she is and the students' thinking they wish he or she were.

Advocating that courses are not necessarily the way to teach thinking does not rule out or diminish the importance of courses in philosophy, psychology, communications, and other disciplines that deal specifically with practical and theoretical aspects of thinking. Nor does it oppose such useful classroom practices within science and engineering as embodied in Wales' "guided design" (Wales and Stager, 1977) or described in Stice's *Developing Critical Thinking and Problem-Solving Abilities* (1987). If it were possible that formal logic or Wood's (1980) logical thinking skills could be uniformly taught in ways that engaged the students, that had genuine impact on their own thinking, such a course might be reinstated in the required curriculum. But the present faculty and even the present students do not seem sufficiently receptive to justify that or any other mandatory "thinking" requirement.

In practice, it may be that the economies of large classes, our time's preoccupation with bodies of knowledge, and the need to cover material are major impediments to giving thinking the attention it deserves. If "writing across the curriculum" proves successful (and it faces the same impediments), then something like "thinking across the curriculum" is an obvious corollary and an even more important reform.

PART TWO

The Skills of Teaching

4

Why the Classroom?

No one has demonstrated convincingly that the classroom and
the fifty-minute hour are the best arrangements for learning.
Clearly, the majority of teachers accept them, no matter how
much they may complain about noise and heat and light and
lack of erasers. Among some college students and teachers, however, the freedoms of the sixties included freedom from the
classroom. The classroom stood among the repressive forces in
higher education, that establishment space that most confirmed
the authority of the professor. On many campuses, classes moved
into professors' homes or students' apartments. On most, both
students and professors developed a more permissive attitude
toward promptness and attendance. Even such a simple act as
moving chairs from orderly rows to the discussion circle marked
a change. Disarray typified many of the classrooms I visited in
the early seventies, partly because of cutbacks in janitorial services but also because of the preferences of students and faculty.
Finally, the bells and buzzers that summoned students to class
and cut off professors' monologues were silenced. Students
showed up about a designated time; professors looked at their
watches or the students at theirs to end the hour.

Much of this ended in the eighties. Students bent on pursuing careers seem to prefer a well-regulated academic life. New
faculty seem to be a pretty tame breed, anxious about their
own careers and almost as conservative in academic matters as
those political conservatives academics commonly deplore. If

the classroom has any academic rival, it is the computer stations harboring row on row of students, and the personal computers in faculty offices which make it difficult for some professors to go to the classrooms at all. The replacement of the classroom by a computer network, however, is a futuristic dream, and probably only of a certain kind of dreamer. The classroom, like the college campus itself, is likely to remain central to formal higher education.

What does the classroom offer? What does it take away? How can it best be used? The first two questions are part of the general questions teachers carry with them through their careers; the third is the practical question a teacher faces every day.

Obviously, the classroom offers a gathering place for a specific activity at a specific time. In most subjects, the teacher gets little more help than that from the average classroom, which rarely defines the learning it houses in the way that a basketball court or a swimming pool or a pool parlor defines the activities for which it provides space. As a consequence, the teacher might give some attention to providing more definition. Changing a college classroom physically raises some difficulties. College professors don't have home rooms, and one professor's decorations are not likely to be welcomed by other professors. Pressuring administrators to put more thought, imagination, and money into classroom design is every professor's business, but that doesn't change the classroom one is in. The situation for most professors is classrooms they didn't build, wouldn't have designed, can't find alternatives for, and must occupy for the term. What then?

First, I wouldn't entirely abandon attacking the institutional sterility of most classrooms, even if only for the brief duration of a class. Posters are cheap; artifacts clutter faculty offices; and students and teachers can bring interesting objects into the classroom, even for each separate hour, that help indicate how the ten-o'clock enterprise differs from the nine-o'clock.

Second, a teacher shouldn't be cowed by custom, colleagues, or janitors into accepting the neat rows and files of chairs that are the classroom norm. During the late sixties, I came upon the story of an inconclusive war between a janitor and students over whether their pillows and pads were to replace his chairs. More recently I found a written note on my own classroom door saying: "Professor in the ten-o'clock class: Please leave the chairs as they were before vacating the room!" Actually I had been leaving the chairs as they were; some class before mine was moving them around. I tried to explain this to my disturbed colleague, but that only led to a discussion of the merits of rectangular seating as against roughly round and to an argument about "square" teaching versus other kinds. Despite some shouting and redness of necks, the confrontation served a purpose: This was the first time in twenty years that we had talked to each other about any educational matter, about the norm for professors in the same building in the same college in a large university.

Third, instead of individual and fitful complaints about heat and light and air and noise, faculty members might mount concerted attacks on the chronic shortcomings of classrooms. In putting up new buildings in the last decade, universities have been more likely to consult the faculty than in the past. Even so, the classrooms probably get the least specific attention. Occasionally faculty members become sufficiently ruffled about these matters to specify their complaints, as did A. L. Herman, a professor of philosophy, in the *Journal of Higher Education* in 1968. He creates for the faculty a philosophic architect who will deal with the ugly classroom (pp. 379-380):

> The question we pose for him is just this: In what kind of atmosphere can instruction be most effectively carried on? Our philosopher-architect will respond with questions, of course. He could suggest free and open instruction in a free and open oat field or apple orchard, with a student-teacher ratio of five to one. After we explain to him our campus and physical plant realities, the state laws relating to our buildings and rooms, and our reluctantly accepted presupposition or assumption regarding classroom instruction, we return again

> to the question. The stage is now set. He under-
> stands that we operate on a thirty to one student-
> faculty ratio in the classroom, that most of the
> rooms in which our students meet are like most
> classrooms in most class buildings throughout most
> of the campuses across the country. We have no
> money to round off the corners, tear out the walls,
> or introduce one-way glass windows. The problem
> is simply, what the hell can you do with an old
> classroom to make instruction more effective?

Professor Herman envisions pictures on the floor, rheostats on the light switches, swinging doors, and the professor teaching from a giant swing attached to the ceiling. Bizarre as these proposals may appear, teachers must continue to make such suggestions if classroom design is to improve.

One can dream still more and go beyond classroom design to envision buildings that create a variety of spaces for teaching and learning. Why should classrooms march up and down sterile corridors chiefly designed to handle large volumes of traffic? Shouldn't there be informal places for gathering intermixed with the classrooms? Classes and classrooms do get in the way of learning. And many professors need help to break away from the restrictions implied by rooms and hours. Conversations begun in a class can be carried on after the hour when there are informal spaces where students and teacher may sit and talk freely. In these respects, corporate headquarters as well as conference centers embrace design features and comforts far superior to what pertains in most educational classroom buildings. Commons rooms, for example, should not be regarded as frills but as necessary places where, by design, students, faculty, and even administrators are brought together. In some of the sciences, laboratories are focal points around which classrooms and classes function. Similar attention to providing focal points in other disciplines might stimulate better overall arrangements of classrooms, library collections, commons rooms, office spaces, and the like.

Classroom design, like much of the teaching that goes on

inside of them, has seemed to exhaust the innovative spirit of the sixties. What has happened, I wonder, to those very large classrooms in which individual chairs were equipped with a simple electronic device so that students could make instantaneous responses to questions posed by the instructor? Where are the classrooms which, for a time, had state-of-the-art audio-visual equipment? On my own campus, dozens of overhead projectors are consigned to storage, and on any given day it is a question whether enough shades will be in repair to even darken a room sufficiently to show slides. We fail to keep up even with the past; in the sixteenth century, in Rabelais' Abbey of Theleme, "all the halls, rooms and closets were tapestried in various manners, according to the season of the year" (Rabelais, [1534] 1946, p. 209).

But the classroom is more than its physical configuration, and teachers and students together can create good classes even in poor rooms. If exchange of information, clarification of concepts, and stimulation to further study do take place in the classroom, they must commonly overcome the limitations that confine learning to a designated space, that place the student before or below the teacher, and that set a fixed period of time at fixed intervals as the norm for learning. The gifted teacher may find ways to work effectively within these limitations. Imaginative and impatient teachers may seek out ways of getting around them.

What are some of the possibilities? One is to give some relief from the fixed space by occasionally moving classes to more appropriate settings. Small classes permit the flexibility of meeting in student or faculty residences or in a library, laboratory, or gallery. Even large classes might be accommodated on occasion in a concert hall or museum. In any size class, putting students on their own during some class hours both expands the classroom and works against the students' dependence on the teacher as sole source and authority. Merely examining the time period in relation to one's teaching strategies can be the first step in breaking free of the confines of the fifty-minute hour. Discussion classes, for example, need an expanse of time in which to develop profitably. A general scheduling of classes in larger blocks of time would not be an impossible demand, and could better suit individual class needs. In one form of team teaching, teachers of two different classes plan their work together and teach the two courses back to back. Block scheduling of a group of related classes for a full morning or afternoon would be a natural extension of that arrangement. Such arrangements would also help get around the difficulty of team-teaching arrangements using two or more teachers in a single classroom. As another example, freshman composition has limped along for decades as an isolated class rather than one that might establish useful relationships with other subject matters or dispense with the classroom altogether. Interestingly, using word processors in writing instruction may result in the added advantage of creating for students new kinds of workplaces and relationships. Similarly, seminars and discussion groups might emerge more stimulatingly if they followed directly from related classroom lectures, discussion, or other presentations, in informal settings such as are consciously built into conference center physical arrangements.

   The Changing College Classroom (Runkel, Harrison, and Runkel, 1969) gives detailed examples of how college teachers in a variety of subject matters have tried to use basic classroom patterns more effectively. In a fairly large philosophy class, for example, the teacher set up a small discussion group that occupied chairs around a table at the front of the classroom. Ten or twelve students from the whole class opted to be in the discussion group each week. They were honor-bound to read at least that week's material and to take an active part in discussing it. All students had one or more chances to be in the discussion group during the term, but participation was at the student's option, with a few students choosing not to participate at all. Most of these students, it turned out, came to the instructor outside class and received personal attention that way. Students not in the group provided an audience for the discussion, and they were permitted to participate by raising questions if they wanted.

   By treating class instruction in a slightly unusual way, this teacher solved a number of recurring practical problems:

Why the Classroom?　　　　　　　　　　　　　　　51

how to get students to read material; how to get them to discuss
what they have read; how to respect students who prefer to remain silent and to give such students a chance to exchange
ideas; how to deal more individually with students in a large
class; and how to inject some drama into classroom proceedings.
Maryellen Gleason Weimer's recent book, *Teaching Large
Classes Well* (1987), offers a wealth of suggestions for handling
this vexing aspect of classroom teaching.

I learned of another way of better adapting the classroom
to the realities of teaching from J. Barre Toelken, a teacher of
literature and folklore at Utah State University. Toelken is a
professional folk singer as well as a teacher. His classes are popular, and through the years he received the usual reward of popularity: more and more students. Yet, as classes grew and moved
from small classrooms into auditorium-type halls, Toelken's personal satisfaction in dealing individually with students diminished. Drawing on his professional singing experience, he
equipped himself with a lapel mike and moved off the podium
to conduct much of his class in the form of give-and-take with
individuals and with groups of students.

It is commonly forgotten that the classroom offers the
rudiments of a stage. In auditoriums used as classrooms, everything is there, including curtains and lights. There is little to be
lost and much to be gained in using the classroom, when appropriate, as theater. Teachers of drama very naturally force their
students out of passive roles into reading parts and acting out
scenes. Rehearsal rooms commonly have no more appurte-
nances than a classroom. It is surprisingly easy and effective to
adapt specific content to dramatic presentations. My experience has acquainted me with professors dressing up not only as
Dickens and Emerson and Thoreau and a variety of Shakespear-
ian characters, but Newton and Marx and Beethoven as well.
Putting students into roles and playing out encounters and conflicts before other students may be even better.

Leaving the classroom altogether for more educationally
stimulating environments is the basis of my final example of
getting past confines of the classroom. An ingenious professor
in Oregon developed a self-guiding "course" on environmental

pollution (suggested perhaps by the self-guiding trails in the national parks) by carefully mapping a route from one city to another with various stops along the way, each of which highlighted some environmental abuse. Students were given a guidebook and allowed to take the tour alone or in groups. For their culminating assignment, the students were asked to write an intelligent report on what they had seen, drawing on other classroom resources to examine cause and effect, detail economic and political relationships, and pose possible solutions.

These hardly startling examples provide teachers' individual answers to basic questions: What is a classroom for? What is a class anyhow? What am I trying to accomplish in and out of class? Is my schedule appropriate to my teaching? Are there some forms of learning, like gaining a command of a language, where saturation over a fairly short period is a better arrangement than regularly spaced classes over a longer period? Are regularly scheduled classes necessary to all those subjects in which large amounts of reading appear to be central? What does a class, dependent upon large amounts of reading, do before the students have had a chance to read? Would I be less tempted to lecture if I did not feel obligated to fill up classroom space and time? Given my university's resources for independent study, how might bringing students together in a formal class best foster both independent and collaborative learning?

There is a paradox running through much of the use of the classroom. Though it is a place for gathering it is not necessarily a place where students learn together, much less with the teacher. There is an air of competition that infects the classroom as it does the entire campus. Teachers know and expound and depart; students don't and passively ingest and elbow each other while doing it. One of the few hopeful signs of changing perspectives in a generally static time is the movement toward *collaborative learning*. The 1987 conference of the American Association for Higher Education gave much attention to this movement. "American higher education by nature promotes competition not cooperation, and may fail in its own ambitions as a result" (Heller, 1987, p. 17).

A group reviewing recent critiques of higher education

and drawing on research which poses ways of meeting these criticisms strongly emphasizes the need for reciprocity and cooperation among students as well as among students and faculty. "Good learning, like good work, is collaborative and social, not competitive and isolated" (Chickering and Gamson, 1987, p. 4).

Much of collaborative learning has been focused on teaching writing (Castelucci and Miller, 1986; Kraft, 1985), but the usefulness of cooperation among students is obviously not confined to skills subjects. Fundamental to breaking out of a strictly competitive model is to revise our ideas about the classroom. It is not a black box, a place for encouraging passive learning inside, mere gathering and memorizing information outside, and reinforcing an individually competitive model for learning overall. As classrooms could well be improved in terms of furnishings and design, so could our conceptions of their functioning as places for learning.

Despite my reservations about classroom use, I see little likelihood that the classroom will be rendered obsolete. Classrooms are too much a solid part of the university's accumulation of buildings, rooms, chairs, and lecterns to change greatly in the next five years or even twenty-five. In addition, the phenomenon of one person learning from another, of many persons wanting to learn something and seeking out a single person to teach them is too deeply imbedded in human conduct to be put aside lightly. The classroom provides a place for such gathering, reinforcing both good teaching practices and bad. So long as the classroom doesn't rule out other possibilities and so long as it stimulates human interactions in contexts that matter, it will remain a central place for instruction.

I have seen, in the course of my visits, bad classrooms, crowded ones, dingy ones, dirty ones, and, infrequently, inviting ones. All things considered, though, it's apparent to me that the classroom is where the excitement of teaching is. I am not sure it is that exciting for students, and I sympathize with the laxness of regulations that let students attend or skip classes as they will. At best, for both teachers and students, the classroom can somewhat approximate those more exciting places where people willingly come together. There is nothing odd in the classroom's attraction for the teacher. For the athlete, performance on the playing field justifies all the grueling work of practice and conditioning. The courtroom, the board room, the stage and playhouse, the church and pulpit—all are places of coming together for exercising private summonings of strength. In all of these instances, the performance represents but a fraction of the long hours of hard undramatic preparation. The students' immediate responses to the teacher are often gratifying, but the true criterion for judging classroom happenings lies in the learning that largely takes place outside.

5

Making Classes Work

There are some no-nonsense teachers who start class right at the bell, hold every class the full fifty minutes, never relax their grip. Such tight control may foster the delusion that every class is going well, and some of these teachers succeed or succeed often enough to look past the bad days. I prefer and advise more looseness in trying to make classes work. Maybe the best advice is still the phrase I once saw pasted on the inside of a chemistry professor's door: "Never have two bad ones in a row." Establishing a good atmosphere for a class is an important aspect of teaching well. Getting off to a good start is as important to that atmosphere as what comes after, and most of this chapter will focus on trying to define a class at the outset.

Skilled teachers know that any audience, even the captive one in the classroom, needs a short period for settling in. An anecdote connecting the teacher's and learners' lives to the subject matter is one of the best of many settling-in devices. Something read or seen, a movie, an item in the paper, a conversation, a trip remembered—the teacher should have a constantly renewed supply of associations to draw on. Ideally, they should be spontaneous or so well contrived as to appear offhand. While such anecdotes obviously and usefully help create the teacher's personality, they also define the subject matter and even the method of inquiry. A geologist bringing in a rock he has just found, an English teacher citing a particularly offensive jingle, a physicist reacting to a current example of an assault on the environment—these are not time-wasters, gimmicks to establish a false camaraderie, or digressions from important matters. They are necessities for establishing an atmosphere in the classroom that may make the rest of the hour reasonably productive.

There is another reason for stressing the importance of defining a class at the outset. Unlike most faculty members, students come into one class from other classes far removed in kind, character, and subject matter. The student who has just gone down the tube in a chemistry test is not immediately (or very soon) receptive to the events of the Napoleonic Wars. Or consider the student who gets a ticket on the way to school or who has to park in a faculty zone to make class at all or whose sex life is going well or poorly. Whatever a teacher can do to provide an easy transition from the student's real world to the artificial world of the classroom is likely to be appreciated and to aid learning.

The partial, often misleading impression the teacher makes at the beginning of a course may establish the attitude, response, and even tempo of the class for the rest of the term. Few teachers escape the disturbing experience of having a class take a set that makes both teaching and learning difficult. Often, it is difficult to determine why one class jells favorably, another adversely. Unable to discover a cause, the teacher has that much more difficult a time trying to get the class back on the right track. Faced with just such a situation some years ago—after many years of teaching and a dozen years of working with this particular course—I dismissed the class for a week, expressing as bluntly and dispassionately as I could my feeling that neither I nor the class was accomplishing much. I didn't know the cause, I said, welcoming anyone who disagreed to correct me. No one corrected me, and we all went off to meditate for a week. When we gathered again, we made a new start. Attitudes had changed, and the atmosphere improved markedly for the rest of the course.

Lest this example reinforce myths about the unfathomableness of teaching, let me specify some things I think went wrong (written comments from students at the end of the course supported my hunches). For one thing, although this was a class I had long been teaching, that year marked my return to the classroom after two years' leave. Second, this was 1972-73, a year marked by a change in the attitudes of students to college, authority, and their own futures. Third, it was spring quarter. Thinking back on it, I can readily see that I didn't pay enough attention to any of these things at the outset. Moreover, I didn't realize how firm an attitude I was bringing to the class. Part of the change I had experienced in those two years of leave was to become impatient with most of the written work I had customarily required in the course. Within a wider range, I shared with students of the sixties a resistance to teaching as it commonly went on: the teacher as authority figure, heavy emphasis on cognitive learning, a lack of independence and imagination shown by the students and accepted by the teacher. So my bias was plain enough to me: I wasn't going to hand out tough written assignments, force the students into the library, award and punish by the professional standards of my discipline. The students were going to have to use their own imaginations and intellects and desires to demonstrate that they were getting something out of the course.

I might have succeeded if I had made my attitudes sufficiently clear to the students, but making things quite that clear also went against my stance. As I found out after the class resumed, the students' attitudes were set just as firmly. Although the campus revolution was over, the Vietnam War was still dragging on, and these students hadn't been a part of either. They were bright students who had proved their ability by their high school grade-point averages (GPA's). They seemed to want a teacher who would lay it out and pour it on; they'd do everything asked and do it well, all the while making it clear that they really didn't give a damn.

A tortured analysis? Maybe. Oversimplified actually, if one considers for a moment the complexities of relationships among any group of humans brought into forced association for institutionally designed purposes. The main lesson I drew from the experience was the need to establish an understanding with a class at the outset.

Part of this can be done in a routine, check-list way, through providing and discussing a course outline that sets forth aims, requirements, and procedures. Students will invariably miss the teacher's loftier objectives and focus their questions on what the tests will be like and how the teacher grades. The teacher will have to mention the texts, find out whether students have them or can get them, talk about reading lists and library work, and take up other details of the course. Like it or not, the teacher will have to make periodic reminders and clarifications of all these things throughout the course. And even then, some students will never get the word. More and more, I think that intentions and expectations—stating objectives, if you will—should be written down as well as discussed in a useful give-and-take with the students. What the assignments are, when they are due, how much they count, what the tests will be like, what a given test will cover—these are matters worth putting down, so that both teacher and students are working under the same rules toward similar ends.

Important as these matters are, they are fairly easy to deal with. More difficult is the way in which a teacher establishes the temper of the class by walk and look and gesture, by anecdote or offhand remark, by the handling of questions—a temper for which the teacher is greatly, if not entirely, responsible. Here, I think, no check lists or set patterns or mimeographed sheets define the impression the teacher wants to make. Spontaneous actions are as telling as prepared statements. I don't intend to make new teachers terribly self-conscious about a matter ill-served by self-consciousness, however. "Be yourself" is as good advice for approaching a class as any. And if you have a crumby self? Then there's only one thing to do: Stay away from teaching.

But if you have a reasonable presence, a personality you and others can live with, is there anything else to be said? Some things may be useful, I think. Openness, for example, is good for teaching, and it has ways of making itself apparent to others. Some deliberate candor about likes and dislikes in classroom matters can go beyond course outlines and statements of objectives. Leaving a part of the class procedures open for students to decide is a defensible technique at any time, not just when students force the issue.

On the whole, teachers are too little aware of the expectations students bring with them. Not long ago, I established myself with a class far more firmly than I intended by casually saying that Thoreau's *A Week on the Concord and Merrimack* wasn't much of a book but I was assigning it anyhow. Two students came up after class to say they'd had teachers assign poor books before, but this was the first time they had ever heard a teacher admit it. That led to an excellent discussion in the next session of Thoreau's first book, written while he was still in his twenties, and, in later sessions, of these questions: What makes first books poor? What kinds of books might twenty-year-olds write? How do strong books follow from weak starts?

The fresh pleasure of beginning a new class makes it unnecessary to stress ways of welcoming the students in. If teachers find teaching pleasurable, they probably communicate that sense in one way or another to students. Small acts of grace like seeing that latecomers find a seat, acknowledging the confusions that go with beginning a class, dismissing the first session early, respecting the difficulties of getting texts, acknowledging the high costs of books, opening windows or pulling blinds —there are dozens of ways, by nature or by design, a teacher can establish a pleasant atmosphere. Ideally, I would have a teacher approach a class as a student of mine described her approach to a book, "as a well-wisher," an anticipator of pleasurable experiences.

At the University of Southern California, I once read, the faculty of psychology included a former gag-writer who promised to sprinkle dull lectures with chuckles. Both gag-writers and professors should be more respectful of stand-up comics if not of college teachers. And, as everyone who laughs should know, humor isn't that simple. Canned jokes, inappropriate jokes, old jokes, corny jokes, not just bad jokes, are no funnier in the classroom than anywhere else. Instead of shared pleasure, they create embarrassment, unease, and hostility. A sense of humor, which almost everyone prizes and claims to possess, is tricky to define. Indeed, the joke, as such, is somewhat suspect as part of the teacher's repertoire.

Nevertheless, humor is an excellent way to establish rapport with an audience, provided the humor is not forced, inappropriate, too obvious, or too subtle. Being funny is serious business, and guidance is as difficult as telling someone how to tell a joke. Probably the best general advice is to avoid telling "jokes." The best kind of academic humor grows naturally and spontaneously from the situation. Two recent and sensible attempts to discuss the use of humor in teaching and containing many references to other literature are Jean Civikly's "Humor and the Enjoyment of College Teaching" (Civikly, 1986b), and Howard Pollio's "Everything You Always Wanted to Know About Humor in the Classroom But Were Afraid to Ask" (1985/86).

Since teaching is so verbal, opportunities for verbal humor are always present. Anecdotal humor arises naturally from the necessary use of examples and illustrations. Self-disparaging humor particularly reaches student audiences because much of learning is solemn, professors often are pompous, and colleges presume to embrace a *higher* learning. Like many other forms of humor, the teacher's self-disparagement acknowledges the students' own difficulties, anxieties, and shortcomings. If a teacher doesn't enter the classroom with a quickness of mind, an eye for the incongruous, an ear for wit, a store of varied experience, and a spontaneous delight in the ridiculous, his or her teaching performance is not likely to be improved by a gag-writer's efforts. If a teacher has a too-ready wit, he or she may need a gag more than a gag-writer. So don't expect any further advice from me about how to be a genuinely humorous teacher. Use humor if you can, but only if you can do it well.

One of the most valuable lessons I ever learned about teaching was how to treat serious things lightly, without doing them disrespect, and thereby adding to their import. The lesson was particularly valuable to me since it spoke to my native facility for parody and satire, the range of comic effects that center on making fun of those things other people view seriously. The lesson came not from one teacher, but from several over a period of time, until in some reflective moment, I saw what was being done and how useful it was for a teacher. Gilbert Highet was a master of this technique, partly because he was both a serious

and a comic man. His Scottish background gave him the necessary grounding in solemnity; his studies of Juvenal grew out of
his own affinity for satire. He could be wittily and aptly dis-
respectful of many of the classics, but he never used wit for its
own sake. Rather the wit served to lay bare some vital aspect of
a work, some universal imperfection, to be laughed at to be
sure, but also to be sympathized with and recognized as part of
our own imperfections. Thus my own seriousness profited from
being able to see my struggles in perspective, forgiving of my
sins but inciting me to risk exposing myself to more.

A teacher, if it can be managed, should leave a student as
little confused at the beginning of a class hour as at the end.
Deliberate confusion, while it may be legitimately introduced
into a course, is seldom useful or excusable at the beginning of a
course. A common kind of confusion, which the teacher often
creates inadvertently at the beginning, is a disharmony between
the instructor's manner and his or her demands. A casual, welcoming manner may stamp the teacher as an easy mark until later
experience proves that he or she is both demanding and rigorous.
A more serious disharmony occurs when the teacher is one whose
words and manner suggest that he or she is open to student suggestions but who in fact runs the course strictly by his or her
own rules. There is also the teacher who preaches order and objectivity but who proves to be both disorderly and unfair. Grades,
more than anything else, are likely to cause students to feel that
a teacher has betrayed them, or, less often, has treated them
better than they deserve. Ideally, teachers should be sufficiently
self-aware to maintain some consistency between their manner
as persons and their conduct of the course as teachers.

Forms of address between students and teacher help
establish the classroom atmosphere. Individual campuses usually have their own customs, although these customs change with
the times and no campus maintains consistency among the
myriad classes, courses, and professors. The new teacher arriving
on campus will simply have to find out what form of address
fits the local customs, suits his or her own ease and style, and best
serves to create a useful relationship with students. My own custom, picked up in an earlier day in a variety of schools, was to

use Mr. and Miss, but the advent of Ms. and changes in the kinds
of students as well as in their attitudes make me less certain
about terms of address. When I was young enough to call students by their first name that was not the custom. Having
passed through a period when the whole world seemed to be on
a first-name basis, I use first names more often now and my advancing age probably sanctions it. But I am cautious here, for
few things irritate me more than telephone solicitors starting off
by saying, "Hi, Ken. This is Ralph . . ." As to what students
should call the professor, I have let them wander among Professor, Mister, Doctor, Sir, and the right and wrong last name. I
give cues, express preferences, occasionally discuss the question
as a relevant matter of language and social behavior, but I seldom prescribe, since the matter of addressing me and my colleagues is the students' problem and part of their learning. Former graduate students, now close personal friends, still call me
Doctor, just as some current undergraduates use my first name
without, apparently, feeling that is improper.

In truth, I am bad at names, first or last, a defect more
easily acknowledged than corrected. Remembering students'
names is a desirable professional skill, but how one acquires facility has its mysteries. There is, however, no dearth of suggestions of how to go about it. The seating chart is the handiest
way, almost indispensable for large classes if keeping students
straight seems desirable at all. For me, however, the seating
chart is too mechanical; its small gain in identity is offset by the
reminder of mass education it reinforces. The seating chart puts
all the bodies in their proper places for systematic, regular learning. Somehow, learning students' names under these circumstances seems less than personal; prisoners and army recruits may
be just as happy when the warden or sergeant doesn't know them
by name. At least two other alternative ways occur to me. One
is to practice the names assiduously at the outset of a course
and to use mnemonic devices well known to psychologists: placing students in a context, setting up associations, forcing oneself to use names even at the risk of making mistakes. The other
method is to strengthen physical associations by acquaintance
with the students' work. My own powers of memory, I am now

convinced, are visual and verbal. If I get large quantities of written work from students, I tend to remember their names. Getting the students into the context of discussing their work has the advantage of going beyond remembering names toward actually knowing them as individuals.

Closeness and intimacy may not be precisely the goal of remembering names or of establishing rapport with students. One justification of institutionalized education may be the separation it provides between student and teacher. If it were not for this separation, some teachers would be swallowed up by students. Other teachers are well served by structures that inhibit their own compulsions to identify with particular students. Maintaining a sensitivity that keeps one from intruding into the students' personal lives without appearing to be aloof, cold, or uncaring is a manner that has much to recommend it. Considering the number of students most teachers encounter, close personal acquaintances with many of them is impossible, regardless of the teacher's manner. Some students will break past a formidable professional reserve; others will remain unapproachable. Being available to students is still the best way of signifying the teacher's genuine concern. The teacher whose door is open, literally not figuratively, some hours of every day; who is even on campus every day; who willingly talks with students after class; who is not always hurriedly rushing to or from important concerns that crowd students out; who finds ways of affecting students' learning outside the classroom—such a teacher's acts will speak louder than any testimony.

Outside of oxygen and maybe light, the two most important things in a classroom are teachers and students. Of course, books and other such equipment are important, but they can be more profitably encountered and put to use outside of class. As for the ideas generated, information exchanged and absorbed, a subject matter in its abstract form, they are dependent, within the classroom, on teacher and student.

I don't intend to contribute to arguments about teaching students *or* subject matter. Strong opinions on either side miss the point. Any teacher must embrace and contend with both. The classroom remains the place where both teachers and students get most of their ideas and impressions about each other. Students have a variety of ways of describing a teacher's characteristic way of going about his or her tasks. When they identify a professor as laid back, or a warm and fuzzy, or a hard-nose, they are probably saying more about a teaching style than about specific practices.

I have written at length about teaching styles in *The Aims of College Teaching* (1983), and edited a collection of essays by others in *Improving Teaching Styles* (1980). In the former I have linked *style* with *character,* endorsing Gibbon's phrase, "Style is the image of character." Nor will I back away from my own assertion: "Without character, a teacher is more ill equipped than if he or she had not mastered particle physics, Shakespeare's tragedies, or harmony and counterpoint" (Eble, 1983, p. 18). And if both these make contemporary teachers uncomfortable, then at least let them heed Carlyle's words: "Make an honest man of yourself, and then you can be sure there is one less rascal in the world."

Here, I will merely emphasize the important points made elsewhere:

- The characteristic way a teacher goes about his or her work may be usefully regarded as a teaching style.
- A teaching style is a matter of both one's natural bent and consciously developed attitudes and actions.
- The intersection between a teacher's style and the disposition for learning that students bring to a classroom is an important consideration for teaching effectively.
- Acquiring a teaching style or adapting or changing one's style can be assisted in many ways: from the literature identifying teaching styles, from observing and being observed by other teachers, from videotaping one's teaching performance, from giving attention to the many ways students respond to one's teaching, and perhaps most of all from giving the way we go about teaching the attention it deserves.

Inquiries into teaching styles may acquaint one with related attempts to classify personality types. The Myers-Briggs

Type Indicator, derived from Jung, may be the best known (Myers and Myers, 1980). Starting from basic divisions between *extroverts* and *introverts, sensing* and *intuition, thinking* and *feeling, perceiving* and *judging,* the inventory arrives at sixteen types. A description of one category, taken from *Introduction to Type* (Myers, 1980, pp. 6–7), indicates something of the complete typology:

"ISTJ means an introvert liking sensing and thinking and a mainly judging attitude toward the outer world. . . . Serious, quiet, earn success by concentration and thoroughness. Practical, orderly, matter-of-fact, logical, realistic and dependable. See to it that everything is well organized. Take responsibility. Make up their own minds as to what should be accomplished and work toward it steadily, regardless of protests or distractions. Live their outer life more with thinking, inner with sensing."

The usefulness that this may have for teachers is both to help see ourselves as others see us and to make us more sensitive to students' being like us or unlike us in these respects. Obviously, if there are patterns of ways in which we perceive and react to the world, such patterns affect both learning and teaching.

The most influential book of the past twenty years with respect to studying even more closely the way college students respond to learning is William Perry's *Forms of Intellectual and Ethical Development in the College Years* (1970). By now Perry's "scheme" has become well known among college teachers. It too has the attraction of ordering the splendid but troubling diversity with which students confront their teachers in and outside the classroom.

In a very simplified brief form, Perry's findings are that college students develop both cognitively and morally from a position of dependence upon authority and a tendency to see their learning in terms of Right and Wrong to one of commitment in which relativism has replaced absolutes. Dualism gives way to multiplicity, diversity supports relativism, commitments get made in the face of both multiplicity and relativism.

To put this in terms teachers may find easily recognizable in their students, the beginning student often expects the professor to be the authority, and easily remains dependent on factual information presented in the most organized, authoritative way. He or she may be troubled by a very characteristic remark of many professors, "It all depends." At the same time, there are great gains for many first-year students in finding that the teacher is not always right, that there are matters that are neither wrong nor right, that teaching and learning break out of previously constraining patterns.

The classic meaning of *sophomore* anticipates by centuries Perry's major second stage. Past freshman year, the student may be so exhilarated by being freed from "yes" and "no," "true" and "false" answers that he or she begins to sample and then wallow in relativism. "So the prof admits there are no right answers, then anyone's opinion is as good as anyone else's." Perry traces the transition to and embracing of relativism (the acceptance of "multiplicity" is another way of describing it) through four or five progressive "positions."

By the junior or senior year, the simple hold on either of the first two stages is being replaced by recognition of the complexity not only of how and what we know but of what may or should follow. This leads in the final positions of the student's development to a commitment, tentative, changeable, but capable of being acted on. "Contextualism" is another word introduced in this position, standing for the student's recognition that as students develop, knowledge takes on contexts and they see themselves in contexts.

One of the engaging things about Perry's book is the transcripts of the responses Harvard students made to their education, the basis of Perry's work. To reinforce the descriptions just made, here is a sampling of these comments identified with the student's class and Perry's positions:

Freshman: "When I went to my first lecture, what the man said was just like God's word, you know. I believed everything he said, because he was a professor and he's a Harvard professor, and this was, this was a respected position" (p. 61). Position 1.

Sophomore: "And now I realize it . . . as I say, there's a lot of answers for a certain question, and ah, by reasoning things out you can come to a variation of the answers, uhuh, and—ah, it depends upon which way you're looking at it. That's right. I mean there's no . . . you can't come right out and point to one thing and say this caused the Industrial Revolution. And that's what I was looking for last year—one sentence that would tell me what caused the Revolution" (p. 102). Position 4.

Senior: "There was one other thing I expected—I expected that when I got to Harvard—I was—ah slightly ahead of my time in that I was an atheist before I got here—I came up here expecting that Harvard would teach me one universal truth . . . (pause). Took me quite a while to figure out . . . that if I was going for a universal truth or something to believe in, it had to come from within me, and I don't know whether Harvard taught me that or not" (pp. 137-138). Position 6.

Like all development theories, Perry's raises many questions. That it describes every student and every stage and a uniform path of development is not to be expected. That it confirms many teachers' observations is obvious.

Its specific usefulness for teachers may be these:

It reminds one that resistance to learning may be other than to a teacher or a subject or the fact of going to college. It may be that students are likely operating at a different position from that of the teacher.

A teacher has both an obligation to respect the stage of development a student may be in and assist that student in moving to the next stage.

A teacher needs to recognize that while cognitive and ethical development do not necessarily go hand in hand, they are often related. A student is at most times wrestling both with a subject and with personal values.

A teacher can use many of Perry's insights in many ways. Unity and multiplicity, challenge and response, fact and opinion, degrees of truth and belief, relativism, commitment, procrastination, avoidance, retreat are all related to teachers teaching and students learning. The more we know about how students learn, the more likely we are to teach effectively.

6

The Lecture as Discourse

The best general advice to the teacher who would lecture well is still, "Don't lecture." That is, for most of teaching, to think in terms of discourse—talk, conversation—rather than lecture. Second, respect silence, both the teacher's and the student's. Third, shift from a total dependency on verbalizing to other means of animating, illustrating, and reinforcing talk.

The lecture has persisted in college teaching because it is the easiest thing to do; it is the accepted thing; it is the safest. For these reasons, professors are likely to go on lecturing. Fortunately, lecturing does shift to many forms of interacting discourse. Some of these forms are already formalized into standard procedures as common as the formal lecture: the lecture-discussion, the lecture-laboratory, the lecture-recitation, the lecture with problem sets, the lecture-demonstration. All of these procedures use the lecture as only one part of a basic teaching technique. There are times when the teacher had best be talking, when, for example, setting forth information with precision and economy is better than trying to elicit such information from the students. Mediocre discussion classes, poor individual student reports, ineffectual panel presentations are no improvement upon a teacher's mediocre lecturing.

As has been pointed out countless times (for example, by Gerschenkron, 1976), the lecture was outmoded by the invention of printing and by cheap and easy access to printed works. But four hundred years later, the lecturer is still accepted and

68

casually adapted to classroom television. The book did not sweep out the lecture any more than television has swept out books, for the simple reason that human beings remain responsive to all forms of intercourse with other consenting humans. The book lacks what television lacks: face-to-face confrontation with other talking, gesturing, thinking, feeling humans. Thus, the live lecture, despite its shortcomings, has reason for its continued use.

Teachers need to recognize the basic attractiveness of the lecture before they attempt to attack or defend it. University lecturing of the commonest kind is not the meticulously composed public address, nor is it even the speech that demands extensive advance preparation or the use of visual aids and demonstrations. No, it is the bare lecture, what a skilled teacher carries to class inside his or her skull with nothing for support but a book or two under the arm and notes in hand. The lecture has the same primitive simplicity for the student as for the teacher. It guarantees a stated amount of academic credit if the student will but sit still so many hours a week for so many weeks and do such work as required. Administrators find it easy to accept the lecture, for it keeps track of students and faculty and can be expanded and contracted at will. Delivered by a professor with a high degree of competence, classroom lectures may well achieve the objectives peculiar to their substance and impact: conveying information to a large audience with some expectation that this information is being received, and stimulating students to pursue specific or related learning on their own.

Of the professors I had at Columbia Graduate School in the fifties who taught almost exclusively by lecturing, I can single out only two highly effective lecturers. Most of the others were passable; some few were awful, though not in all respects. In many years of observing teachers since, the skillful lecturers I have observed were above all keenly aware of and responsive to their audiences. I cannot think of many lecturers who didn't know the subject matter immediately before them, though I could have been spared some lecturers' dwelling on how much other scholars didn't know. Most were reasonably well organized, and in one instance, a night class, a student helped out a professor who wasn't by shouting out, "What the hell are you talking about?"

What distinguished the most highly skilled lecturers was their ability not only to embrace content but to justify the enterprise by their skill in projecting both content and presence. Their priceless impact was to stimulate and renew, making up for much else that was drudgery, turning for a time solitary pursuits into social occasions. Though some of these lectures were essentially formal and delivered to large numbers, they had the effect of enlightened and spontaneous discourse.

For the most part, teachers everywhere enter into lecturing too lightly, pay too little attention to what good lectures might accomplish. They are even more remiss in failing to consider what makes up the skills of a really good lecturer. Perhaps the reason for this is that college and university teachers show a marked suspicion toward rhetoric, accord a low ranking in the academic hierarchy to speech teachers and speech subjects. These attitudes persist despite the fact that most teachers can't escape being rhetoricians of sorts. "Too often we lapse into thinking that because we communicate," Jean Civikly writes, "we necessarily do it well. We stop questioning or reflecting on *how* we do it and stop evaluating *how well* we do it" (1986a, p. 1). Speechifying is equivocally regarded only when someone else is making the speech.

Speech is a basic tool, the chief means by which teachers attempt to reach students, and command of voice is as serviceable a part of professional competence as command of subject matter. Still, I think Lowman (1984, p. 75) is right in saying, "Almost all instructors take their speech for granted" and "few college teachers evaluate the effectiveness of their speaking voices or actively work to improve them." If an effective manner of speaking must be worked at, so must any other aspect of professional competence, and the work necessary to bringing voice qualities to acceptable levels requires but a fraction of the time customarily given to gaining mastery of a discipline. Teachers should obviously have voice qualities and diction that are reasonably effective—even pleasing—to others. Persons proposing to earn a living by using their voices have obligations to develop force and control and to overcome stridencies, nasalities, and the like.

No one is demanding an orator's voice or even the smooth delivery of the ordinary television announcer. One can get by with a higher pitch than one might desire, with less force than would fill an amphitheater, with some peculiarities of dialect, and with less than impeccable diction. But there are limits to the allowances that should be made:

- Students should not have to strain all the time to hear what the speaker is saying.
- Students should not have to puzzle over just what it is they have heard.
- Students should not have to guess at stress and emphasis and organization of sentences.
- Students should not be maddened by verbal tics nor dulled by repeated *uhs* and *ers,* the most common verbal affliction.
- Students should not be able to make book on the number of pet words, cant, or jargon that will occur in a class hour, or if they can, the odds should be more like 5 to 3 than 6 to 1.
- Students should not be subjected to a voice emanating from the blackboard or the far windows or the recesses of a suit or dress.

Pace and timing are important qualities of verbal delivery as well as aspects of shaping lectures and classes. Timing is probably harder to develop than a reasonable pace for normal speaking. Professional comics all possess remarkable timing. Delivering a successful monologue, telling a joke, building on a single joke all depend upon timing. Teachers should back off from saying "I'm no comedian," and recognize that a teacher's verbal art shares the basic necessities of catching and holding a listener's attention, of providing emphasis and direction, and of leading up to a key moment and striking home. Teachers I have observed strike me as often being too static, or too little aware of the impact that gestures and other movements of face and body can have.

I am not trying to conjure up mechanical men and women

with trained corporation voices and gestures. That specter is more imagined than real anyhow, for that supposedly indistinguishable array of M.C.'s, announcers, stand-up comics, and other entertainers speak in no single pattern. The best of them rise to prominence on the strength of their individuality. So teachers need not worry about effacing themselves in finding an individual but effective range of voice, diction, gesture, and movement.

There is no easy way of separating preparing a lecture from lecturing. Often the best time to prepare a lecture is immediately after a class. There is a good reason for seizing on this opportunity and a justification for not having two classes in a row. The realities of a class are most apparent right when it's over, realities far different from a lecture on paper or even a tape-recorded lecture played back later. What worked, what didn't, what one wanted to do, what one will do next time—all these are vitally important to shaping effective lectures. And considering everything that can get in the way, preparing classes when the urge is strongest is virtually a necessity.

Preparing the lecture is important, but it must accommodate spontaneity as well as planning. A written script intended to be read is the worst possible preparation. "Written things," Mark Twain advised, "are not for speech; their form is literary; they are stiff, inflexible and will not lend themselves to happy and effective delivery with the tongue" (Neider, 1959, p. 176). If one has time and can work that way, preparing a formal script may be excusable, but only as a first step. Certainly a script should not be read, and committing a script to memory is both impractical and unwise. Reducing the text to a timed outline or sketch is probably the best general practice.

A working sketch for a good lecture should block out a small number of points to be emphasized—two or three points can be sufficient; a dozen is surely too many. Selecting effective illustrations and examples is of great importance, for they add interest and variety as well as substance. A generous amount of time should be set aside for them, for too often much of the work of gathering excellent materials is wasted in having to crowd them into the lecture. Time should also be allowed for responses from students, and the pace of the lecture can be set by anticipating where these responses are likely to be most effective. We almost always tend to include too much in the lecture and force ourselves to discard some materials, rearrange the outline on the spot, or hold it over for the next hour, thereby getting farther behind day by day. Or, more commonly, we crowd it in, losing focus and emphasis. The classics scholar who, according to Nicholas Murray Butler, covered only 246 lines of *Medea* in a term (Highet, 1950, p. 75) still has his or her descendants among us. But they are probably less numerous than the professors in almost every field who cover the first half of a course in a decent way but then cram the rest of the course into the last week or two of class.

Even then, the results may be no worse than those of the mechanical ticking off of necessary topics that constitutes "covering" the material. Coverage deceives the teacher about learning as much as it aids simple organization. A good part of the college curriculum and the teacher's efforts are weakened by the assumptions made about the topics that must be covered and by the expedients adopted to get them all in. The preparation of an individual lecture, like the harder task of preparing a class through a term, demands an intelligent, imaginative, and ruthless power of selection. No good teacher ever included everything that should have gone in the course; wisdom is in part learning what to leave out. "Every year," a biology teacher told me, "I teach less and less." As surprising as that statement is in an explosive field like biology, I do not doubt that the teacher was both honest and wise. She was not merely keeping up with her field, but keeping her field, or the part of it she was teaching, cultivated and in bounds. The most successful language teacher I ever had spent perhaps fifteen minutes of each class telling us what we had to know and answering such questions as might stand in the way of learning it by the next class period. Thus he pared away unnecessary learning, the stuff of little use and much confusion which can plague beginning language study. The rest of the period he talked, mostly about France, more as a good conversationalist than as a lecturer. We had the feeling that we could talk, too, and we did talk when we had something to say. Almost offhand, we learned French.

Sound preparation involves not only gathering material,

but also throwing it away. It involves some attention to beginnings, even though the specific beginning of a lecture may occur on the way to class or arise from a lucky accident or exchange. But beyond these opening grace notes that allow a class to settle in, there should be another beginning, the setting of the topics for the day or the posing of leading questions that might be answered during the hour. The ways of beginning a lecture are as numerous as the ways of beginning a sentence. Notes in handout form, a sketch of the day's work on the blackboard, a jotting down of key points—these are all useful to setting a direction at the outset.

Lack of preparation can undermine students' confidence in a teacher, but overpreparation can have adverse effects as well. Every teacher remembers splendid classes that were put together at the last minute and on the run. The phenomenon is not as mysterious as it might appear, for somewhere prior to that hasty gathering together of today's materials usually lies a long and arduous preparation, not just for one class, but for the learning that is within an experienced teacher's command. Similarly, the common fault of overpreparing consists of having too much to try to get across and having too much that lacks the vitality of knowledge "fresh drawn from the sea." Beginning teachers may be comforted by hearing from experienced teachers that there never is sufficient time to prepare. Early or late, teachers will find, whether they admit it or not, they never will be able to keep up, never read all the books they need or want or plan to, never will write out all the things they have in mind, never will feel quite comfortable that they know enough, and never know much.

Now, almost at the end of the century, is a good time to add something about the explosion of knowledge which is another aspect of never being able to keep up. The metaphor is an interesting one. Like "the cutting edge," and "the fast track," all are horrifying in their implications if one considers how explosives blow people up and knives cut them apart and speed shatters tranquility and order. Yet academics treat them as benign and lending excitement to a choice of life not exactly on the fast track.

As related to lecturing, the point is that everything cannot be included, never could be included, the state of knowledge at any one time outrunning the capacity to reduce it to words. A lecturer has to be ruthlessly as well as wisely selective. There *are* facts and ideas and examples that are more important than others, just as there are books and subjects and whole areas of knowledge more important than others. The lecturer's specific task, like the scholar's task at large, is to bring some part of knowledge, too big in its unselected vastness at any period of time, into a manageable form. For on the other side of this equation are the human beings listening to someone lecture. There is only so much that can be absorbed, whether we are in some imagined time of comfortably controlled knowledge or in one where it is exploding all around us.

Once begun, the lecture must have a body. The human body will do as an analogy to describe its proper kind. It should have a variety of parts both independent of, and dependent upon, other parts; much substance; density and lightness; its own pulse and rhythm; warmth—all the parts and attributes constituting a distinctive whole. We can usefully expand the analogy beyond human forms, for some lectures should be shaggy monsters, sports, and freaks. Above all, the lecture must live, vigorously, engagingly, and surprisingly.

I am reluctant to go much beyond this analogy in offering advice about the body of a lecture. The subject makes a difference, the audience too, as do the weather, yesterday's lecture, and the one to follow. But as general advice applicable to a wide range of college teaching, I suggest that the body of the lecture be broken into distinctive parts. For example, ten minutes of precisely defining, exemplifying, and relating a basic concept might be followed by ten minutes of questions and answers about the concept followed by ten minutes of applications involving both teacher and students. The chances are that a planned-for thirty minutes will fill the hour, particularly if time is reserved at the end to bring things together, to recapitulate main ideas, and to set directions for the next session. It requires rare eloquence and a particularly good day to spin out fifty minutes straight without some division of the lecture into parts.

Even then, the teacher needs some concrete evidence that the students are really along on the teacher's trip.

Lecturing creates the temptation to set one's voice on "play" and forget everything else. Chronological, historical, and connected discourse still needs the breaking up that necessitates headings and paragraphs and topic sentences in writing. Again, in preparing such a lecture, one should plan for pauses and interruptions and a diversity of presentation. The instructor should have thought out where and how far he or she wants to go, calculated that there is a reasonable chance of getting there, and accepted as a part of the plan that other ideas, objections, preferences, and confusions will arise.

The blackboard is still the handiest complement to the lecture, so commonplace that we may forget its importance. An early enthusiast, Josiah Bumstead, wrote in 1841, "The inventor or introducer of the blackboard deserves to be ranked among the best contributors to learning and science, if not among the greatest benefactors of mankind" (Anderson, 1952, p. 18). The blackboard provides the simplest means of on-the-spot organization and emphasis, with which the teacher can focus and shift the class's attention. It forces the lecturer into physical movement, and remains the best of audio-visual aids, not as flashy as slides or film strips nor as neat as an opaque projector, but less likely to tax a professor's ability to use and even to master it. And, except for want of chalk and erasers, the blackboard never breaks down.

Endings are, like beginnings, necessary parts of any composition. Most lectures are too long, and stopping before the hour should be a much more common practice than it is. Even the most fascinating lecturer cannot get away with always holding students after the bell. Students often have classes back to back, and it's an act of courtesy as well as wisdom to stop on time. Though I am as much an offender in this respect as anyone, I have come to realize how little students gain by my earnest attempts to fill out a last sentence. I cannot think of an instance when the students would not have been better served by my simply stopping at whatever noun, adverb, verb, or preposition happened to coincide with the ringing of the bell.

Even informal, discursive class hours need to come to an end. That is, the students need a sense of having reached some destination, even though, as is the case in most college lecturing, it is a temporary one. The ponderous summary, the "Now, what have we learned, Dick and Jane?" is surely to be avoided as much as giving no signal at all or having the class drift off by ones and twos. My most embarrassing moments as a speech-maker have usually involved endings, promising to be brief and not being, coming to the dying fall and feeling compelled to add one more thought and provoking a tentative scattering of final applause from a sentence that is still a paragraph or two from the end.

The kind of informal, discursive lecturing I have been discussing, varied during the term by other means of stimulating learning, is likely to be a college teacher's main standby. Let me move to the end of this chapter by telling of an attempt I made to deliver a deliberately bad lecture.

Clearly, the attempt provided the most entertaining morning I had in my years as a supposed expert on college teaching. I considered doing it because I felt obligated to demonstrate effective ways of teaching as well as to talk about them. But I also did it because I had long been delighted with Mark Twain's account of a performance he included in his lecture repertoire. The entire lecture consisted of an anecdote leading to a single lame joke, earnestly and desperately repeated to make the audience get it. Twain describes his technique (Neider, 1959, pp. 144-145):

> I told it in a level voice, in a colorless and monotonous way, without emphasizing any word in it and succeeded in making it dreary and stupid to the limit. Then I paused and looked very much pleased with myself and as if I expected a burst of laughter. Of course there was no laughter, nor anything resembling it. . . . I tried to look embarrassed and did it very well. For a while I said nothing, but stood fumbling with my hands in a sort of mute appeal to the audience for compassion. Many did pity

me—I could see it. But I could also see that the rest
were thirsting for blood. I presently began again
and stammered awkwardly along with some more
details of the overland trip. Then I began to work
up toward my anecdote again with the air of a person who thinks he did not tell it well the first time
and who feels that the house will like it the next
time, if told with a better art.

Later in his life, he tried the trick on a New York audience (p.
146):

It was as deadly an ordeal as ever I have been
through in the course of my checkered life. I never
got a response of any kind until I had told that
juiceless anecdote in the same unvarying words five
times; then the house saw the point and annihilated
the heart-breaking silence with a most welcome
crash. It revived me, and I needed it, for if I had
had to tell it four more times I should have died—
but I would have done it, if I had had to get somebody to hold me up.

In my own case, I wanted to show convincingly that
there is much agreement about what constitutes effective and
ineffective teaching and even more agreement about what is a
good or bad lecture. I had experience enough with bad lectures
—my own and others—to sketch out the rudiments of one a
half-hour before I was to speak. The audience was right, about
two hundred college teachers at the third session of a two-day
conference. I was following two other experts who had spoken
the previous day on aspects of teaching. Few in the audience
knew me or had any reason to suspect that I might set out to
deceive them. Nevertheless, delivering a bad lecture by design
is no easy matter. For one thing, not making contact with the
audience is a necessity, yet maintaining that contact is the only
way you have of knowing whether you have established the
authenticity of the lecture or are just making a damn fool of

yourself over an extended period of time. Length also contributes to badness. The purposely bad lecturer must drone on long
enough to suggest the interminability of bad lecturing, but
briefly enough to escape physical harm. The rest, I think, comes
distressingly easy, the *ahs* and *uhs,* the dwelling on insignificant
details, the circumlocutions and imprecisions. In fact, that part
has its difficulties, too, for as one goes along, the deliberately
bad parts begin to sound just like one's ordinary manner.

In any event, this lecture began as an excursion into a
wholly fictitious historical account of efforts to evaluate teaching. I only got to the eighteenth century, had to skip the seven-
teenth century altogether. The audience was taken in. After
eight or nine minutes, I pulled my head up out of my notes and
said in a normal tone, "Have you ever heard anything like this?"
Someone in a far corner of the room said loudly enough for
everyone to hear, "Yeah! Yesterday afternoon!"

As a part of this exercise, I compiled a list of characteristics that distinguished the badness of this lecture. They can
serve as a framework for my concluding remarks about lecturing
well:

1. Lack of introduction to the subject or to the speaker's
    style, attitudes, or objectives.
2. Lack of contact with audience.
3. Fixed posture with attention fixed on notes.
4. Monotonous voice with little emphasis and force.
5. No references to present context or broader subjects.
6. Failure to respect audience's knowledge or interests.
7. Displays of false modesty about self and subject.
8. Repeated hesitations just short of fumbling.
9. Little sense of time passing but insistence upon proceed-
    ing in an orderly manner.
10. Preoccupation with historical background to neglect of
    subject at hand.
11. Use of arcane terms whether or not the audience is famil-
    iar with them.
12. Appeals to historical, classical, and expert authority.
13. Use of learned quotations.

14. Excessive qualification of terms.
15. Reference to materials not available to audience.
16. Private quarrels with other authorities over esoteric points.
17. Sense of audience impatience with performance, gestures toward doing something about it but with no real modification of voice, pace, emphasis.
18. A dutiful interest in subject conveyed as expertise in trivial matters.

There are other possibilities for lecturing badly, a splendid variety of bad lectures to be given. But in concluding this chapter, we face the question directly: How does one lecture well? I have not often let myself be pinned down on this question, both because I distrust the lecture as a generally effective form of instruction and distrust myself whenever I am tempted to say, "This is the way to do it." Nevertheless, lecturing well is certainly preferable to lecturing poorly, and there are some teachers who may be served by undisguised "how-to" advice. Asking only that the reader recognize the limitations of simple, direct answers, the following points are the ones I think most important to lecturing well.

First, fit the material to the time at your disposal. Restrict your aim to less than a handful of primary topics and consider specific ways of engaging the audience in each one. Do not elaborate overly much nor introduce important matters that leave the audience grasping for particulars. Conduct your scholarly arguments and pursue your peculiar obsessions in places other than the lecture.

Second, seek hard and unrelentingly for precise examples and illustrations and for ways of breaking up a single presentational mode. Take advantage of physical presence and movement, and employ the blackboard and other such devices.

Third, begin by stimulating the interest of the audience. Alluding to the personal or to the world outside, arousing curiosity, providing surprise, and using casual humor are some of the ways of enhancing beginnings. What might work for an opening day of class may not work the day after a tough exam. Sensitivity to the mood of the class and a variety of ways of responding to that mood increase the chance of involving an audience day after day.

Fourth, in following the sketch that comes from advance preparation, develop an ability to improvise and to sustain an improvisational quality even in a carefully structured presentation.

Fifth, provide the audience with frequent breathing spaces and opportunities for questions. Better to talk too little and stop short than go on too long.

Sixth, provide an ending for every lecture but maintain a continuity with what has gone before and what lies ahead.

Seventh, develop and use a range of voice, gestures, and physical movement that is appropriate to your style, to the material, and to the occasion and that reinforces content, fixes attention, and stimulates an audience. Listen to yourself and root out mannerisms and affectations.

Eighth, be guided by the living audience and the most pressing need of striking up discourse with as many as possible. You are both host and guest.

A final word should be said specifically about the audience for our lectures. Perry's work, cited in Chapter Five, should remind a teacher that students vary widely in their responses to what we teachers do. A professor capable of well-organized lecturing may find students, particularly beginning ones, quite willing to accept that mode of teaching, not because he or she does it particularly well, but because it matches their stage of dependency on authority and a wrong or right world. How different this is from a young English professor's opening of a class described to me by one of his students. On the first day, he came in with a heavy lecture meticulously penned on note cards. After a brief introduction, he began reading through the cards, and the students began taking notes as fast as they could. Suddenly he stopped, threw the note cards in the wastebasket, and said that if that was the kind of class they wanted, they should check out at once. Then he turned to a live discussion which forced the students out of their passivity, and pushed them at least one step toward engaging not only with the subject matter but with their own learning.

I am not saying a lecture is incapable of stirring students out of a passive stance, of moving them forward in terms of Perry's stages of intellectual growth. But when everything is in the hands of the lecturer, it is easy to forget not only what the audience actually is, but that the lecture in mode and style and substance should also stimulate students' general intellectual growth.

I am still struck, after two decades of making speeches across the country, by how often a good speech prepared in my own study is not quite the right speech for an in-fact audience somewhere else. That has caused me to build in some looseness, some ways of quickly testing the audience and of adapting on the spot. I recommend the practice to any classroom lecturer.

All of what I have said applies equally well to discussion, the subject of the next chapter. In discussion, the group itself can help determine how this method matches any participant's stage of development. But insofar as discussion does not proceed in a linear fashion or deal with certainties, it may be difficult to initiate among those more comfortable with the lecture. Deciding on the appropriateness of either method then is both a matter of respecting where a student may be in his or her response to learning and of encouraging a student's intellectual growth beyond what he or she may be most comfortable with.

7

Discussion

Discussion covers as wide a range of teaching activities as lecturing does. I have seen some very good discussion classes and some very poor ones. I think that developing the ability to conduct effective discussion classes is even more difficult than learning to lecture effectively, although that belief may simply reflect my own preferences and abilities.

One can begin thinking about discussion techniques by first clarifying one's teaching aims and then asking how discussion can help achieve them. In some classes, discussion will dominate, to be set aside only occasionally for other ways of exchanging and transmitting information. In other classes, discussion may be a weekly opportunity for students to deal with course content. In many classes, lecture and discussion will be mixed according to the instructor's judgment and the temper of the class.

There are a number of common reasons for using discussion. All relate to moving the student from passive learning to active participation. "Other things being equal," Wilbert McKeachie writes, "small classes are probably more effective than large, discussions than lectures, and student-centered discussions more effective than instructor-centered discussions for goals of retention, application, problem solving, attitude change, and motivation for future learning" (1971, p. 7). It is a good idea to give serious attention to McKeachie's conclusions, which are based on careful examination of numerous studies. The outcomes he singles out are basic to the aims of many classes in many different disciplines. In addition, students prefer discussion in one form or another, a fact that is doubtlessly related to the effectiveness of learning. Observing teaching as I have arouses my admiration for the millions of students who sit before professors day after day. I wouldn't do it, not without getting paid. Being able to take part in a discussion relieves some of the tedium that lecturing forces upon students. For an observer, staying out of a discussion is almost as hard as sitting through a lecture.

The place of discourse in education has been eloquently described by Michael Oakeshott in "Poetry as a Voice in the Conversation of Mankind" (1962, pp. 198-199):

> As civilized human beings, we are the inheritors, neither of an inquiry about ourselves and the world, nor of an accumulating body of information, but of a conversation begun in the primeval forest and extended and made more articulate in the course of centuries. It is a conversation which goes on both in public and within each of ourselves. Of course there is argument and inquiry and information, but wherever these are profitable they are recognized as passages in this conversation. . . . Conversation is not an enterprise designed to yield an extrinsic profit, a contest where the winner gets a prize, nor is it an activity of exegesis; it is an unrehearsed intellectual adventure. . . . Education, properly speaking, is an initiation into the skill and partnership of this conversation in which we learn to recognize the voices, to distinguish the proper occasions of utterance, and in which we acquire the intellectual and moral habits appropriate to conversation.

It is in this spirit that I would advise teachers to develop the vital skills of talking and listening to others.

Only if one holds to the extreme view that the teacher's role is one of unquestioned authority and expertise can one rule out discussion. But even then, the need to clarify concepts with the students and to ascertain whether signals sent are in fact being received moves one away from being strictly a transmitter of information. Discussion, properly speaking, may not be necessary, but interaction with the learner is hard to avoid, and that interaction is the cornerstone for discussion. Few teachers confine their role to either transmitting information or establishing authority. Providing a context where the students can voice their specific questions, confusions, and doubts and where they can put ideas together, frame hypotheses, and be assisted in their ability to learn on their own is a responsibility all teachers must accept.

Admittedly, discussion as a central teaching method better fits some classes and some disciplines than others. In the humanities, the essential humanistic posture is discursive. Discussion is an essential part of the social and political process. Not having discussion in the social and political sciences would be like ruling out hook or line in fishing. In the fine arts, outside skills courses, discussion is as important to students as an audience is to a performer. Even in the theoretical sciences, discussion is necessary not only because of the difficulty of understanding theoretical concepts but also because in many basic areas the concepts themselves are still in the stage of being discussed. Even in studio courses, where the teacher enjoys a dialogue with individual students who are focused on the work at hand, discussing the current work with the group is a commonplace of instruction.

I am not primarily concerned with discussion as the most common or most appropriate mode of teaching a given subject. Rather I am interested in setting forth some general suggestions about the effective use of discussion regardless of subject (see also Hill, 1977). Basic to using discussion at all is consideration of goals. These may be long-range, general objectives of the kind I've just described: involving students; providing a socializing mechanism; examining, clarifying, even confusing concepts; raising value questions. But goals also need to be examined in much more specific ways: What are the goals for the individual class period in which discussion is central? What are the goals of that class in relation to the larger aims of the course?

For example, consider a class in a technical subject with a

difficult textbook. The teacher's general goal is to get across a body of information, most of it involving the application of theoretical concepts to an understanding of specific physical or chemical behaviors. A class in thermodynamics might fit such a description. An instructor in such a course might obviously choose to emphasize his or her role as elucidator of concepts, who demonstrates and clarifies text material, and his or her role as disciplinary agent, who, by assigning problems, testing, and repetition and review, would move students toward a command of the material. Given these roles, the teacher could easily operate as expert and authority, and be only as close to the class as these functions require. But few teachers could escape the realities arising from the diversity of students and their different aptitudes, understandings, and motivations. Thus discussion might be a way of facing these realities. A teacher might plan weekly discussion sessions in preference to lectures. The objectives of such discussions would be at least twofold: to clarify the subject matter for individuals and the group and to provide motivation through participation and involvement. Another teacher in the same course might pursue the same objectives but with a different structure. A weekly discussion period might not fit this teacher's style, and discussion, brief but purposeful, might be deliberately introduced at those points in the class period where there seemed the most need and opportunity. Nor am I denying another possibility, that whatever the instructor's plans, the needs of the class come to the fore and discussion occurs as the situation brings it into being. I have seen a very skilled teacher teach a technical class of this sort almost entirely by problem sets. But every class I witnessed involved not only the working of problems at the board but also a continuing discussion of these problems with individual students and the class.

    I do not believe that everything in teaching can be planned or should be. Discussion is so associated with spontaneous, free activity that planning may seem to be in conflict. But discussion in teaching is a clearly identifiable technique, and therefore does involve decisions on whether or how to use it in the classroom. A teacher might find, upon examining actual outcomes of a course, that the objectives sought were not being achieved. Perhaps the cause is that students have too little opportunity to

voice their confusions or lack of understanding. Or perhaps the
general discussion sessions are taking time that might better be
spent in tutoring individuals.

In some classes, discussion seems to be the most appropriate technique. An example would be a thematic course of a
common kind, say on personal freedom and social responsibility. The substance of the course is probably a set of readings;
the objectives are exposure to these materials and the development of the students' abilities to reflect on the material, to
exchange opinions about it, and to see its personal and social consequence. Most often, such courses are tied to freshman composition or speech, with the gaining of writing and speaking skills
as a principal objective. Here, the teacher must decide not so
much whether to use discussion as how to make the discussion
effective, again in terms of the individual student, the class as a
whole, and any one class period in relation to the course. As
with the technical course, the teacher has a hand in what happens. Facing class sessions in which the discussion suffers for a
want of common information, the teacher may give up some
discussions for activities specifically aimed at acquiring information: lectures, group readings, sessions in the library, the preparation and presentation of reports. Once again, my point is that
the teacher has the responsibility for considering both before
and during the term what method of instruction best fits which
topics and which students at what periods of time.

As general propositions, the following may be useful to
teachers:

—Discussion is not very good for dispensing information,
but it is useful for fixing and relating and promoting thought
about information that has already been acquired.

—Discussion may be useful for clarifying information and
concepts, but the instructor may have to play a more directive
role if clarification is his or her main goal.

—Discussion is the primary way to raise the level of student involvement in the classroom. It follows that using the discussion for establishing rapport, for motivating individuals and
groups, for suggesting directions of further inquiry, and for raising the interest level is highly legitimate.

—Discussion provides one good form of feedback about

the progress, attitudes, and aims of individual students and the class.

—Discussion develops the individual skills of formulating and expressing ideas and opinions.

—Discussion offers the opportunity for widening the student's perception of learning and of ways of learning and for making distinctions in the use of fact, opinion, belief, rumor, proof, value judgments, and the like.

—Discussions need time to generate. The hour is rarely enough; a span of two hours is likely to be better.

Within discourse, whatever form it takes in the classroom, asking and answering questions is essential. Punctuating one's discourse with pauses for questions is a very rudimentary act of teaching, and eliciting good questions is a skill that expert teachers are always striving to develop. Shaping questions, persisting until answers are gotten, guiding questions to some end—these are matters of great importance in trying to carry on good discussion classes.

The teacher's general stance can invite or discourage questions. A skillful teacher may need nothing more than a gesture, a turn of head, a singling out by hand or look, even a pause, to elicit questions. If one wants more than random questions, moving toward an individual is one way to begin. Real conversations do not take place with one person sitting on high and the others at his or her feet. As conversations grow more intense, speakers tend to move toward each other. Around a discussion table, people shift forward discernibly and pull up their chairs.

The art of asking questions, eliciting answers, and moving with both to understanding is the essential art of those who deal with the discussion method. It is essential to the dialogue, to the seminar, to the larger discussion class. In all forms of questioning, there appear to be at least three cardinal principles.

First, ask real questions even though they may seem offhand, simple, or imprecise. Nothing is more dismaying to the student than the canned question, of which the worst sort is the question picked up from a teacher's manual (or a book like this) and ill-suited to the teacher's own style. Such questions generally have canned answers, ones that the teacher alone knows and that students shoot at forever, scoring many near misses but never hitting the bull's-eye. Moreover, such questions often are, or appear to be, invested with too much significance by the teacher. And worst of all, they are artificial. Teachers are better off sticking to questions that for the moment, with a particular student in the context of the discourse, really interest them. Real questions, however trivial, have the effect of grounding the dialogue or discussion in a reality that will gain attention and interest, even respect. From there, one has a chance to move on to big questions and perhaps make big questions seem real.

Second, be ingeniously responsive to the students' answers and questions. In conversation, no utterances are wrong, though they may be false, off the mark, vague, wandering, irritating, or whatever. So it is with dialogue. All answers are good answers; even dummying up, bullshitting, and smart-assing can be turned to account. A smart-ass answer may deserve a smart-ass reply, or it may not. The simple "I don't know" deserves respect, but it shouldn't cut off dialogue. The teacher can shift the question so that the student can respond, and thus, through a series of such questions, demonstrate that students do know things they don't think they know. Enthusiasm for all responses, not just for right answers, is both a courtesy and an incentive. Never deliberately ignore a question or demean the questioner.

A long-remembered experience of mine seems to violate this principle though actually it supports the point. I was challenged in a question-and-answer session to support my claim that characteristics of good and bad teaching could be identified. "Can you give even one example of bad teaching?" this faculty member asked. I thought a moment, then said abruptly, "That seems to me to be a trivial question," and turned to another question from across the room. I went on for some moments, keeping the first questioner in the corner of my eye to make sure that he wasn't stalking out of the room. Then I turned back to him, apologized for my rudeness, and said, "That's your example."

Third, try to achieve a rhythm in a series of questions so that the group arrives at moments of larger understanding. If you're lucky, a single student may provide the culminating answer and stitch the parts together for the whole class. If you're not, you can legitimately move in to underline the big question and the tentative answer. By establishing such sequences and rhythms, questions and answers can define the larger purposes of a class.

What I have put down is based on my own practices, which are central to the kind of teaching I prefer. Like other specific techniques of teaching, techniques of questioning have been investigated more within secondary and elementary schools than in higher education. Still, a professor of education can write, in reviewing research: "In sum, we do not know much about questioning and discussion" (Dillon, 1984). Since questioning was a way of learning long before systems of formal education, I think that if we don't know much it is because we don't read widely enough. The research literature I have read is not so much uninformative as it is unenlightening, though it is often both. It tends to investigate questioning within narrow confines, and to be preoccupied with defining and classifying its parts in relation to one or another system of learning objectives.

A little book, *The Art of Questioning* by Josiah Fitch (ninth edition, 1879), originally aimed at British Sunday-school teachers, is sufficiently knowledgeable about questioning that it might well be reprinted as a manual for college professors. It begins, as many subsequent books have begun, with exemplifying from a Socratic dialogue. From there, Fitch offers his own advice. "First, then," he writes, "*cultivate great simplicity of language* . . . connected with this is another hint of importance: *Do not tell much in your questions* . . . It is of great importance, also, that questions should be *definite* and *unmistakable,* and for the most part, that they admit of one answer. An unskilful teacher puts vague, wide questions." He observes that vague questions will bewilder the thoughtful, encourage the clever in guessing, and lead the sly and knowing to give back what the teacher expects. No college teacher should need help in identifying these kinds of responders among college students.

He calls attention to "the order and *arrangement,* which should always characterize a series of questions," but cautions that the teacher "must not attempt, even for the sake of logical consistency, to adhere too rigidly to a formal series of questions, nor refuse to notice any new fact or inquiry which seems to spring naturally out of the subject." There is other good advice: to avoid "all monotony of voice, or sluggishness of manner," to apportion questions among all the students, not penalizing or shaming students for wrong answers, and to work to get students to ask questions of one another.

Fitch's peroration is worth quoting entire (pp. 138-139):

> For indeed, the whole sum of what may be said about questioning is comprised in this: It ought to set the learners thinking, to promote activity and energy on their part, and to arouse the whole mental faculty into action, instead of blindly cultivating the memory at the expense of the higher intellectual powers. That is the best questioning which best stimulates action on the part of the learner; which gives him a habit of thinking and inquiring for himself; which tends in a great measure to render him independent of his teacher; which makes him, in fact, rather a skilful finder than a patient receiver of truth.

Most teachers are concerned with getting a high proportion of students involved in discussion. That number will probably always be somewhat fewer than the total number in the class, though when a class is going well, a skilled teacher should be able to make every student feel he or she is involved, and over the period of a term, that every student has participated. An attention to how the class functions as a group as well as to how each individual is taking part offers good guidance. The research of social psychologists adds to what experience can tell a teacher about how seating arrangements, distances between speakers, presence or absence of overt direction, and the like affect group behavior. A cocktail party probably succeeds as the small size of the room relates inversely to the number of people; intimacy of conversation is directly related to closeness between speakers; hard chairs may or may not be more conducive to discussion than soft chairs; the pattern of discussion is different with a leader than without one.

The gains attributed to student-centered discussion probably refer to shifts in attitude more than to acquisition of information, even though attitudes do greatly affect the gaining of both skills and knowledge. Certainly, it is evident that individuals can learn from each other, but also that structures to bring people together, to decide on focus and direction, and to provide extrinsic as well as intrinsic motivations are useful. Where discussion is the method, it is helpful to have participants who know something.

Thus, if one's aim is to reduce the reliance on the teacher, it is still wise to define goals, set agendas, arrange rooms, and provide for the tea and cookies. If an institution serves well at all, it provides informal means by which bull sessions are a recognized part of learning. Bull sessions should not be formalized. Students resent discussions that are really lectures, but they also resent discussion classes in which they are expected to profit solely from the half-baked ideas of other students, with no correctives from facts, experiences, and hard exacting thought.

Much of my greatest success with discussion has resulted from becoming more confident about letting things happen. Teachers should probably give up the notion that discussion sessions will meet their fondest hopes very often. They should be concerned, work at their skills, but not feel personally defeated when discussions come up short. The good discussion is not entirely within the teacher's control. Why some discussions go and others fall flat is one of those engaging mysteries of teaching. The following additional propositions, observations, and suggestions may shed some light.

1. Getting a good discussion going is seldom easy. The test is not what happens in the first fifteen or twenty minutes but what goes on thereafter. Good discussions can be generated within the class hour, but being able to go over into a second hour is more satisfactory. Specific problems and ideas, particularly ones students have already shown an interest in, generally provide a good focus for discussion. Such problems and ideas

set in personal contexts are probably better ways of getting a discussion started than are broad questions and definitions. "Do you consider yourself a romantic?" is better than "What is romanticism?"

2. The teacher makes a difference in who responds and who doesn't, in what gets covered and emphasized, in what attitudes are created. Being open to a class does not rule out having directions in mind or taking responsibility for providing directions. Joseph Axelrod (1973, p. 37) describes a student's response to a highly successful discussion leader who let students do practically all the talking: " 'He doesn't have to say anything. Just having him there is important to us.' " (An unusual aspect of this professor's technique is that he refrains from personal reactions or criticisms during the discussion. Instead, he jots down notes, and at intervals of two or three weeks, he organizes his impressions and allots a class hour to an exchange about the preceding discussions and the individual students' part in them.)

3. Avoid semantic tangles at all times if possible, but most certainly at the beginning. Though it may seem necessary to spend time with the person who says, "But what do we mean by a (book), (chair), (desk)?" it may be better just to hit him or her with a (book), (chair), (desk) and get on with it.

4. A discussion leader cannot avoid dealing with individuals who block discussion. There are three ways of handling them. First, put questions off on the promise that they will be answered in the course of the discussion. Second, bluntly rule out quibbles as less than crucial at this point in the discussion. Offer a temporary resolution, a working definition, gain assent from the group to set the matter aside, and proceed. Third, if it begins as, or moves toward, a quibble between two persons, step in as a referee and move the discussion away from the quibblers.

5. If the discussion is to deal with substantial matters, have things at hand to refer to. In English, for example, poems that can be examined easily by everyone in a group are better discussion material than the novel. If the discussion cannot be tied to a text, use the blackboard to show visually where the group has been, what it has arrived at, where it is going.

6. Break the subject into parts, consolidate, clarify, and move along. You can be blunt, forceful, yet tactful. Being shocked, outraged, struck dumb, or bowled over is a legitimate response. So is humor, praise, or astonishment. Use all the resources you have.

7. Clarify at the outset what the discussion is trying to achieve. If the dialogue is to be open-ended, it is better to make that clear initially than to disappoint participants who are looking for firm conclusions. On the other hand, some very good discussions proceed under the gun; that is, everyone is informed at the outset that there is a fixed time in which to achieve specified objectives.

8. Clarifying the kind of discussion and its objectives will help you decide how firmly to guide the exchange. Since the leader tends to play a prominent part, probably he or she should give more attention to holding back and shrewdly observing, participating only when needed to check digressions, clarify positions, and give a sense of progress.

9. Constantly but unobtrusively try to shape the discussion as it moves along. Anticipate the end well before the discussion gets there so that some kind of conclusion can be achieved, even if it is only that sort of finale in which everyone is at a high pitch of excitement amidst issues still unresolved.

10. Open discussions from which the teacher is absent may have some specific uses. At the beginning of a unit or segment of the course, such a discussion may be a way of bringing out what the students are most interested in or puzzled about. In midcourse, it may be a way both of putting students on their own and of finding out what in the past has engaged their attention, what needs further clarification, and so forth. A tape recorder can capture the discussion and give the teacher guidance for future class work.

Most of these suggestions pertain to leading a discussion, a skill all teachers should acquire. Whitman and Schwenk (1983) have prepared a useful handbook for discussion leaders for use in medical schools but applicable to general teaching practice. In general, careful planning, a willingness to intervene, and an ability to hold back are preferable to having to continually prod the discussion along. To me, the ideal discussion is one in which invisible strings guide a varied and vocal group during a period in which most of the participants sense the worth of their own ideas, experience some visceral excitement, and arrive at some destination. This is a high ideal. At the sinking end are the discussions that waffle off, the ones dominated by a handful of students, and the ones in which the invisible strings are all too visible—and resented.

One knows pretty well when a really good discussion comes off. But discussion as a regular technique makes it possible both to underestimate and to overestimate its impact on students, for teachers, despite their professional expertise and their role as discussion leaders, themselves get involved in discussions and may lose awareness of whether their intentions are being carried out and may even forget what those intentions were. Some cues are obvious enough. Surely the most bothersome are the students who never open their mouths. Running a close second are the students who never shut up. Many years of trying have made me less nervous about getting silent members of a class into a discussion. Some students prefer to be quiet and learn that way. Privacy deserves respect, but patience, enough time, and some specific invitations and incentives often bring such students into a discussion on their own. A teacher can devise specific strategies: ask direct questions, shift seating positions in the group, shut off students who dominate the discussion, create subgroups and subtopics, and find other ways of talking with silent members.

Dealing with compulsive talkers is less difficult than dealing with one's own natural tendency to accept a discussion between the teacher and a select handful of students as a good discussion. One simply and firmly shuts down the compulsive talker in any of a variety of ways. But the dialogue between the instructor and a select few raises questions of whether it's better to settle for a good discussion among a few than to risk a poor discussion involving more. At times, one may want to pass over the student with the ready response in favor of trying for a less successful response from another student. In encouraging reticent students, however, one does not want to exclude the more responsive ones. It is a tricky business. If discussion is going to be the dominant mode of a class, it may be worthwhile spending some time at the outset to go over the necessities for a good discussion. It may be possible for the class itself to make up the ground rules, establish a collective responsibility for not making speeches, coming forth at some times, and holding down private quibbles and pet notions. It may be equally useful to establish other discussion leaders and let all members of the class face the difficulties and opportunities of that position.

Sometimes, perhaps only in a group in which both familiarity and trust have been established, the group itself will check excessive behavior. I have had a class in which the class itself reduced the tendency of a single member to dominate discussion. Groans, audible comments, "Hey, let John answer it," and a variety of gestures and grumbles got the point across without my intervention and without, in this instance, reducing the talkative student to silence. I have also had students express privately their own anxieties about whether they were speaking up too often or too little.

Something very important is happening when students thus become conscious of their role in discussion. Apart from the subject matter, they are becoming aware of their own and other students' responses to learning. The kind of growth Perry describes (see Chapter Five) has a greater chance to take place in situations where students become aware of their intellectual positions. Discussion clearly suits the advance from absolutes to relativism, and it widens a student's awareness of contexts for subject matter as well as for learning.

The hope of arriving at good discussions is reason enough for developing skill at improvisation. Underlying this skill is an attitude toward truth that stops well short of certitude. This view holds that truth is not static, that it is not an absolute waiting to be exposed little by little to the seeker's view. Truth is various and changing, whether illuminated by lightning flashes and candles or by the steadier lights of human contrivance. The student who learns in discussion sees learning as it really goes: fitfully, haltingly, speedily with one set of things, stumblingly with another, now following logical pathways, now connecting at unlikely points. Viewed in this way, both truth and learning may seem less forbidding. The pursuit of truth is anyone's game, a game with very old general rules and penalties for setting those rules aside altogether, but a game that gives room for error, scope for the imagination, and many different rewards and satisfactions.

8

Seminars, Tutorials, Advising, and Mentoring

The opportunity for teachers to work with individual students is limited in large American colleges and universities. Small classes afford some opportunity, and the seminar designation has been a way of recognizing the value of small classes. Tutoring in a systematic way has not been a feature of many colleges or universities, though informal tutoring goes on in many schools. Independent study is still a permissible option for students, its usefulness often depending on the kind of tutorial arrangements that accompany it. In a small number of colleges, advising may be such an integral part of academic work that it contributes greatly to the student's learning. Despite the dominance of fairly large formal classes, the general preference among students and faculty for small classes suggests that teachers need to give attention to the demands that more individualized instruction makes. The relationship of teacher to student in tutoring and advising is also an aspect of teaching that skillful teachers should explore.

Seminars

The seminar is as much an accepted part of college and university teaching as the lecture. It would not be precisely true for me to say that, as student or teacher, I have never experienced a good seminar, but I have been disappointed more often than not. The ease of dealing with small numbers of students is a main reason that professors are fond of seminars. There are fewer papers, fewer tests, fewer grades, fewer names to remember. Moreover, seminars characterize graduate instruction and therefore carry greater prestige.

Why my distrust of seminars? First, as with the lecture, strong assumptions about the value of the seminar keep teachers and students from examining whether or how seminars work. Second, seminars lack definition. In undergraduate work, almost any small class is called a seminar. As graduate classes, seminars seldom achieve the lofty research aims they purportedly serve. "The only way in which a teacher can make his students begin to do original research without very extensive preliminary investigation," Ian Watt writes, "is to allot them either incredibly minute or indefensibly esoteric topics" (1964, p. 384). Third, seminars are not often what seminars should be: a small number of intensely interested and knowing individuals letting their minds play on a common topic.

Where and how might seminars work best? I have no quarrel with the general assumption that seminars are most appropriate to upper-division and graduate courses. But the fact that Harvard and Stanford could conceive of freshman seminars, using that name and following a graduate-research model, underlines the points I have just made. Graduate seminars commonly fall short because of disparity in the students' interests, competence, past experience, and information. The freshman seminar faces even greater difficulties in this respect. Senior seminars are reasonable possibilities only if close attention is given to focus and outcomes. Watt concludes that if the seminar is to be an effective undergraduate teaching method, "it must, merely to provide intellectual cohesion, lose much of its research character" (p. 385).

The "how" of a seminar should follow from its specific aims and focus. The structure should allow each of the participants to contribute knowledge and to reflect with the others on the relationship of that knowledge to the controlling topic. The structure of most seminars contravenes both of these elementary purposes: the seminar takes up discussion before an adequate base of information exists, and it ends with the delivery of formal papers crammed into the last weeks of the term. Indeed, the preparation of papers might be the proper beginning of a seminar, thus giving the meetings and discussions a content, focus, and meaning now often lacking. If even this injunction were heeded, the seminar would do more than merely provide a framework for individual exercises in gathering and presenting information. There are cheaper and more efficient ways to do that. Rather, the seminar would produce outcomes closer to those implied in the dictionary definition of the word: "a small group of students, as in a university, engaged in advanced study and original research under a member of the faculty and meeting regularly to exchange information and hold discussion." As seminars are commonly conducted they conform to a much looser definition: "any meeting for exchanging information and holding discussions." Such useful words as *colloquium* and *symposium,* describing less focused, more discursive, less purposive gatherings, have very little academic use. But whether we use other terms or not, the teaching of seminars should be more than just a way of getting a light work load.

If one were a Socrates, the smallness of a seminar might permit the introduction of the symposium into undergraduate education. The ability to conduct a Socratic dialogue is essential to working with small groups of students. The major aspects of the technique should be familiar to all teachers. Ethan Fishman (1985) has described the method well as it might apply to a political science class. Within a Socratic dialogue, a series of questions moves the participants in discernible steps to a larger understanding. One does not have to be a Platonist and believe in preexistent knowledge to demonstrate that more answers reside in students' heads than can be brought to bear on any one question a teacher asks. Nor should one be upset to discover that Socrates often seemed to know full well where his questions were leading and even took his adversaries there against their will. The teacher who masters the Socratic dialogue must be as aware as was Socrates that dialectic can impose a deceitful tyranny on the student. But it can also draw forth true understanding. What redeems it as an honest intellectual procedure are the human qualities that make it a drama as well as an exacting exercise in following a pattern of thought. Wit, irony, indirection, persistence, self-recognition, humility, exaggeration, puzzlement, a sense of purpose and of play—one draws on all these in using the Socratic dialogue.

A seminar is often the name attached to any small discussion class. Most college teachers tend to worry about having too many students to make good discussions possible. Seminars are closed at ten or twelve participants; students are discouraged from discussion classes that get beyond fifteen or twenty. I don't think there are any exact figures here, but experience tells me that too few should be as much a source of concern as too many. In the undergraduate classes in the settings where I teach, twenty or twenty-five students provide better discussions than do ten or fifteen. One reason is that the absence of some students does not affect the larger group as it does the smaller one. Another is that a dozen students coming into a class at random may not represent the diversity and competence useful to good discussion. The small group does not really remove the difficulties of getting all students to respond; the intimacy may, in fact, inhibit some students. Similarly, the very small group may encourage monologues by the teacher or a continuing dialogue between teacher and one or two students.

In the very smallest seminars, six or eight students for example, it seems advisable to break up the formal pattern of group meetings. More is to be gained by working with students individually or having students work together on related projects or conceiving of a common project to be worked on at and outside of class meetings. Whatever the size of the seminar, I think it should be goal oriented. But saying that does not lead me to endorse the goals most common to seminars: the preparation of individual papers or projects and their presentation to the group. The practice is flawed in two ways: the time for preparing the work is too short, and the time involved in presenting it is too long.

I can think of a number of remedies, all of which have been put to use by some teachers. Seminars might well carry over into a second term where the carefully done work of a first term becomes the object of more informed discussion and actual revision during the second. By using two terms, I once had a small seminar write a genuine book, from arguing out a table of contents and choosing chapters to be written to editing and duplicating a final draft. It was not a great book; it made no argument for writing books that way; but it did expose the writers to the actualities of fashioning a book as against doing and presenting a seminar paper. Seminars might make more of a group's collective strength, perhaps in carefully selecting a common topic and working collectively to explore that topic both in discussion and writing. At the end might be a single product, a document arising from both the individual contributions and careful revising and editing by the group.

Seminars might candidly examine the practice of students' reading their papers. In some disciplines, architecture for example, the presentation is a professional expectation and as much attention is given to method as to substance. Generally, however, oral presentations are more of an academic habit, contributing a little to future appearances at professional conventions but very little to actual teaching or research. Circulation of duplicated papers and discussion after is an obvious way of saving time and getting better results.

Tutoring

Tutoring is not very prevalent in American colleges and universities, surely more because of cost than merit. Given the size of our classes and institutions, the teacher who can find some place for individual instruction, despite its difficulties, enhances his or her effectiveness. More than anything else, tutoring requires that professors be willing to give up large parts of their time to work closely with individual students. Before cynicism and defensive adaptation set in, teaching assistants in charge of English composition and basic mathematics often give this kind of attention, which is missing almost everywhere else in the program of instruction. The acquiring of skills is particularly served by a one-to-one relationship between teacher and student. Mathematical ignorance and incompetence in writing both owe something to teaching-learning contexts that seldom enable teacher and student to work closely enough together. Tutoring in any subject at any level is a luxury American institutions seemingly cannot afford, and few faculty members are likely to engage in it freely.

Giving up some formal class time in order to find time for individual tutoring is one way of facing these realities. Teachers cannot expect an exact exchange of time. Individual conferences simply consume large amounts of time, more than one saves by not having to prepare an individual class. One expedient is to keep a strict watch on time per student, not an easy thing to do, but preferable to giving up altogether the idea of seeing students outside the classroom. Even if one is willing to take the time, setting time limits on tutorial sessions probably serves both teacher and student. It keeps the professor from that common vice of teaching more than the student wishes to learn, and it saves both student and professor the embarrassment of looking for excuses to get away.

Another expedient is to schedule office sessions with two, three, maybe a half dozen students. Some students are always going to privately ask questions that should have been asked before the whole class, just as some students are always going to engage in their most animated discussions after the bell. An announcement of specific times when particular matters in the course will be discussed may capitalize on these habits and bring in more than one student for this kind of tutorial. I have had some success in encouraging two or three students to sign up for the same hours of independent study, largely a directed readings course, and to meet together in regularly scheduled tutorial sessions.

I have heard of some attempts to adapt the tutorial to mass instruction by reducing the demands of independent study and allowing the students to range on their own. Under one scheme, a humanities professor let students prepare their own reading lists, suggest how many credit hours they wanted to receive, and how long they would take to complete their work. Freed from other classwork, the professor kept much of his day open to talk with students about their reading as the students came in on their own. Large numbers of students chose to work in this way, to the seeming satisfaction of both teacher and students.

Independent study has always been an option that moved in the direction of the tutorial. Ordinarily, faculty are reluctant to take on too many independent-study students, for required assignments and tests, whether oral or written, demand too much time. Administrators are nervous about independent study "classes," which seem to put one professor before a single student. But since independent study should aim at truly independent learning, a more casual conference might suffice to guide and motivate the student. Moreover, if some of the constraints of class packaging and specialization were lifted, faculty members might venture into guiding students in materials suggested by the students but outside the individual teacher's specialty.

The teacher's role as tutor in both colleges and universities in this country is bound to be limited. Demands on teachers generally preclude leisurely office visits. The closed office door is much more the norm than the open one, and despite the expansion of buildings, faculty and students share few amenities of space and decor. Moreover, right now, both sides seem to accept these conditions. The students don't show up; faculty members are glad they don't, or are not in their offices if the students do. Perhaps we are witnessing an adaptation to university life not unlike that toward urban living. One aspect of this adaptation in the universities is an increase of privatism, the narrowing of the individual's attention to the personal and professional matters he or she can most easily control. In addition, the individual identifies only with those subgroups that are very near at hand and undemandingly congenial. If this is the case, the teacher's satisfactions may come from teaching fairly large groups that make very few personal demands. In such a climate, faculty members are not likely to seek to affect an individual student's learning in the tutorial. What tutoring there is will probably grow from informal contacts and find its own patterns and time.

Advising

Supposedly, in some hallowed past, teachers and learners mingled intellectual and personal development so closely and so happily that there was no need for special counselors and advisers. The small, rural, residential college tried to approximate that condition. (In some New England prep schools, the headmaster personally bid each student good night every evening.) But accurate accounts of such colleges suggest that students and faculty maintained their distance even then and that the intellectual and personal lives of neither group ran smoothly side by side. Only in unusual times and under unusual circumstances is there great harmony.

My point is that only in theory has there been much effective concern for knitting formal campus learning together with actual campus life. Living-learning arrangements that sprang up in the sixties have fallen short of becoming established campus patterns. Some cluster colleges and small colleges within larger universities have survived, but only as a very small part of higher education.

What might an individual teacher do to go beyond keeping regular office hours and not brushing students off after class? I have tried a good many of the usual devices: sponsoring clubs, taking students to lunch, having them into my home, arranging picnics and parties, worrying about formal counseling procedures and trying to find better ones. I have drawn the conclusion that nothing works very long, that very little works without careful attention, and that students vary as widely as faculty in their need for enhancing institutional learning relationships and in their responses to ways of meeting that need.

Nevertheless, an education that purports to contribute anything to a person's life must surely deal with the relationships among the varieties of human beings that make up students and faculty and the varieties of activities they engage in, both as learners and persons. I am not talking, for the moment, about formal counseling; rather, about ways of advising and counseling indirectly, maybe no more formal than providing excuses and opportunities for easy talk.

One overall way of improving advising is to keep insisting on the idea of collegiality and to keep trying to provide structures through which students and faculty can have associations outside the classroom. Colleges and departments, in themselves, no longer provide these possibilities. Any such association will probably have to come from the students and faculty on their own, perhaps when a few like-minded individuals set out in a variety of ways to form informal collegial structures quite apart from those that now define campus teaching and learning.

Another way is to expand the opportunities for individual attention within the classroom. Class time used to help students see their own growth in relation to classwork is seldom wasted. From conscious efforts to identify students as something other than social security numbers can develop associations which have some chance of enduring beyond the twelve- or sixteen-week term.

The discontinuities of learning are a marked feature of mass education. Beyond the separation of classwork from out-of-class activities, of one class from another, and of one discipline from another are the larger separations of parents from the college and of alumni from the academic work they might have pursued. Again, I would suggest, probably in vain, more efforts to let parents see and enjoy some of the academic life they are paying for and to invite alumni back to share their after-college experiences with students and faculty.

A final suggestion is to continue with something of the spirit of the free university, a by-now-forgotten relic of the sixties, but still surviving in adult and continuing education and in other structures of some colleges and universities (Graber and Jones, 1987). Faculty members and students know many things outside their own disciplines. And though free learning has a hard time competing with credits and grades, it does have its attractions. Indeed, the kind of trust and friendship and expanded understanding that can grow out of learning with others something one really wants to learn is seldom approximated in a regular class. A weekend that a faculty member might spend with students rock-hunting or fly-casting or prowling some odd corners of a museum could be free learning in its best sense.

Within the present climate, my suggestions have about as much to do with the actual academic programs as with actual formal advising and counseling procedures. Yet, such attitudes and activities bear importantly on both. Formal advising is right now and everywhere in pretty much of a mess. The doctrine of *in loco parentis* having been swept aside, other ways of substitute advising have shifted or disappeared. The counseling functions taken over at one time by professionals in guidance and counseling appear to be coming back as faculty responsibilities. The venerable office of dean of students, which in small schools and in the past was intimately connected with the academic life of students, long ago lost that connection. Students developed their own agencies to cope with academic and nonacademic needs, which became separate provinces of the office of student affairs. In large universities, the sheer size of such functions as management of housing, health and psychological services, placement, and the student union has turned each into a separate operation. Nevertheless, there seems to be a persistent desire to unite academic concerns with something approximating the whole life of the student. This desire accompanies a recognition that what students learn depends on many factors outside the teacher and that some total development of the student is still a legitimate aim of the college and a responsibility of the faculty as well.

Thus, a teacher may have to add a basic competence in counseling and advising to his or her professional skills. One gains such competence in much the same way as other skills: by learning through study or instruction or practice. Little skill is gained unless the teacher accepts the responsibility, gives attention to its details, and intelligently engages in doing it. The University of Michigan's Memo to the Faculty no. 69 (Ericksen, 1981) wisely addresses many aspects of this formal and informal responsibility: "Students seek out the teacher as a person whose judgment is respected, whose confidence is trusted, as a counselor, advisor, and friend."

The patience to listen and the willingness to have routine

information in the head or at hand are minimal qualities. Patience may develop from the recognition that listening gives a teacher legitimate respite from talking. The willingness to provide information is more a matter of will, of resisting cant as much as vowing a positive effort. The cant is that professors are incapable of keeping details straight and that petty details are beneath their dignity. It is odd that an institution would trust professors to master the details of vast and complex subject matters and not trust them to convey accurate information about requirements for a major. Admittedly there are degrees of competence in these respects as there are degrees of inclination. But the general tendency to relegate advising and counseling to only a handful of faculty is wrong, ultimately doing no favor to those teachers who at first escape drudgery but in the end perpetuate ignorance.

Advising and counseling are part of the necessary interchange between teacher and student. If a student makes the first step into a professor's office to find out what courses he or she still has to take, that step may lead to an exchange as important as that day's classroom lecture. Until a campus creates an ambience that expands these moments, both artificial and artful ways will have to serve. The teacher's responsibility is to tolerate the one—the obligatory advising, which may mean the mere getting of a signature—and to develop the other—ways of making embarrassing, trivial, mechanical, dumb queries lead to real questions. From that beginning, a teacher can contribute much to learning outside the classroom.

There is a great deal to know in these matters, and faculty members who feel uneasy about counseling may be deferring to the greater wisdom of the professional clinician. The disturbed, the depressed, the paranoid, and the suicidal students are not screened out at admissions time. Teachers help create them. It may be better to be informed about where help is available than to try to handle a situation by oneself. I am thankful for living within a university community and knowing its resources in the times (still few in number) when I have been responsible for dealing with suicidal students or deranged faculty members. Teachers live among these responsibilities, and they should no more expect calamity every day than disregard the possibility that it might show up some day. So, although an open office door may be an invitation to trouble, the literal and figurative opening of office doors might be the best single step toward improving that part of out-of-classroom learning and of counseling and advising for which teachers have responsibility.

Mentoring

"Mentoring is a slippery concept," Pat Cross writes in a recent book (Daloz, 1986, p. ix) on that subject. "Most people think of a mentor as a person, usually older and more experienced, who is able and willing to help a protégé get where he or she wants to go." The concept is not so much slippery as fallen into disuse for being deliberately shunned. Neither the conditions which pertain to most American college students nor the inclinations of most professors are favorable to mentoring, though students will continue to find mentors and professors will become mentors despite forces that work against mentoring relationships.

One measure of how mentoring is perceived within formal higher education is the fact that Daloz's *Effective Teaching and Mentoring* is based on and aimed at adult learners pursuing academic work in adult and continuing education contexts. Few references to mentoring are to be found in writing aimed at the traditional college-age population, despite the fact that the term *mentor* arises from the character of Mentor, the guiding spirit for Telemachus, who was just coming into adulthood. It alters Homer's concept considerably to think of Telemachus as middle-aged, immersed in adult responsibilities, and with no father to search for or mother to defend.

I am not implying that adult students do not need mentors; rather that there should be more mentors in all our colleges and universities and among all ages of students. But college and university teachers, it must be acknowledged, do not uniformly accept the importance of even being role models for students, of trying to affect the development of the whole person, of helping shape lives as well as develop competences. In the universities particularly, the career ambitions of professors as scholars within their separate disciplines can outweigh the wise and active caring for students, which is at the heart of mentoring. In all institutions, the fragmenting of classes and subjects often works against an individual student even becoming very closely acquainted with an individual professor. And there are many aspects of the formalizing of higher education that cause both students and professors to shy away from mentor relationships, to feel unwilling, perhaps, to let education become personal, to think of teaching as anything more than imparting useful knowledge and developing useful skills.

The uneasiness that professors show toward advising and counseling, and the placing of these functions entirely or in part with a professional staff, constitute other barriers to mentoring. Should we be assuming responsibilities, professors may ask themselves, in an area—personal development of students—in which we are not experts? The answer is likely to be no, especially when such responsibilities may cut heavily into work deemed more important. Those who advise and counsel may feel that they are cut off from actual teaching and therefore cannot act as academic mentors for students primarily intent on doing well by the requirements attached to their majors and future careers.

The difficulties of mentoring as an identifiable mode of teaching reaching great numbers of students are probably insurmountable. Bradley (1981) points out that mentoring was most prominent in the late 1960s and 1970s and probably arose as a response to students' demand for more individualized instruction. As formalized within institutional practices, mentoring hardly exists today. Nevertheless, a lifetime of teaching might not seem fully rewarding if something like mentoring relationships did not now and again arise. The self-selecting process by which a relatively few students seek mentors may make mentoring within most colleges possible at all. Daloz's analysis of the activities of those who become mentors squares with my own observations about teachers who make an extraordinary impact on students. He writes: "Mentors seem to do three fairly distinct types of things. They *support,* they *challenge,* and they *provide vision"* (1986, p. 212). Daloz's full discussion of mentoring is valuable to any teacher, and I will set forth here my own brief observations within the framework he provides.

Supporting, challenging, and providing vision all depend on a willingness to give oneself to the student without imposing oneself upon her or him. *Caring* may be the essential if one is to arouse or to accept a mentoring relationship. Caring must be an embracing concern, not just for what the student achieves in a course, not just for how a mentor succeeds in drawing the best out of the student, and not even wholly focused on caring for the student. It is also caring in some way about the consequences and possibilities of human development within the broadest of outlooks, ultimately caring about civilization itself and the part educating plays in it.

If one enters into a mentoring relationship or is sought out as a mentor, the first demand it makes is probably on one's time. The teacher who rushes out quickly after class, who is seldom available to students or who, when he or she is, is still engaged elsewhere, is not likely to become a mentor. The student who feels the closeness necessary to mentoring will find it necessary to draw upon the mentor's time, even as a respect, a shyness perhaps growing out of admiration, a reluctance even before a compelling urge to ask for attention, may protect the mentor's time.

Much of that time will probably be taken up in listening, the need a student feels to find a sympathetic ear having helped create a desire for a mentor in the first place. Mentoring, I think, implies a nondirective relationship. That is, as Mentor in the *Odyssey* did not so much tell Telemachus what to do as give him the courage to do it, so the teacher/mentor will let the student voice his or her hopes and doubts and conflicts and directions. It is not easy for teachers to listen; for one thing it takes time, time better spent, some teachers say to themselves, telling students what to do and getting them to do it. For another, what is the use being a professor if you can't tell people what you know and what they should do? Nevertheless, if one would be a mentor, would teach in the light of mentoring, he or she must, as Emerson said, "listen greatly."

Support of students comes in many forms. Within the framework of competition and evaluation which rule over college and university teaching, conflicts are hard to avoid between supporting a student's efforts and yet rendering judgments on performance. I think it is possible to work within that conflict, but not easy. The key may be that of taking a genuine interest in the student's strivings beyond what is being achieved in a given course. That fact may be why mentors often are identified outside of a student's major and why mentoring relationships develop after being in a future mentor's class. In both instances, the teacher is free to give support unencumbered by the necessities of passing judgment. In any case, a mentor's responding to a student-mentor relationship is more than simply accepting whatever and however the student performs. Again, the context which surrounds mentoring does not leave the student free to accept as mentor someone who does not acknowledge the realities of both the student's and the mentor's situation. That may be why it is possible to accept the student's strivings without qualification, and to support those strivings even within the necessity of rendering judgments about the performance.

Support relates closely to challenge. A very appealing kind of teacher is one who may seem to withdraw support in confronting the students with challenge. But support is still importantly present in the mentor's assuming that the student is capable of meeting the challenge. Our previous discussion of achievement motivation in which the teacher picks tasks that are hard but not too hard supports this aspect of mentoring. Perhaps mentoring differs in that the challenge a mentor provides may embrace a wider range, not just the challenge of immediate tasks but challenges which involve the person's attitudes, stages of growth, values, life itself.

Daloz speaks of the highest kind of challenge as "the challenge to become more fully ourselves *through* them [the mentors]. They call forth the best we have. They invite us to transcend ourselves. They personify our highest aspirations" (p. 231). In such aspiring, students clarify not only their own visions but those their mentors have helped hold before them.

In my own past experience, I can think of only three

teachers that I regard as mentors. Only one was within the major I was pursuing, and with only one of the others was I a student, in the sense of having a fairly close classroom acquaintance. What all three had in common was that they both articulated and embodied a larger vision of academic work and by implication of life than any of dozens of other professors. They were demanding in the sense that I could not fall short without a sense of not being up to what I had idealized in them. They were supporting in that they were in a sense smiling on me, urging me on, when I found myself going in promising directions. They were supporting in a different way in the letter one wrote me when I was struggling with the dreariness of graduate work and voiced some complaints over that struggle. The message was longer, but what it said simply was, "Don't whine." And most of all, they justified what I had chosen to commit myself to, an academic career with which I often found fault, with which I still question and quarrel, but which their very presence justified.

I conclude with this personal experience not only because mentoring is a very personal matter but also because I was able to encounter this vital experience within and in spite of the prevailing structures of higher education. None of these teachers had any more time, was less devoted to his own scholarship, was any more seeking students to mentor than other equally skillful and knowledgeable professors. But above all else they conveyed a feeling that what they were doing and how they went about it mattered greatly not just to them personally but to the world, and that world somehow included me.

Mentoring, it may be argued, cannot be adapted in any serious form to the realities of mass education. I do not argue that it can, though I think thoughtful consideration of mentoring should be expected of all teachers. Given the variety of students, it is hard for any teacher to escape being regarded as a mentor by someone. Given the variety of teachers, it is not surprising that some shy away from the role. The difficulty of being wise indicates that true mentors will be few, and the presence of fakery and vanity among those posing as mentors justifies a teacher's reluctance to embrace mentoring. Nevertheless, in those modes of teaching we have been discussing, in small groups like the seminar and in tutoring and individual study, and in the role of adviser and counselor, teachers are drawn closer to conditions that foster mentoring relationships. Most important of all, many of the characteristics one identifies with mentoring are also characteristics one finds in effective teaching of many kinds.

9

Teaching Without Teachers

Most teachers, I suspect, feel reasonably comfortable in the classroom. But there is a serious concern within the teaching profession for increasing the quality of those many acts, structures, and devices that lie outside the confines of the classroom. I will not feign an enthusiasm for nonclassroom teaching that I do not feel, but I will try to set forth information about teaching that moves away from the classroom and the classroom teacher. I will begin with describing the most successful forms of individualized self-pacing instruction, turn to instructional systems dependent largely on technology, and conclude with some observations about the relation between the teacher and these mostly teacherless means of instruction.

Programmed instruction is the name commonly given to college and university materials that students work through on their own. These materials are largely texts, though other hardware—slide projectors, film strips, audio and video tapes—are easily incorporated. There is nothing very new in the concept of programmed instruction. Learning the piano by ear in ten easy lessons has a long history, as does correspondence study of various kinds. If carefully put together, programmed materials can be adapted to many college courses. The chief principle behind this method is reinforcement, and a good learning package organizes its material so that a logical progression of subunits leads to mastery of a total skill or body of information. The package presents information and concepts and tests the student's learning directly, without the presence of a teacher. Whether this package takes the form of a booklet, uses computer input and response, includes resource material, or provides some access to teachers along the way, the basic structure and theory behind all programmed instruction remain much the same.

The method has had considerable success, particularly since it readily adapts to introductory materials that faculty members tend to shun but still feel are necessary for the students. A good self-pacing system is certainly preferable to poor teachers and bad conditions for handling masses of students. Such systems can perform very well the task of sorting and ordering a body of material in ways that can lead students to mastery. They also offer the great opportunity to accommodate instruction to individual differences. They can draw on a wide range of technological aids to learning, and they can help students develop the useful ability to learn on their own. Where programmed instruction falls short is in motivating the students. The self-pacing learning-center campus depends altogether on the willingness of students to show up and work. I doubt that great numbers of students will take advantage of obvious opportunities to learn without some varied, immediate, and human incentives. The college campus itself may seem to be at odds with a kind of instruction that could be easily carried on elsewhere.

I see this kind of instruction remaining, even expanding, as an adjunct to live teaching (Knapper, 1982). I do not see its being more than an adjunct except in concepts like the British Open University, where the learning packages are highly sophisticated, where most of the work is done at home, where a convenient network of teachers is available, and where the individual experience is capped by a short residence on campus. Although adaptations of this model have been established in this country, the great numbers of campuses and of faculty members seem to work against any large-scale transformation.

Nevertheless, to many of those professionally involved in education, perhaps more in the public schools than in higher education, technology has a great appeal. In some parts of the college and university, however, the systems approach has been given an enthusiastic reception. Arising from the simple ideas of behavioral objectives and Skinnerian reinforcement, various types of self-pacing instruction have taken on formidable names: contingency management, precision teaching, personalized system of instruction (PSI), computer-assisted instruction (CAI), self-paced supervised study, mastery learning, modular instruction, contract teaching, positive learning reinforcement system, and performance-based instructional development. A jargon has sprung up, and a literature has come into being. I respect the central ideas and some of the refining of details; I react adversely to the inflation of small truths and the distortion of both common sense and learning theory into a pedantry of technological learning.

The Keller Plan, named after Professor Fred Keller (1969) and dating from the mid-1960s, is a full and sensible system of individual self-pacing instruction (for a short description and appraisal, see Ryan, 1974; Milton, 1974). In the Keller Plan, students work at units of a course on their own in sequence. They must master each unit before moving on to the next, ordinarily demonstrating that mastery by perfect or near-perfect performance on an examination. Such examinations—Keller preferred the short-essay examination for his basic psychology course—may be taken whenever the student feels ready; failure imposes no penalty on the student, and the test may be taken again and again until passed. Noncompulsory lectures and demonstrations are provided as sources of motivation. Students who have finished the course assist in testing and scoring and in the incidental tutoring of individual students.

Keller-Plan courses and various modifications now have hundreds of users in many different disciplines. Reports evaluating the results of these methods indicate that students find such courses to be demanding, that those who finish (and some studies report fairly high dropout rates) do as well on final examinations as students taking the same course in the classroom, and that students completing the course strongly prefer such instruction to the conventional course.

Obviously, this method can be adapted to a good many courses. The kind of involvement it demands of the teacher may well suit some members of a faculty. Developing and supervising an appropriate course can be a satisfying part of a teacher's work. Just as this kind of instruction requires increased self-motivation for the student, so does it raise the instructor's need to find satisfactions other than those that ordinarily come from live classroom interaction. Student achievements are an obvious source of those satisfactions, though a high dropout rate would undercut it.

The Keller Plan may succeed in part because it still provides a place for active interchange with students. Some kind of involvement of teacher with student is, to me, a basic necessity of instruction. One of the great weaknesses in preparing teachers for the public schools, a weakness that will not be offset by systems or research or professionalization, is that college professors of education lose contact with public school students. The exciting books and pioneering discoveries in public education in the last decades have not come from departments of education but from individuals within and outside professional education who have been in the classrooms alongside the students. Thus, it is fortunate that college and university teachers are not swept into becoming solely creators and managers of systems, but rather remain instructors who may wish to incorporate self-paced instruction into their teaching repertoires.

The fourth revolution, according to Eric Ashby (1974), springs from developments in electronics, notably the radio, television, tape recorder, and computer. The first revolution was the shift from parent to teacher as the central agent of education. The second was the shift from spoken to written word; the third, the invention of printing. Ashby's book, the two volumes edited by Sidney Tickton (1970), and the Carnegie Commission's volumes *The Fourth Revolution* (1972) and *Computers and the Learning Process in Higher Education* (1975) are recent enough to have measured the initial impact of electronic technology. The development of the computer, however, has been so rapid in the last decade that print publications can scarcely keep up with the newest developments in hardware and software. Nevertheless, what these earlier surveys observed still seems pertinent: that the possibilities for teaching and learning offered by technology still must recognize the limitations in their use created by costs and by necessary adaptation to established educational practices. There is still a lack of research that demonstrates convincingly how much of what students learn can be attributed to specific technology. In one of the early evaluations (Magarrell, 1978, p. 5) of computerized teaching systems on a broad scale, the conclusion reached was that neither of two systems had "reached the potential so long claimed for this form of instructional technology." The PLATO system, one of the earliest developed, "had no significant impact on student achievement." Chambers' and Sprecher's (1983, p. 21) review of studies to 1981 concluded: "CAI either improves learning or shows no differences when compared to the traditional classroom approach . . . reduces learning time . . . develops more positive attitudes toward computers" and perhaps toward subject matters. Sullivan and others (1976) studied the relative effectiveness of instructional television and Kulik, Kulik, and Cohen (1980) have made a number of studies of various technologies.

This is a good time, therefore, to discuss in practical terms a teacher's competence with the use of technology. The first and simplest competence is knowing what is going on. Colleges and universities, internally or from one to another, are remarkably bad places for effective exchange of information about matters of instruction. With respect to aids to instruction, a partial cause for infrequent use may be the common separation of audio-visual services from academic departments. Try as media centers will to make their resources easily available, they simply cannot compete with these things within a faculty member's reach. The blackboard and book still remain the most widely used technological aids to instruction, largely because they are at hand and are utterly simple to use. No electronic device has yet become as available as either blackboard or book. Until electronic technology becomes that commonplace, the faculty member has the responsibility of finding out what is available, obtaining it, and putting it to use.

The growing demands of the present time cannot help but unsettle faculty members. In most disciplines, access to printed research data is available through long-established, definitive bibliographies. In many disciplines, more sophisticated information retrieval systems are also in use. In addition, resources are expanding in both print and nonprint forms. All of this adds to the scholar's basic job of keeping up with his or her field. Keeping informed about the range of technological aids to instruction is an additional job the individual faculty member may not be willing to accept. Finding one's way among unfamiliar materials is an invitation to avoid them altogether. The previewing of a film, for example, is a less-than-natural act, I suspect, for most professors. Yet, previewing is hard to avoid if one is careful about what goes into a class hour or course. The difficulties in using local materials are compounded in trying to find out about resources on other campuses and arranging for their use. Thus, the simple competence of being informed about available resources is not as simple to develop as it sounds.

In addition, teachers need to keep informed about the technological resources available to students. Since the faculty member has no personal need to use these things and does not participate directly in preparing media materials, he or she may still think that a university library is a collection of printed works only. Firsthand acquaintance with learning-carrels is a necessary part of a teacher's competence, as is awareness of the availability of computer terminals or microfiche readers and the extent of slide, tape, and record collections.

"Computer literacy" is a catchphrase on most college and university campuses. At its simplest level this seems to mean all members of the university community being able to use a computer for purposes relevant to their work. A decline in "computer literacy" interest on some campuses suggests that this level has been reached in many places. At the far end from such relatively simple adaptation of an obviously useful technology is the disappearance of print and classrooms and libraries in their present form and the emergence of the fully automated comprehensive electronic teaching and learning system.

"Totally electronic instruction," Linda Fleit, president of EDUTECH International, observes (1987, p. 96), "has been predicted for at least 20 years, and yet several studies have shown that an electronic classroom may be no more effective for learning than the traditional non-computerized one." Despite such cautions, there are few areas in which computers have not been introduced for instructional use. Science, engineering, and business are probably the biggest users, and in all areas more use is made of computers for the faculty member's research and writing than for instruction.

Within instruction, CAI (computer-assisted instruction) defines the most common practice. Faculty members, whether in economics or music or engineering, seem to still prefer maintaining control and using the computer as it can assist them in teaching and learning.

I will not attempt to list all the ways the computer has been made to serve students, faculty, and administrators. Its potential for self-learning is probably as great as its current capacities for record-keeping and communicating. Nevertheless, I doubt that the computer will materially improve teaching in its complex and personal and educational dimensions. But whatever its effectiveness, computer technology must be added to the many things a teacher must know about.

Since 1970, probably no subject category in the library card catalogue has expanded more than "computers." Many of the titles focus on applications within specific disciplines and in the public schools. The following are some titles of broader interest to higher education: Bork (1981, 1985), Carnegie Commission on Higher Education (1975), Chambers and Sprecher (1983), Gagné (1987), Hawkridge (1983), Kepner (1986), Maddison (1983), Masat (1981), Merrill (1986), Rushton and Reid (1985), Ryan (1974), Sloan (1985), Tashner (1984), Tucker (1983–84).

I will not dwell long upon the responsibilities that are closely linked with knowing what is going on: actually using technological resources and becoming involved in the production of software and hardware or in the study of their adaptation, use, and effectiveness. Surely, by now, some such basic competence might be expected of teachers, ranging from changing a record or tape to programming a computer. Universal competence is no more to be expected than is universal incompetence presumed to be the norm. The best way to develop relevant skills is through repeated use. And repeated use develops from an initial act of will and from continuing satisfaction with results. Short courses in how to run a projector or a computer will do little good if one does not follow the course with purposeful use. And only by repeated use does one get the "damn thing" to work often enough to put down one's reservations about using it at all.

In sum, technology offers the teacher a vague promise of increased effectiveness at the price of having to know and do more. Teachers will continue to do the easiest thing, both because of natural inclination and because of the many demands on their time. Slide and computer freaks will continue to put on dazzling shows; some of their expertise will rub off on other teachers. But we have a long way to go before any of the electronic media—even the tape recorder and the projector—become natural parts of instruction.

PART THREE

Grubby Stuff
and Dirty Work

10

Texts

I have given so much space to the classroom because it is there that so much of the pleasure of teaching is to be found. I have also underscored the probability that the classroom is not the place where most learning occurs. Much of both teaching and learning is underground, perceived only by the teacher and the taught, seen dimly by family and friends but seldom sympathetically enough by anyone. It is the grubby stuff, the dirty work.

First, a number of things that are part of the classroom and that the instructor must take class time to use or explain are affected by the way they are handled as well as by what they are. Textbooks are an example. There are three important questions about textbooks: which ones to use, how to use them, and whether to use them at all. The answers are so individual and changeable as to support an imposing textbook industry. At the same time, there appears to be some widespread agreement about texts that accounts for those "standard" or "definitive" textbooks, which are the equivalent of best sellers in trade publishing. With the multiplication of texts, the presence of paperbacks which go in and out of print rapidly, cheap photo duplication, and computer software, the problem of getting appropriate texts grows more complicated every year. With rising costs, the number of students who can't afford texts is many times greater than faculty members imagine. For most courses, there never has been such an abundance of useful text materials. Faculty members tend to take advantage of these riches, may total the costs for an individual course, but fail to consider that students are expected to buy books for four or five courses.

Costs do not make a very lofty beginning for a discussion of textbooks. Still, costs are a chronic as well as a current reality of instruction. If students are not buying all the assigned texts, then some thought should be given to arriving at better expedients. Costs, for example, may rule against opting for a collection of paperbacks over a comprehensive and up-to-date text or anthology. Costs may force a teacher into greater use of the reserve reading room. Costs may even foster more exchange of books among students, with the faculty encouraging such exchange. Costs should certainly make a faculty member wary of assigning texts that are rarely put to use in class. And costs should make a teacher even more sensitive to lecturing that merely repeats the text.

All of these considerations would be important even if costs could be set aside. In most courses, the choice of one standard text as against a number of texts involves real choices, from the obvious advantage that the single text affords continuity and consistency to the disadvantage of having to lug a seven-pound anthology to class every day. The choice of textbooks should be recognized as a way of clarifying objectives. If a teacher stresses highly organized mastery of a body of information, a single text is probably the best choice. If one wishes students to develop a facility for weighing evidence, for comparing points of view, and for theorizing on matters of opinion as well as fact, then a collection of text materials may be justified.

There are bad texts—which someone else writes—good texts—which we write—and perfect texts—which we plan to write some day. The first consideration in choosing texts is whether students are likely to read them, work with them, and learn from them. Achieving this is not as easy as it sounds, and the teacher has a specific responsibility to go beyond assigning a text and testing on mastery. This responsibility is particularly important when a number of texts are assigned and only certain parts of them are used or stressed. It is always good to choose a text that can be read in a reasonably systematic way and understood without the help of the teacher. A text that stimulates the student's interest is usually better than one that merely satisfies the instructor. Second in importance in choosing texts is justifying their use by accompanying assigned readings with specific amplifications or explanations, discussions, assignments, or tests. It is advisable at the beginning of a course to acquaint students with the nature of the text and to indicate specific use in the course outline. Considering the comprehensiveness of many texts, a teacher should help focus the students' reading, perhaps assigning both required and optional readings from the text. Third, and probably the most vexing problem to both students and faculty, is learning to use the text without merely repeating it. One way is to devote a small part of class time to clarifying or supplementing textual matter, and the balance of the time to discussion, application, and amplification of text materials. A useful strategy is to deliberately choose texts that offer a different kind of material or a different emphasis from that of the instructor. The definitive text from a disciplinary point of view may not be the best teaching text. It may, quite simply, leave too little for the instructor to do.

An important consideration in using a text well goes back to the teaching stance. If the teacher considers transfer of information the primary objective, then it may be the teacher who is redundant, not the text. If, on the other hand, stimulating learning through interaction between student and teacher is the chief aim, then what the teacher does in class differs in kind and substance from what the text does.

If one does not want to use a text, the best general advice to follow is to emphasize the value of original sources. Amid the overpowering abundance of secondary materials, the classroom teacher has an obligation to work with, sort out, and bring attention to primary sources. Sometimes the teacher's published scholarly work will coincide with this need. For the most part, the work that scholars publish has little direct bearing on teaching. It is read, if at all, by other scholars working the same narrow vein. There are few honest opportunities and little need for forcing such research on students.

Teachers who work almost entirely with primary materials still face the problem of judging the quality of editing, printing, and annotation. In the anthologies, the editor's selection is critical. In general, largely because of scholarly zeal rather than out of consideration for the student, many anthologies include much apparatus—textual notes, annotations of all kinds, study guides—much of it designed more for the scholar than the student. The fault of texts too encumbered with apparatus is that they draw the students' attention away from their own exploring, criticizing, thinking and toward accepting someone else's.

Most new teachers have to resolve doubts about the teacher's presence with respect to texts. Being overly dependent on a text is probably no better than persistently disdaining the use of texts even as one is using them. Even the best of texts does not guarantee a common learning among students in a class, but it does offer a basis for independent reading, questions, and discussion that may lead to a common learning. The text may usefully appear (and often is) more authoritative than the teacher. The teacher need not be defensive, antagonistic, or servile to the textbook's superior command of a subject. Wise teachers will take advantage of it by not hiding the fact that the text furthers their learning as well as the students'. The kind of suggesting, questioning, and responding that a good teacher can supply is superior to the best of texts in that the teacher offers a wider range of useful and immediate guidance, stimulation, reinforcement, and challenge.

Texts vary greatly in difficulty. The best way to find out whether a text is too difficult or too easy is to ask the students. A small amount of time spent in filling out an informal questionnaire or in discussing such matters as we are discussing here —choice and use of texts, testing, grading, assignments—is seldom wasted. Nor is the discussion in text-selection committees a waste of time. The only such practice to which I take general exception is the selection of texts by teachers not actively teaching a course. The person who is likely to have something specifically useful to say about adopting a text is the teacher who has used it with a variety of students. Otherwise, one's remarks lack the benefit of page-by-page, class-by-class experience.

By the way of useful general advice, I will add some do's and don't's about textbook choice and use:

—Do keep in mind alternatives to assigning a text. If the class engages students in reading and thinking about a variety of verbal as well as nonverbal materials, if the class hour provides ample space for the kind of accurate guidance good texts give, then a formal text may be superfluous.

—Do find ways besides periodic review and tests to encourage students to use texts. Reviewing and testing are so common, so easy—the instructor's handbook even provides the questions—that they are virtually inescapable. If done well, they are supported soundly by learning theory. But a teacher should find more varied motivations. Selecting passages of interpretation from several texts and duplicating them for thought and discussion is one way. In my own work, I often give students examples of how different English translators have dealt with a major work in another language. The differences speak for themselves and lead to my asking students to try their own hands at translating a passage into an idiom they might better understand. Teachers in mathematics and the sciences invent their own problem sets as well as use those in the text.

—Do try to show both respect toward, and independence from, the text. If you've chosen it, you can't always be knocking it. But you may view a historical development or an economic theory differently from the text, and students can benefit from your bringing these differences out accurately and fairly.

—Do consider both cost and size in selecting texts. Can the student be reasonably charged with keeping up with the text assignments? Is the text easy to carry around? Does the use of the text justify its cost?

—Finally, don't inadvertently confine a student's reading to the text. College, as many students keep repeating, often stands in the way of learning. There is so much valuable current reading in every area of university study that a teacher should feel guilty about crowding it out of the students' lives by always giving textbook reading first priority.

This last piece of advice warrants some further discussion. It is not easy to get students to read beyond the text or to free

them from the duress and compulsions associated with required
texts. All teachers should seek to foster a habit of reading
throughout college. In part, the trick is to get books out of
their confines in bookstores, libraries, and faculty bookcases
and into the hands of students. Dan Fader's success with supposed nonreaders in *Hooked on Books* (Fader and McNeil,
1968) rested on the simplest of expedients: placing boxes of
books where students could get at them. For a number of years,
I consciously pursued two strategies. The first was to set aside
a shelf of books in my office and announce that all these books
were there to be borrowed as the students wished. If they jotted
their name down and stuck it in the space where the book had
been, all the better; if they didn't, all right. I could always lo-
cate missing books by asking my classes. A few books did get
borrowed that way, some made enough impact to arouse a discussion when they were returned, and the losses were negligible.
The second strategy was to increase this kind of reading by
bringing to class specific books and articles selected for brevity,
interest, and relevance to what we were studying. The rate of
borrowing went up greatly, and almost all the students return-
ing borrowed materials indicated that they had read them profitably. This second strategy had to be worked at, and I have
never been able to maintain it as a regular practice. Nevertheless, I keep it in my mind as a workable way of getting students
to read beyond the text.

For that, surely, is the central point about using texts.
Textbooks are academic. Their impact on learning beyond the
academy may well be negative. Since so much textbook reading
is done under duress, reading either seriously or casually may be
one of the casualties of a college education. The enormous resale
and turnover of textbooks suggest the lack of permanent value
that students attach to them. Few texts become permanent parts
of a student's library. If texts play any part in the lives of people outside college, it is in the form of how-to books usually designed for simple satisfactions of specific needs. The teacher's
highest aims in respect to the use of texts may be those of not
turning students away from reading, of illuminating the range of
experience and pleasure that can come from the written word,

and of keeping alive curiosity and a willingness to learn by whatever means the real world offers.

One last reflection, aimed at teachers more than students. The practice of selling textbooks to used book dealers is a small manifestation of disregard or disrespect for college and university education. The high cost of texts and the rising expenses of going to college may justify the practice for some students. But it may also thrive because teachers produce and assign the kind of texts that aren't worth keeping. Confining learning to bits of courses and certifying them with grades add to a feeling that a course has no existence apart from work done under compulsion and the outcome of passing the course.

It would be ideal if a great many of the texts used in college became the basis for personal and family libraries. For some students, they undoubtedly do. I have been cheered over modest efforts to encourage students to build libraries, in one instance, to award prizes to dormitory occupants for the best personal library. But for too many students, textbooks are merely a somewhat bulky form of exchange.

The practice of faculty members selling textbooks back to used book dealers is another matter. Trimmers tend to defend the practice by purporting to sell back only those books which publishers have sent without their being requested. Very few textbooks get into faculty members' hands that way; that excuse is hardly better than blaming such petty venality on low salaries. The practice is both unethical and cheap. And if faculty bookshelves get overburdened with books, there are a good many places in this country and the world where books would be welcomed.

11

Assignments

I will use the term *assignment* to cover the widest possible range of requirements teachers make of students beyond coming to class and keeping up with the textbook. These requirements include outside readings, book reports, short and long papers, projects of all kinds, team investigations and reports, and even such things as collages, light shows, diaries, journals, and meditations. While I take a dim view of some of the things my colleagues have accepted as course work in recent years, I completely agree with their intentions, for there are few assignments worse than those that satisfy nothing but the teacher's demands. The borrowing, buying, or stealing of term papers is only the most conspicuous manifestation of this kind of assignment. The fault lies with teachers as much as with the students—good assignments elicit good work; bad assignments, bad work.

In general, the term paper is a bad assignment. Teachers rarely think through their reasons for assigning papers, take too little account of the demands papers make on the students, and are too sanguine about the results. All of these facts explain why commercial term-paper outfits flourish. The product is easy to mass-produce, a more than sufficient labor force is on hand, and the market is reliable. There is a long shelf-life for stock like: "The History of .... from .... to ....," "The Rise (Fall) of .... and its (Social) (Political) (Economic) Consequences," "A Comparison of ....'s and ....'s Views of ....," "The Early (Late) Work of

132

................," "A .... Solution to .... Factors in
a .... Analysis," and "The Behavior of .... under Conditions of ...." If one feels a need for jazzier packaging, certain titles fit all manner of content: "Peace and Repose,"
"The Quarrel with Time," "Ecological Privation," "The End of
Rainbows," "Conscience in the Community," "Ethnic Impera-
tives"—the list can be expanded as far as the writer's vocabulary
permits.

So what is wrong with the term paper? It inflates into the
doctoral dissertation and becomes the ballast of the weightier
think-magazines. Surely thinkers and writers become better
thinkers and writers by thinking and writing just as students become better students by that same process.

We have mentioned the first thing wrong with the term
paper, that teachers don't give enough specific attention to its
nature and aims. A second wrong is that too much weight in the
course is given to the term paper. A third is that it is too easy for
students to get term papers done for them by someone else. A
fourth is that students often face too many papers within a
brief term to do any of them justice. And a fifth is that faculty
members don't commonly provide the feedback that serious
written work deserves.

If one is going to argue for the term paper's worth, one
must first get students to do their own work. In this respect,
faculty members will probably have to accept the responsibility
for some surveillance and sleuthing. Asking for note cards and
drafts as well as for the final product is a useful check. Topics
can be defined so as to outwit some students or at least to drive
up prices in the term-paper factories. Some faculty members
can even bring moral suasion to bear to get term papers honest
enough to warrant careful reading and response.

Still, none of these—outguessing, anticipating, sleuthing,
and catching and punishing—are very satisfactory for either
teacher or student. A more promising move is to get away from
the term paper itself: its research data, its length, its time of
completion, its ubiquity. A realistic appraisal of the term paper
from the point of view of a publishing scholar would bring some
sensible recognitions. Few scholars who carry heavy teaching

schedules can research and write more than one publishable piece per term. If they could, the journals would be even more flooded than they are now. The truth is that scholars have summers and sabbaticals to attend to these obligations and they do not have to face incompletes or failures at the end of each term. Nor can one argue that faculty members have more obligations than students. Students almost everywhere carry more classes than faculty members teach; many have jobs (assigning term papers, teaching, writing scholarly pieces *are* the faculty member's job); students' lives, too, are full of personal distractions.

But, it may be argued, professors don't require publishable work from students. One can as quickly reply that professors don't produce publishable work a good part of the time. The important point is that doing a good term paper probably puts just as much strain on the student as writing a professional paper puts on the teacher. Both require the same physical format: typed, double-spaced, clean, fully documented, with proper footnotes and bibliography. The professor probably expects no less of the student than the journal editor does of the professor. A good student might do a creditable job if he or she gave one paper per term all the attention. As it is, students do the one that counts and may feel forced to buy or borrow or plagiarize the others. Perhaps the term paper is realistic compared with life's performances—you do some and fake the rest. But that argument is not sufficient reason for depending on an assignment that invites such misuse. If the term paper is to be used at all, the faculty should cooperate to reduce the number of papers. Even two or three good papers a year stretch reasonable expectations, though that number would constitute a big reduction for many students.

But what of the aims and intentions of term papers that, teachers will argue, cannot be served better by other assignments? Posing questions, stimulating inquiry, developing techniques of investigation, and broadening the student's knowledge of resources are surely defensible aims. Stimulating inquiries in ways appropriate to the subject at hand and related to other objectives of the course as well as to larger educational aims appears to be sound teaching strategy. Developing powers of analysis and synthesis is likewise an objective served by assigning the term paper, and the demands of appropriateness, reasonableness, and relevance should be placed upon these assignments. Teachers can use their own command of specific fact, research competence, and broader knowledge to shape topics that will reward analysis. Obviously, there is a progression from simple inquiry to sophisticated analysis and synthesis, from the shorter papers in the first years of college to the full-blown term paper in the last.

I object to none of these aims, nor do I question the claim that term papers can serve them. But I do object to the failure to recognize practical objections to the term paper and to see other possibilities for fulfilling these legitimate aims. The alternatives to term papers are many. If one of a teacher's aims is to develop the inquiring mind that will pose questions as well as seek answers, then much of the stress on the correct format for lengthy research papers could be laid on finding answers to real questions and reporting them in whatever ways seem appropriate. I do not mean that the teacher simply backs away and says, in effect, "Go find out something and bring it back," though, in its way, that is about as good as assigning a term paper and wastes much less class time. Rather, a teacher can suggest pinpoint questions, indicate where answers might be found, and move students to the leg work that accompanies real investigations. As a practical matter, shorter, focused assignments in which the teacher's expertise plays a significant part offer more chances for learning than term papers do.

The aims sought in the assigning of term papers need not be met solely in research or in individual work. The communication of research findings is but one limited kind of communication. More encouragement should be given to group investigations intended to cross disciplinary lines and arrive at finished reports that make an impact on a public rather than merely add to the stock of inert information. Much of the real work of the academic world itself goes on in committee, just as it does in the real world. Why can't a group of students be charged both with researching any of the hundreds of problems that professional societies, citizens' groups, public commissions face every day and with contributing something to that problem's solution? Keeping these points in mind might offset one of the common weaknesses of term papers, which gives the student a choice of taking a trivial topic and expending on it more critical intelligence and energy than it's worth or of attempting a large topic that simply expects too much of the student's knowledge and technical command.

Inquiry, analysis, and synthesis attached to a base of knowledge and formal research methods define only one kind of term paper, anyway. Imagination, grace, and force of expression are just as worthy of development. The first inclines toward formal scientific research, while the other inclines toward literary creativity. One does not necessarily exclude the other, and both can be of use in many different disciplines. This second kind of paper shares much with the essay—a trying out of ideas, information, and experience to illuminate the subject at hand. The essay form forces students to stretch their powers of thought, feeling, and expression to arrive at something they can truly call their own. The spirit and intent of the written essay can be legitimately extended to any creative response, such as pantomime, painting, dance, or even to the gathering of objects and actual demonstration of findings appropriate to a subject under study.

Essays can also be plagiarized or done sloppily. Substituting another person's style and stance and substance for one's own, however, may appear more foolish to the student and more obvious to the teacher than appropriating impersonal data for the standard term paper. The weaknesses in an essay assignment are no greater than the weaknesses in an assignment that implies that informed expression only comes by hunting out facts, authoritative opinions, and the thoughts of others. The term paper, in short, depends too much for its substance on our collective scholarly vanities. Although "Look it up" is not bad advice, "Think about it" is even better. The one, of course, need not exclude the other. The teacher's choice and management of assignments might be considerably improved by considering the separate as well as common objectives of "looking it up" and "thinking about it." Clarification and interest established in *pithy*

these two activities, "expressing it" might yield more learning than seems to reside in finishing four or five term papers at the eleventh hour.

Yet, regardless of the care one puts into devising assignments, students' questions invariably come down to: "How long should it be?" and "When is it due?" And every new class is going to be as anxious about "How many papers do we have to write?" as about "How do you grade?"

I suspect the best answers are the arbitrary ones: four pages, six pages, eight to ten pages, twelve pages; eight A.M., 5 P.M., midnight; April 15, April 21, May 1; and whatever numbers are required. The only useful pieces of advice I have ever given about length are three: first, that anything called a paper must be more than one page; second, that a handwritten paper should not end at the bottom of a page; and third, that papers of any length beyond three or four pages should be thought of in terms of blocks of material.

Behind the first piece of advice is no hostility to concise, pithy expression. With most student writing, however, brevity is not synonymous with either conciseness or pith. The consequences of facing a second page are sufficiently important to warrant this arbitrary, mechanical rule. The writer of a single page too often expires at the end of it. Forced to carry a sentence over to a second page, the writer may just find another sentence or two possible, may even find something valuable to say.

The second piece of advice further confronts the temptation that besets all writers to stop at the first opportunity. It was Hemingway's practice never to stop a day's writing on a full page. That practice can be applied here. Since a blank piece of paper is the hardest thing for a writer to face, a full one provides the easiest excuse to stop. Too often, papers end at the end of a page rather than at the end of a subject.

As to handwriting, much of the market in term papers would shrivel if students were required to submit handwritten papers rather than neat, typewritten manuscripts. Typewritten copy is still a great convenience for teachers, editors, and printers. For all the marvelous things word processors can do, much of what they do comes after both thinking and writing. A pencil and paper is still a marvelously portable, inexpensive, and fundamental writing tool. It ranks right up there with the sentence-forming brain that needs only such a tool to get down things while they are hot. So while we are moving students who haven't yet mastered the typewriter on to the word processor, we might also be encouraging them to learn to write with the hand.

To me, writing is muscular as well as mental. An unacknowledged reason that college students don't learn to write is that they don't, in fact, *write.* They put down something in writing and then have obliging friends, relatives, spouses, or sweethearts type it up. No student learns much about writing this way, nor is typing nearly the common skill we assume. Insistence upon typed papers is simply and importantly wrong. Rather, the teacher needs to consciously work against stated and unstated rules that only typed papers are accepted and against the accurate gut feeling of students that typed papers will get better grades. The availability and use of word processors undoubtedly makes writing papers easier, but it probably increases the chances of someone else doing much of the work. Now, any copy becomes indistinguishable from the original. The word processor also makes it easier to produce written work that looks so much like a good term paper as to deceive both the student and professor. Word processing, as I have observed it so far with students and faculty, tends to increase length without necessarily increasing quality.

The third piece of advice, to think of longer papers in terms of blocks of material, is designed to make the labor of writing easier. Paragraphs are probably more useful to the writer than to the reader. And beyond the paragraph in most kinds of student papers are three or four or five—rarely more—blocks of material. If the writer sees these blocks, gets the sense of not having to write a whole long paper every time out, feels the satisfaction of getting one block of work done, then the task of writing is greatly simplified.

In this respect, word processors do have a specific utility. They enable writers to shift material, to respond quickly to the common experience that this block of material really belongs somewhere else. In general, the word processor makes revising easier in all ways. Getting students to recognize that revising is important is a gain most writing teachers acknowledge. But learning to revise is more than being handy with the cursor. The *ease* of revising is secondary. Whether the student submits work done by hand or word processor, the teacher's responsibility is to help the student grasp the necessity for, results from, and techniques of revising. Thus, the very ease in using a word processor may lead both students and teacher away from such useful strategies as assigning shorter and more frequent papers and providing more interchange between teacher and student at various points of composition.

My final comment on written assignments is that teachers who expect good written work are obligated to read it promptly and well. Few student complaints are as justified as those against professors who give perfunctory attention to papers students have worked hard over and who return papers only long after they are turned in. Professors rationalize at length about their failure to meet these obligations of diligence and promptness: "Too many students," "Too many dummies," "Too little time," "They've probably cribbed the papers anyway," "Besides, I'm no English teacher." Poor excuses one and all. The same habits that cause editors of academic journals to take months to read manuscripts lead to sloppy handling of students' papers. It takes no more time to read papers now than later, and no unsuspected abundance of free time will appear in the future. There is no way to require assignments without committing oneself to responding to them. Putting them off is a dodge, using readers a dodge, offering excuses a dodge.

Facing these harsh words, the teacher may reply that the alternative is to assign no written work. That's not the only alternative at all, and not even an acceptable alternative if a teacher's honest appraisal of learning values written assignments. One of the advantages of sorting out what one is trying to do in every class is the possibility of arriving at a mix of classes in which the necessary grubby stuff varies enough from one class to another so that all of it can be handled decently. As I ask teachers making assignments to be aware of the students' other assignments, so I advise teachers to look to their own schedules in relation to the kinds of demands various classes make. Some classes may not require large amounts of written work as a first objective. Other classes may profit most from short written exercises. Still others may demand substantial written work.

In addition to planning written assignments into one's own schedule, the teacher can gain some ground by informing students what they can expect as responses to written assignments. Better to be honest and admit that papers will be read hastily or tardily or by someone else than to let all of these happen as if it didn't matter. The practical difficulty of reading papers carefully is another reason for avoiding the standard, long term paper and assigning instead a number of shorter papers. With a number of papers, a teacher can assure students that all papers will get read and that at least one will receive painstaking attention. Asking for long papers at the end of the term is a generally shoddy practice. Professors say that only at the end of the term will they have time to give papers the attention they deserve. But the end of the term is filled with getting ready for the next term or turning to the Christmas holidays or getting off on spring break or summer vacation. Occasionally, if students furnish stamped envelopes, they may receive months later sandy and soggy papers brilliantly critiqued, treasures to be mounted and hung. Far more common are the papers that get done immediately in haste or done well at leisure, both placed somewhere in departmental offices for students who never pick them up.

What I have said about written work applies to other kinds of assignments. Problems in mathematics and the sciences, case studies, reports, and the like can be considered in a similar way. The teacher's responsibility is to clarify what the specific aims are, how they can best be carried out, and how prompt and careful feedback will be given to each student. Practical considerations of the other demands on students' time, of independence and honesty in carrying out the work, and of avoiding deception by busy-work and show also enter into making the most of assigned work. The best general stance to take toward assignments is to expect no more from them than the teacher puts in. Though I haven't stressed them, there are many frivolous, witty, whimsical assignments that can well act as seasoning for a course. Contests and games and puzzles with real prizes are possibilities. The serious and demanding gain in contexts in which the not-serious-at-all has a respectable place.

Finally, with fewer college graduates finding employment in lower and higher education, teachers might begin to think of course assignments in less academic terms. A great many opportunities can be provided for students to practice academic skills, acquire information, and exercise critical faculties through real "assignments" in the community. There are adequate institutional models for such activities, from Antioch working from a small college base to Northeastern using the resources of a major city. But outside these specific milieus and such departments and schools as social work or business, many college teachers are not in close touch with nonacademic work. They have no experience and no lines of communication. But these lines are likely to be opened up, and teachers need be aware of these opportunities. Credit for job experience is only cheap credit, unwarranted credit, when faculty members fail to be involved in examining and judging its worth.

Underlying almost everything in this chapter is a distinction between useful work and busy-work. Theory and conscience contribute to the teacher's failings here, for both tell us that students should be doing things that cause learning, that they should not just be passively studying or listening to teachers. Assignments are ways of getting students to do things. The catch is that good assignments are so hard to find and ordinary ones so readily available. My examples of busy-work come from both public schools and college, and many from what my children have brought home as they passed through sixteen years and more of schooling. I have contributed to it. Busy-work includes most looking up of facts; most book reports; most fill-in-the-blanks aids to mastery of historical events, biological classification, social structures, literary terminology, and the like; most research papers and project reports—in short, most homework not carefully thought out both in the assigning and the doing of it.

As to advice I might give, an unremitting attention to fashioning useful work for students and a distrust of routine assignments are places to begin. Defining assignments carefully and connecting them with clearly defined aims are of first importance. Borrowing ideas from others, exploring the pedagogical literature for ideas, and adapting such ideas to one's specific needs should be standard teaching practices. Trying out assignments on ourselves and getting students' views about the worth of an assignment are necessary correctives to a teacher's one-sided view. Making assignments is among the most difficult of a teacher's routine duties. We know the worth of what we ask the students to do, but, for students, almost any assignment may seem to be busy-work if they don't see what purpose it serves.

12

Tests

"The obvious method of discovering whether the class has studied its work," Gilbert Highet writes, "and of prodding them on to study in the future, is to ask them questions. Written questions with written answers are 'tests' and 'quizzes,' or 'examinations.' Horrible words. My soul sickens at their very sound. I sat so many scores of them, and I have marked so many hundreds of them. . . . Yet I have never been able to think of a substitute, and have yet to meet anyone else who has" (1950, p. 133).

Would we give tests or take them if we didn't have to? Oddly enough, to judge by newspaper quizzes, electronic genius calculators, television quiz programs, and the game Trivial Pursuit, we probably would. Perhaps all of these are evidences of a trivial and misplaced regard for learning, or in the case of quiz programs, so nakedly attached to greed as not to count as learning. I don't think so. Rather, they all go back to a basic pleasure in finding things out, and among those things is the question, "What do I know?" Like grading, testing makes teachers uncomfortable because it threatens an amicable relationship. That threat is most prominent when one person seems always to be the one who tests and grades and the other the one who is tested and graded. In part, that is the reason why I am such a strong advocate of student evaluation of teachers. Student evaluation is the one situation in the whole university operation where roles are somewhat reversed. It is also the reason why I advocate that students make up tests as well as take them and that teachers themselves take such tests.

Tests almost always have some impact upon the students' learning, but a great deal of sloppy testing exists because the true purpose of tests is to arrive at and defend a grade. The cart is before the horse, and most of this discussion aims at getting the horse in front again.

The first questions a teacher should ask are, "Why am I testing?" "How am I testing?" and "What results am I getting?" The complaints students voice among themselves and sometimes with the teacher are more pointed, but they fall within these categories. The complaints include an irritation with trivial quizzes, a confusion over just what the teacher wants, objections to what the teacher accepts as good or poor answers, and a sick stomach both before and after going down the tube. Keeping these responses in mind, let us explore the broader questions.

"Why am I testing?" I have already spoken against the practice of using tests chiefly to arrive at grades. It is an indefensible practice, except as grades are firmly established in the students' minds as measures of learning. Even then it is indefensible unless the grade and the test point out what has been learned, what remains to be learned, and what is vaguely comprehended or wholly misunderstood. In this limited sense, all tests are diagnostic, telling the students some very specific things about where they stand with relation to the development of skills or the acquisition of information. This diagnostic function is legitimate. Recognizing it may help a teacher prepare more sharply focused tests, use them to build specific competences, and adapt them to individual needs.

Tests, like grades, can be given for simple motivation. Most often they represent the stick rather than the carrot. A science professor told me that, as a regular practice throughout a term's work, he constructs some tests on which the slow students will do well. "They need to win one once in a while," he said. The trick in constructing these tests was to disguise the fact that they were easy by design. Since I prefer positive to negative motivation, I wish that more teachers would construct tests with the hope that everyone will do well, not with the more common desire to separate sheep from goats, to establish the curve, or to get the lazy bastards who never show up for class and don't respond to the teacher's brilliance when they do. Much of the motivational impact of testing arises from the relationships among students in a class and the relationship of one test to other tests. Competition on tests and for grades can, up to a point, increase motivation. Beyond that, it can block achievement for certain students and create strong adverse reactions for the class. Giving tests frequently rather than rarely does provide the teacher with more of an opportunity to provide different kinds of motivation and to shape them to the needs of individual students.

Tests serve purposes beyond grades and motivation. One of the most crucial is to select from a large body of information those facts, concepts, theories, opinions and the like that have the greatest importance. Students criticize teachers justly for tests that dwell on trivia or matters little emphasized in class. A widely publicized letter of complaint from a parent to a college president cited a specific final for an introductory philosophy course. "There are seven questions in this final exam," the father wrote, "and five of them deal with Kant. In an introductory course covering approximately 2,500 years of philosophy, how can anyone consider this test to be valid? . . . My daughter had a positive attitude toward philosophy when she began the course, but Professor ——— has succeeded in turning her off" ("A 'Concerned Father' and His Bout with Academe," 1974, p. 8). My sympathies are altogether with the father. Even at second hand, I grow indignant at the teacher's failure to distinguish important information from what was probably the subject of his Ph.D. dissertation. It is not just a matter of the teacher's fairness to the student; it is a matter of his or her basic competence in a subject matter.

That competence lies not only in knowing one's stuff, but also in reflecting on its importance and on ways of conveying that importance to the students. Unfortunately, the professoriate is not very skilled in the mechanics of testing. Nor are many professors more than casually acquainted with the learning theory behind good testing practices. Paradoxically, but not surprisingly, at the highest level of awarding advanced degrees, the tests are probably less valid and reliable than those which accompany lower-level classwork.

Learning theory says that recall is aided by repetition and reinforcement. Hence there is some reason for testing which repeats the items most commonly missed. For the most part, teachers scant the careful analysis that could be useful in shaping the next test. Learning theory supports tests as a means of providing feedback, another confirmed essential of learning. Yet, too little feedback characterizes university testing, a fact most apparent in the practice of giving final exams. By scheduling exams in a final test week almost all the effects of specific feedback are lost. Further, the presence of excessive stress, which learning theory has demonstrated to be harmful to performance, is deliberately fostered by final exams.

In general, the ability to make up tests, like most of the competence acquired by college teachers, develops through happenstance. Common sense often offsets the ill effects of knowing little about test design and picking up that little knowledge from drawing on routine patterns, which relate more to institutions' and teachers' convenience than to the way students learn. Nowhere else does authority sit so heavily on the students, both in the attitude that tests are the way students learn and in the fact that teachers give tests and students must take them.

The ways of testing are many, and since "tests and measurements" are the specific research concern of colleges of education and departments of psychology, there is no shortage of experience close at hand to draw on. I am not advocating that testing be turned over to the experts, nor am I bowing to the quantitative niceties that dominate the field. Instead, I am saying that a college teacher's education should include enough substance and practice to face that question, "How am I testing?" One of a number of simple and reliable pamphlets on test construction should be a basic part of any professor's equipment.

Some useful books on test design and the fundamentals of testing are Copperud (1979), Ebel and Frisbie (1986), Gronlund (1982), and Walsh (1985). Levy (1984) raises many important questions about the use of tests in education. Sarason (1980) is an authoritative source about test anxiety, and Milton

(1982) focuses on college testing in a provocative way in *Will That Be on the Final?*

As a general response to "How am I testing?" faculty members generally arrive at a relatively few common practices that seem most appropriate to their subjects. English professors give essay exams; math professors, objective tests. Examinations can be as dull as lectures, and for the same reasons: a lack of variety, a lack of emphasis, a lack of imaginative makeup. Within the limits of assumed appropriateness, the teacher has much room to create memorable tests. Raymond Weaver, the Melville scholar, is still remembered for a two-question essay test. As I remember the anecdote, the first question asked students to pick out and expound on the worst book they had read during the term. When they had been given ample time to tear their favorites to shreds, Weaver wrote the second question on the board, to the effect, "To what defects in my own perception of literature do I attribute the previous answer?"

The most successful test I have ever used incorporated in the test procedure itself the substance I was trying to teach. In this instance, a class in the history of ideas was reading Aristotle's *Ethics*. The effectiveness of this specific quiz depended on establishing a pattern of quizzes, which were graded by assigning a number of points to each question and totaling the points for a grade. Customarily when I returned the quizzes, I indicated the point value of each question on the board, marked on each student's paper the points received for each question, and entered a total point value and grade. Usually I put a graph on the board showing the distribution of grades. In going over the quiz, I pointed out, as a matter of routine, that while I had read the papers carefully, I computed scores as rapidly as possible. Consequently I asked all students to check my arithmetic and let me know of any mistakes in calculation that might affect a grade. If they wanted to argue about my evaluation of any single question, they were also invited to do so.

For this quiz on ethics, I made deliberate mistakes in calculating points and grades on some of the papers: Ten or so students got grades higher than they should have, while another ten got lowered score. The results the first time I gave this quiz were as I expected, and they have been repeated by subsequent classes. Almost all the students who had mistakes that lowered their grades called the mistakes to my attention, but none of those who had mistakes in their favor said anything. In a subsequent class period, I acquainted the class with these interesting facts, a lesson, I think, in situational ethics, in the realities of ethical behavior at a simple, unthreatening, but memorable level.

Although students can get along without ingenuity in test design, novelty makes an impact simply because so much testing is routine. Tests that have some element of play in them probably help reduce test anxiety over time. As I told the students in the ethics test just mentioned, I recorded no grades nor, certainly, the names of those who came forth and those who didn't. The learning was in the test itself, quite apart from the grades. Not every test need be graded, though any test worth giving needs to provide meaningful feedback to the student. Ungraded quizzes can be reviewed as carefully as graded ones; oral quizzes are as useful as written ones if one can get something like the whole class to participate.

The final important question in testing is, "What results am I getting?" This is, in part, a matter of knowing something about what tests reveal and what they don't, and I refer teachers to the previously cited books for basic advice in these matters. What test results should not tell teachers is what they most often do tell them—that is, these are the bright students, and these the dumb ones. There is no way I know of to prevent such offhand conclusions, but there are certainly ways of rendering them relatively harmless. One way is to think of test results diagnostically and to spend time outside class not only sorting items that everyone knows from those no one knows but also diagnosing individual patterns of performance. Feedback to the whole class can concentrate on known and unknown material, leaving some time for working on individual students' learning in specific ways. Giving feedback on an examination is as necessary and as worthy of care, intelligence, and imagination as making up the test in the first place.

Examinations also commonly give the teacher some awareness of class norms and of each individual's standing or

progress with respect to these norms. Teachers gain such awareness in an imprecise way from their accumulated experience of
giving the same test to different classes. Standardized testing
with great numbers of students produces established norms.
Tests that establish performance levels usually come under institutional sponsorship and are used in various ways for admission,
classification, and exemption or credit by examination. It is
commonly accepted that such tests establish the level of verbal
and mathematical skills. The popularity of credit by examination in other subjects has aroused a fresh controversy between
faculty members and professional testers. On balance, I trust
professionally devised tests more than do many of my colleagues—partly because I respect the complexities of test design
and partly because I think there is as much need for professional competence in designing a test as there is in designing a
chemistry experiment. In general, faculties kid themselves in
thinking that a test devised by two or four or eight of them for
use by thousands of students in their own institution is likely to
be any more personal or precise than one devised by professional testers.

An example of what professional expertise can do for the
classroom teacher is the development by the Educational Testing Service of holistic scoring of writing. White (1985) describes
this development into what has now become a common practice: the controlled reading by multiple readers of student essays to measure writing ability. The procedure is sufficiently
economical and reliable to be linked with the teaching of writing in a productive way for both students and teachers.

The larger issue of the usefulness and advisability of stan-
dardizing such testing arouses strong and contrary feelings
among faculty members. While many teachers think that professional testing proceeds from sinister motives and has dangerous
consequences, they regard their own regular testing, which is
not markedly different in character and use, as by nature benign. Having worked on both sides of the controversy, I conclude that professional testers know more what they are about
and are better able to achieve their objectives than faculty test
makers. The argument is really one of objectives. If the intent is

to process large numbers of students for the purpose of admitting them to, or excluding them from, aspects of learning, then surely the professional tests are an efficient way of reaching that goal. Whether they are a good way or whether they are even good enough to be the basis of screening and classifying is as debatable a question as whether screening and classifying are good for education and American society.

An issue causing much controversy in the eighties is proficiency testing. The idea behind it is as old as any in education: that if learning takes place, the results should be visible, and the learner should be able to do things he or she could not previously have done. A number of states have mandated statewide tests for students in public institutions. *Assessment* is a big word with boards of trustees and legislative bodies. Faculties are probably wiser not to confront assessment as an unwarranted intrusion into academic matters but as an opportunity to inform nonacademics that there is more being learned and to be learned than we can measure in our testing.

A more informed perspective toward assessment is behind the movement known as performance-based education long established at Alverno College, but slow in attracting full commitment from other institutions. This kind of education does not gain easy acceptance from college teachers, for whom so much learning is conceptual, ideational, verbal, and independent of specific doing. One can teach another person how to pull a tooth skillfully, and make performance the test of whether the skill has been learned. But testing performance in that great number of subjects in which the learning is conceptual and verbal is by no means as easy.

A part of professional education, like much of pure science, keeps looking for simple ways of explaining complex matters and, like applied science, developing simple instruments to accomplish complex tasks. These pursuits are not to be deplored, except as they fail to recognize complexities and are deceived by simple solutions. The zeal with which many educators took up behavioral objectives is a prime example. The principle is simple and valid: that defining one's objectives—that is, making clear what you're trying to do—is generally a good idea. The sticker is in turning a common-sense recognition into an educational touchstone. To make behavioral objectives valid, all learning must be defined as behavior. Certainly, much learning has its outcome in behavior, and I am critical of much of higher learning because it is characteristically passive, so deliberately set against doing. But that criticism has yet to convince me that useful learning does not go on internally. Such learning may not manifest itself in behavior.

Performance- or competency-based education is an extension of the interest in behavioral objectives. Like behavioral objectives, performance-based education applies best to those subjects in which clear-cut behaviors are the desirable outcome. Such behaviors might be determined adequately by performance tests. Unfortunately, as performance-based education is applied in a wider spectrum, it tends to increase the tendency to define education as that which can be tested and to narrow a student's learning to that which can be determined on a test. The aim of performance testing is legitimate if it helps students learn—that is, if it provides motivation, usefully identifies strengths and weaknesses, and reduces the chances of marking time and keeping in step. The truly harmful effects of performance testing, as many critics have pointed out, lie in its negative application. Performance testing can discourage, hold back, and discriminate against students, and it can reduce the variety and potentialities of learning. Criticisms that apply with greater force to the standardized, performance-based testing we've just been discussing apply to some degree to all testing, a fact that is reason enough for faculty members to try to do their testing well.

In conclusion, I will set out some concise suggestions that underline some things discussed here and that add some other useful points:

1. Use a variety of testing methods.
2. Always give feedback, promptly if possible.
3. Tests should be more for learning and for motivating than for measuring. All three are useful.
4. Regard the absolute worth and accuracy of testing with suspicion.
5. Reduce in any way you can the threat tests pose.

6. Don't grade all tests.
7. Clarify test objectives both before and after, with yourself and with students.
8. Be honest, open, and fair. Discuss tests both before and after.
9. Let students be makers as well as takers of tests.
10. Don't stress the trivial just because it is so easy to test.
11. Surprise quizzes and tests which can't be completed in the given time may serve the teacher's ego more than the student's learning.
12. Be imaginative as well as careful, balanced, and precise.
13. Be generous.

13

Grades

No matters are more vexing to students and teachers than tests and grades. In part, that vexation arises from the way that teachers often lean on tests and grades as evidence of their worth as educators and the way that students commonly view test scores and grades as synonymous with getting an education. Since there is much that is intangible in human learning, the concreteness of tests and grades is bound to have an appeal. Testing is surely one way of providing emphasis, repetition, and reinforcement, all admitted aids to learning, and grades certainly provide a simple form of motivation. Moreover, customary testing and grading have such a basic appeal to ideas of competition, accomplishment, advancement, superiority, and recognition that I see no way of avoiding either. Still, it is worth continuing efforts to see that some opportunities for learning are honored in which neither tests nor grades are the measure. It is also important that college teachers resist the false security that comes from having too great a confidence in grades.

One of the few books that perceives college grades in a wide social and historical context is *Making Sense of College Grades* (Milton, Pollio, and Eison, 1986). That book reminds faculty that *deflation* as well as *inflation* can apply to grades, that any given letter grade only roughly approximates any other same letter grade, that the practice of giving grades contributes to creating grade-oriented as distinguished from learning-oriented students, and that the grade-point average (GPA) is for the most part a useless and misleading statistic. These and other findings lead the authors to make five recommendations which I restate as follows (pp. 202–203):

1. To make grades primarily serve the purposes of learning and teaching rather than of rank-ordering students.
2. To improve the quality of tests so as to better identify what grades are actually measuring.
3. To give students more and better information about performance than letter grades provide.
4. To reduce the number of symbols in a grading system; to give up the false precision of minuses and pluses in favor of Honors, Credit, No Credit.
5. To abolish the GPA.

It is interesting that grading has so flourished in a society which avows egalitarian sentiments yet lives with a widening gap between failure and success. It is not just simplicity that keeps the grading system in place, nor its usefulness as an admission criterion for further study or the professions, nor even the students' needs to get feedback on learning. Grades probably arise from some basic urge to make distinctions, to sort and rank human beings, to unconsciously operate in harmony with the rest of society. The arguments over the validity of using grades will continue. Averages will go up and down. Faculty and students will continue to tinker with grades, resent them, and search for a better system, but the basic practices will not be greatly changed. Nevertheless, I regard simplicity and flexibility in grading practices as a healthier condition than that in which bell-shaped curves, pluses and minuses, percentages and percentiles are commonplace.

Before going on to give what helpful advice I can, let me offer a few samples of the controversy over grades.

First, from a Harvard senior, quoted from a taped interview in William Perry's *Forms of Intellectual and Ethical Development in the College Years* (1970, p. 140):

You've got to make a choice, let's put it that way, between getting good grades, I mean really

> good grades, or doing pretty much with your life, and even though, if you try to see a perspective, and say, "Well, I'll get good grades now, and I'll have the rest of my life to do what I like and I'll have that *cum laude* diploma under my belt," all right, but these four years are—if you have any sort of intellectual interests—this is the best place in the world to be with it, and the idea that it has to go to waste, that time, time can't be spent in, indulging more in them is unfortunate. But I don't know as there's really any solution to that. I guess you, you've just got to make your choice.

It is a common plaint: Grades keep students from learning what they want to learn. There is probably a mixture of truth and falsehood here, reflecting both a yearning for the free, joyful learning we know exists and a natural disinclination to face up to hard, exacting work. Ohmer Milton and John Edgerly (1976) offer some factual evidence that grading does inhibit students' choice of classes. Of graduating seniors at the University of Tennessee, one-half said they had not taken certain courses because of the possibility of poor grades. Pass-fail, credit–no-credit grading was adopted in part to work against this narrowing of choice, and the change constitutes a real gain in modifying the grading system.

How rigid teachers can be about grading is illustrated by a professor of engineering whose section of integral calculus was composed of students who had received A's in all previous math courses. Although all his students performed well on the examinations, the professor still found enough variance within the group to grade them on the A-F curve. By the end of the term, he relented sufficiently to give 40 percent A's, 50 percent B's, and 10 percent C's. Even though the professor knew the caliber of the students, he still could not bring himself to give all A's.

Various studies of grades—many admittedly looking for pernicious effects—conclude that grades encourage cheating, limit choice of classes, create an unhealthy competitive atmosphere, and promote conformity in learning. (See Warren, 1971, for an excellent discussion and extensive bibliography.) Moreover, evidence exists that grades don't really reveal much about later competence. Donald Hoyt has made the most substantial analysis of the studies researching the relation of grades to later achievement. He concludes: "The forty-six studies examined were grouped into one of eight categories—business, teaching, engineering, medicine, scientific research. . . . Although this area of research is plagued by many theoretical, experimental, measurement, and statistical difficulties, present evidence strongly suggests that college grades bear little or no relationship to any measures of adult accomplishment" (1966, p. 3). For example, an elaborate performance rating of practicing physicians by their peers showed little or no correlation with grades in either undergraduate college or medical school at the University of Utah. This finding resulted in a modification of the traditional, rigorous grading practices in that professional school. Baird's extensive review of the literature (1985) supports these earlier conclusions.

In addition to their general uneasiness about grades, teachers face specific difficulties in arriving at grades which are or seem fair, objective, and helpful to the students. Martin Gold of the University of Michigan sums up, in a more benevolent way than usual, the realities of grading practices across a university (1966, p. 3). "I do not doubt," he writes,

> [that] instructors vary widely in the level of their aspirations for their students. We vary also in the quality of our instruction, so that some of us do better than others in helping students reach our goals. Our students appreciate this; they speak of tough and snap instructors, and of good and bad instructors, and many students select their courses according to the reputation of the instructors. The important point here is that many students set their own levels of aspiration when they elect their courses; and I believe this is as it should be. From the start, then, the instructor and his students often share the task of transmitting education, and *the course grades should be considered as earned by instructor and students alike.*

Sound advice I think, but obviously ignored by teachers who pride themselves on the number of low grades they hand out. Nor can one say that teachers have been other than reluctant in yielding to the pressures of the sixties to accept student evaluations of teaching. The almost universal practice of grading students has not yet led to general acceptance of grading teachers, and certainly not on an A–F curve. Finally, no line of resistance to student evaluation is more common than the flat assertion that student ratings are popularity contests, that the teacher who gives high grades to students is thereby assured of high ratings. The facts, for a variety of fairly simple reasons, support no such assertion. Indeed, there is every reason to believe that, since the usual rating of teachers is an average of the responses of a majority of the students in a class, it is much less likely to reflect personal bias than is the individual grade that the professor alone gives to the student.

For a number of years, I have begun a discussion of grading and testing with graduate students preparing to be college teachers by asking them to put down the most severe problems they have had with grading and testing. As regards grading, the following responses appear with fair regularity:

1. "Students getting paranoid about their grades in relation to other students in class—the Whadyaget syndrome."
2. "How to use grades for incentives and yet avoid punitive effects."
3. "Trying to remain objective."
4. "Arriving at a comfortable feeling about the students' role in determining a final grade."
5. "Working within a system that insists on normative standards of grading—getting nasty memos about too many A's and B's."
6. "Trying to decide how much weight to give to earnest but not very successful effort—also whether to ignore or include things like attendance, attitude, and progress."
7. "Finding alternatives to letter grades."
8. "Making evaluations that include more factors than performance on tests and assignments."

9. "Trying to keep grades from being a judgment on a student's worth."
10. "Resisting tendency to arrive fairly early in a class at firm ideas of who the 'good' and 'bad' students are and to grade accordingly thereafter."

I make no attempt to disguise my own attitude toward grades. I don't like them very much; I distrust their accuracy and their effects; and, after more than thirty years of teaching, I still have problems giving them.

There is no conning students—good grades are better than bad, and wherever grades are given, "Whadyaget?" will always be a prominent part of student conversation. A recent inquiry into the complaints that university ombudsmen receive disclosed that grades were a principal source of complaints. Even the apologist for grades might find his or her defenses weakening in the face of the pettiness, arbitrariness, fuzzy-mindedness, and unfair treatment which provoked these complaints. Of course, the complaints are few in number compared with the total of students, but lucky is the teacher who gives out a set of grades and gets no kickbacks. In the students' eyes, professors are every bit as neglectful of responsibilities, as oblivious to previous agreements, and as unreasonable in their expectations as professors consider students to be.

One recent term I escaped with only two complaints, partly, I suspect, because I posted my grades early and stayed away until the heat was off. One student caught me on a quick trip to the office and expressed with some reluctance his disappointment in getting an A— instead of an A. Up to the last week, he said, I had pretty much indicated that he was going to get an A even though his first papers fell below A work. I acknowledged that I may have misled him, largely because to me an A— is clearly more an A than anything else. He was right, however, in pointing out that an A— is not precisely an A. The student had a point—not that he deserved a full, fat A, but that I had probably not suggested that I was a dealer in pluses and minuses. The trouble was that my university had just swung back to permitting plus and minus grades after five years or more of freedom from dealing in such fractions. I had adjusted perfectly well to choosing between A's and B's and C's, but given the opportunity to weasel, I had done so, and this student had been among the first victims.

The other complaint came from an honors student—bright by test scores and high-school record—who still couldn't organize written expression, didn't take much part in class discussion, and who gave little evidence of understanding important aspects of the material. She had the opportunity to demonstrate her competence in a final exam, but chose not to take the test. She received a C for the course. C's for honors students are traumatic, and our confrontation took the form of a late-evening call expressing shock, dismay, and indignation. I held my ground, and I think she was treated fairly, if more rigorously than she had been used to.

In some freer days of the past I used to meet some grade complaints by saying, "All right, what grade do you want? I'll change it." And some I did change, though for the most part, the result was an embarrassed backing down on the part of the student. I have also, on more than one occasion, given good grades that obviously were undeserved, sometimes because I detected an extraordinary need in a student to luck out, sometimes because it seemed to me that experience doesn't provide enough occasions when people get more than they deserve.

Obviously I refuse to take grades too seriously, and I counsel other teachers to do the same. One risks having playfulness and whimsy judged as irresponsibility, maybe risks being judged unfair though the most serious attention to grading is not likely to arrive at exact justice. And not taking grades too seriously doesn't mean dodging responsibility or being deliberately arbitrary or uncaring.

As to specific advice, I'd advise beginning teachers not to be intimidated by grades. The presence of a grading system and pressures from peers and students make this difficult advice to carry out. Nevertheless, institutional practices, department norms, statistics, and curves can be used as guidance rather than as directives. Knowledge of grading practices is, like most knowledge, useful in warding off intimidation. Trying to find better ways of evaluating student performance, of furnishing useful feedback to students, and of motivating learning are neverending professional obligations. All are related to grades, but they offer a larger scope for the teacher's competence than does ordinary grading.

It is probably better to give many grades during a course than one or a few. Numbers and averages do carry conviction. The teacher who bases final grades on an average of numerical scores on weekly quizzes translated into a previously announced A-to-F scale does not escape problems with grades, but he or she probably does eliminate the common hassle of students' challenging the way a final grade was determined. For the range of subjects I teach in the humanities, I find numerical grading on quizzes too mechanical, though that has not kept me from using numerical scoring when I thought it was appropriate.

But whether a teacher employs numerical scales at all, students can profit from various means of evaluation used fairly often during a term. Such variation allows students to demonstrate proficiency in different ways, and it takes into account the good days as well as the bad. Only with a number of grades in a course is it possible to throw away the lowest score or scores, a practice that has had long and widespread use. Grades do their best work as simple and reasonable motivations when they appear with some regularity. And I think that giving many grades reduces the psychic wear and tear on the students. Everything doesn't ride on the midterm or the final.

In endorsing the giving of many grades, I am not particularly favoring mechanical quizzing and averaging. Instead, I am emphasizing steady and purposeful feedback to guide both teacher and students in identifying the students' needs. Not all of this feedback should take the form of grades. Written comments, self-grading, exercises that are corrected but not graded, individual conferences—all these methods and others can have a useful relation to numerical scores or letter grades. Going beyond fixed scores and averages complicates the act of grading, but evaluating well cannot be regarded as a simple process. And only by demonstrating that grading is not always necessary and that other kinds of feedback and evaluation are both possible and useful can one honestly minimize the importance of grades.

The student question, "How do you grade?" still irritates me almost every time I hear it, which is nearly every time I hold a class. I have played so many games with students over this question that I may soon give it up, type out with the course outline a neat statement of precisely what will count, how much each element will weigh in the final grade, and how the data will be processed. Following that statement will be a long and brilliant description of the psychic processes that accompany my reading of papers and a detailed analysis of the physical and mental processes I go through in arriving at final grades. In truth, I won't do that, though I think some good can result from putting into writing the particulars of how grades are to be handled. I prefer to deal with the question orally, sometimes addressing the matter straight out, other times forcing one student or another to ask the obvious questions.

Grades are not just the teacher's business, though the teacher in most situations has to bear the responsibility. Without shirking that duty, the teacher can share it with students in many ways. I have seldom answered the question, "How do you grade?" without touching upon, in one way or another, another question, "How do you want to be graded?" Students, in truth, are no more ingenious in these matters than we professors, but accepting even our own ideas as the suggestions of someone else has obvious advantages. Accepting suggestions contrary to our own ideas may be an even bigger gain in the development of the teacher if not in the perfection of the grading system.

This apparent yielding to the students with respect to grades is not that at all. Both students and teachers should share the recognition that grades play a part in the students' learning and, grades aside, that knowing how one is doing is a necessary part of learning. Although I have stressed the vexations of grading, I think that students place reasonable demands on teachers —that is, they want to know what the teacher's expectations are, they want to feel that they are being evaluated fairly with respect to these expectations, and they want a final grade to give an accurate and unbiased reflection of how well they have met the expectations. Disagreements are most likely to arise from the question of how expectations for the individual relate to expectations for the group and of how much importance is to be attached to individual effort and progress. In practice, these questions ask whether one grades on the curve and what provides the curve, whether one can do extra work to raise a grade, whether one can redo an assignment or retake an examination or do anything else to raise a grade. These, too, are sensible and natural questions. Good grades are better than bad grades, and a teacher should not act as if he or she alone guarded the treasury and as if students were always trying to trick him or her into turning the back.

"Be generous" is lately acquired wisdom that I do not expect young, fierce instructors just out of graduate school and with reputations to make to pay much attention to. I am content in that I see a balance between miserliness and generosity, perhaps between the old and young, but certainly across a faculty. My soft head is certain to be countered by someone else's hard nose, and the only saving grace I find in the grading system as a whole is that students get many grades from many different faculty under many different conditions. I maintain a faith that, as respects the marks on the transcript and the ultimate GPA, the average results are superior to what the student gets course by course.

Finally, although this discussion accepts grading, it still encourages individuals to subvert the system. The contract system of grading, which moves purposefully to engage students in setting their own goals, is an example of a subversive alternative. In some versions of the system, students can contract only for A's or incompletes. Either they come up to the agreed expectations by the end of the course or that expectation is deferred until they do. In lieu of standard grading, student profiles embracing qualities other than test scores have been adopted in some institutions. Written reports as a substitute for, or an addition to, grades have also appeared with some frequency. Pass-fail and credit–no-credit options, though often unnecessarily restricted, were made widely available in the seventies. I suspect that all these sensible modifications are in less use today and that they have not much altered academic practices in a seemingly grade-dependent society.

Nevertheless, faculty members cannot excuse a supine acceptance of grades, particularly by citing the needs of future employers or even of graduate schools. The individual teacher, whatever the institutional system and however heavy the hand of its administrators, can find ways outside the system to provide students with measures of their performance which are both more informing and reinforcing than letter grades. Where teachers can and need to be inventive is in finding ways to evaluate performance that identify the particulars by which performance can be improved. Experiments with other evaluative procedures as well as with grades are easy to carry out, and they can add to both teachers' and students' knowledge about motivation, feedback, and growth of competence.

The shift from grading to useful evaluating, from classifying and certifying students to teaching them, will begin when we recognize that grades are a peculiarly academic hang-up. Certainly, we undergo job evaluations, monitor our own performances, seek advice about how we are doing for anything we want to do well. But nowhere else in society is such a long stretch of human behavior subject to such excessive piece-by-piece quantitative assessment. The teacher's obligation is to fight it just as one resists any other obsession.

14

Cheating,
Confrontations,
and Other Situations

The situations that follow are certainly among the grubby stuff of teaching. Fortunately, most don't arise daily, though memories of a confrontation with a cheating student or of an entanglement with a bad class can last a long time. The best general advice is not to get into these situations. But that's like saying, "Don't catch cold," when your head's full and chest's rattling. This discussion suggests some preventive measures and also offers some practical advice for dealing with the situations that do arise commonly.

Cheating

Ideally, morally, people should not cheat. However, they do, in marriage as in taking a college course. Teachers probably overreact to cheating, for since it aims at deceiving the teacher, the offense may be taken as a personal affront. By distorting the grading scale, cheating does an injustice to the other members of the class as well. And since cheating only concerns a college course and grades, not life itself, it may seem a mean and sneaking offense. I am not saying that cheating is regarded too seriously; I believe that people should not cheat if they can help it. But I begin by asking teachers to look at cheating in other terms than of absolute wrong. Cheating is natural, common, and greatly affected by the situation in which individuals are placed. Let us look first at some of these common situations and the teacher's responsibility toward them.

First, there is the large objective examination held in a big room amidst many security precautions, from the seating arrangements to the proctors lining the walls. Most of these conditions foster cheating, or at the least, suggest even to the most innocent student that cheating is expected. The less naïve students (in view of their ages and lower-school experiences, close to 100 percent of the group) can hardly escape thinking about the abstract possibility of cheating and about specific ways of doing it. The higher the stakes, the more these thoughts crowd in. Much the same analysis can be applied to term papers. In both situations, a teacher does better to examine the teaching practices than to dwell upon the immorality of students.

I see little reason for classroom teachers to support either practice—tests in auditoriums or routine term papers. The answer to cheating in each instance is similar: Drop bad practices, and find better ones. Such a move means more work for the teacher, but that possibility shifts the problem of cheating on to the moral ground of the faculty, a territory that needs as much examination as does the academic work of the students. There are many alternatives to the impersonal practices that minimize learning and encourage cheating. It is not only physically difficult to cheat within a group of fifty or fewer students when the professor has made up a fresh exam the night before and is certain to read and respond to the students' answers; it is also psychologically difficult. And that is what I am emphasizing as a first point: The wise teacher takes ordinary precautions against cheating, but equally important, uses the kinds of tests and assignments and teaching practices that provide few rationalizations for cheating.

Number, variety, and quality of tests are matters of importance in eliminating cheating. More tests decrease the weight of any one test; variety offsets the students' tendency to try to outwit a professor whose routines are set and shallow; a good test repays a student only as the student honestly masters it. Fresh tests not only stimulate the professor's thinking; they also keep up with the state of knowledge, and they balance out the worst effects of past material accumulated in dormitory files.

Testing, like grading papers, cannot be easily turned over to someone else. The reason is not only that the professor can do the job best; it is that the practice of farming out test papers reduces, in the students' eyes, the value the professor attaches to testing. Professors should be physically in the room in which tests are given, just as they themselves should read the papers they assign. I admit I am talking against very common and long-established practices. For peripatetic professors, giving a test and having someone proctor it is the easiest way of "taking care of a class." And teaching assistants are just as commonly the givers and graders of the professor's tests and papers. Nevertheless, I single both out as expedients which should at least cause a twinge of conscience if not a change in practice.

Finally, elements of spontaneity, immediacy, play, whimsy, can easily be incorporated into tests, not only for the general purpose of reducing tension, but also of specifically introducing contexts in which cheating would not be right or wrong, easy or risky, but plainly out of key. Written tests can incorporate the elements mentioned above; a professor can add them orally during a test period or include them among the varied assignments or tests during a course.

My remarks are not meant to rule out the giving of mass tests; rather they argue that the professor shares with the student the responsibility for fostering cheating. My preferences go to changing procedures rather than increasing security, examining teaching practices rather than sharpening skill in search and detection.

I make no attempt to examine all the varieties of cheating. One form is so common and vexing, however, that my singling it out will not unnecessarily dignify it. That form is plagiarism, one that falls particularly into my province as a teacher of English. One of the many faults with freshman English is that plagiarism is about as certain an outcome of the course as gaining skill in writing. The basic conditions for plagiarism in fresh-man composition are very similar to those for cheating in mass tests: high stakes (a required course that must be passed for all other progress), impersonal conditions (hundreds of sections with a narrow range of expected assignments), faculty detach-ment (the whole job turned over to assistants), and many possi-ble sources for cheating (stacks of themes, thousands of theme writers, libraries full of obscure materials). The efforts freshman-composition programs lavish on security are often contrary to their efforts to teach writing. The common practice of keeping student themes, however effective it may be in reducing the numbers of themes available for circulation, certainly detracts from the purpose of developing writers. Considering the great numbers of themes, the use of word processors, and the avail-ability of duplicating processes, the practice is not very defensi-ble as a security measure, anyway. But the larger point is that written composition, if it is to mean anything at all, needs to be kept by the student, valued, looked back on, and learned from. Even if few students take advantage of reviewing their previous work, many may feel some inclination to cheat because the fac-ulty seems to expect it. Silly business. Perhaps themes can be kept in vaults, but libraries full of materials useful to would-be plagiarists cannot be. Nor can campuses be denuded of students, some of whom can write very well for others who can't.

Obviously, combatting plagiarism by police methods is a dead end. Prudence, reasonable care, even moral exhortation if one is desperate are worth maintaining as standard practices of teaching. It is the obvious and extraordinary measures against plagiarism that are counterproductive. I have already said enough about term papers to suggest alternatives that are likely to in-crease learning and thereby reduce plagiarism. The lesson is the same as for testing: Invest the assigned writing with value for the student, and demonstrate that the professor values it as well. Get close to the assignment, to the processes by which it is carried out, and to the efforts the student is making.

Now, suppose that one has done what all teachers should do, cutting fewer corners in their own teaching practices and demonstrating more respect for learning, and still there arise egregious instances of cheating. What then? Few teachers escape such experiences. Few courses of action are easy.

First, I put some emphasis on the word *egregious.* We teachers operate enough as security guards. I would rather see a teacher put down mild suspicions and run the risk that some student may get away with something than let those suspicions develop into nagging doubts, worrisome anxieties, and into angry and hard-to-prove charges. As a general principle, faith and trust are ultimately beneficial to teaching regardless of how both may be, in specific instances, ill rewarded. There is also a coldly practical reason for following this principle. Proving that a student has cheated on an examination or plagiarized an assignment is often very difficult, and the effort needed to arrive at proof may simply overshadow the gains to be had from bringing a particular wrongdoer to justice. Often proof of cheating comes to the "You did," "I didn't" confrontation, from which student and teacher profit little regardless of who is right.

Real proof of cheating on tests constitutes such a thing as clamping a hand on a wrist with the shirt cuffs exposed and the test answers clearly visible thereon. Even then, the alleged criminal may claim it's his roommate's shirt. Better to give him a try at another test than strip him of his shirt. More commonly, the teacher has only the strong suspicions that arise from polished essays turned in by unpolished writers or from exactly the same test answers turning up in an amazing number of blue books. Asking for another paper or giving another test is a better strategy than bringing charges. If offenses seem to persist, then it's time to face the student, not necessarily with allegations of cheating but certainly with concern about the work being done. Colleges and universities usually have firm policies and procedures for bringing formal charges of cheating, for passing judgment on the charges, and for the severity and execution of penalties. I see little reason why the teacher should not know and use these regulations. In the present litigious atmosphere, it would be more than imprudent not to. Nevertheless, the teacher has many ways of resolving suspicions toward cheating short of moving toward a formal charge. The most excruciating decision may well center on whether to take such a step.

Making a direct charge of cheating should only be done in light of such questions as: Have previous confrontations with the student led the teacher to prejudge the case? Is the teacher's sense of personal injury more the issue than the alleged offense of the student? Has the teacher been guilty of entrapment? Is there an equally valid, honest, and alternative interpretation of the evidence? Has the offense the magnitude the teacher attaches to it? I mention these legalistic questions because the legal framework adopted by university statutes aims at justice, which includes protection of rights of the accused as well as discovery of the truth. It is not out of timidity, fear of legal entanglement, or the difficulties of trial and punishment that I counsel the faculty member to seek resolution short of adversary proceedings. The reason is instead that teaching and learning go better on a nonadversary basis. Exact justice in the sense of bringing an alleged offender to the bar is to me less a goal than maintaining a relationship in which cheating of the common kind would seem about as silly as cheating in trying to learn to play the piano.

Plagiarism has certain peculiarities which teachers should pay attention to. There are more honest differences over what constitutes plagiarism than many teachers acknowledge. The lower schools certainly condition the student to respect the direct transfer of information from a published text to his or her own reports and papers. Teachers murmur things about "your own words" and "paraphrasing," but they rarely face candidly the logic of students who ask why should they change things into their own words when the original is obviously so much better and how they can write their own work on a subject about which they know nothing except what they've just read. Not yet wedded to exact quotation and footnote citation, the lower-school teacher leaves students in considerable confusion. How many of one's own words make something one's own? Isn't it just as much cheating to change words here and there—which is apparently O.K.—as it is to take the whole thing, and if one doesn't understand it very well anyway, what's the point of either one? I have read too many college papers to argue strongly that students know jolly well what plagiarism is and where the lines are to be drawn. Rather, I would maintain that many don't know and that a considerable number will pass through college training in research and report writing and will have learned only how to cheat legitimately.

The fault lies with the overpowering importance attached to locating and transferring facts and opinions and the lack of significance given to thinking and independent expression. The answer is not to move the machinery of formal scholarship down into elementary grades, but to diminish greatly the witless gathering and disguising of facts. Rather than assign a child a report on gold mining in Argentina, assign the lesser task of locating the information, leaving to the teacher the task of duplicating and distributing the material if it appears to be of any general worth. Little writing skill is gained by either paraphrasing or copying encyclopedia articles. Indeed, more skill might be gained by dropping such exercises and making the student's writing dependent only on a blank sheet of paper, a pencil, class time to do it in, and the teacher's encouragement and response.

College teachers need to be mindful of these realities. If one's bag is the formal research writing of his or her discipline, then insistence upon the methodology of quotation and citation will, at the least, clarify how to borrow legitimately. But since the majority of students given the occasion to plagiarize are not envisioning an academic research career, that scholarly bag is a pretty pinched one for an instructor to insist on. I would rather see both instructor's and student's time expended in establishing a common value for written work. Some papers would be trivial by intent, purely personal in execution. Others would plainly involve looking up, putting down, and transferring facts with no need for disguise. Others would be ambitious efforts to clarify one's own ideas or to relate an experience. All of these assignments have their own internal checks on plagiarism. They do not preclude the writing of formal reports and research papers, nor eliminate the plagiarism that arises as pressure increases, stakes go higher, and possibilities expand. Nevertheless, the confusion over what plagiarism is lessens considerably, and the close working relationship between teacher and student, writer and reader, works both for learning and against cheating.

In short, I would not be very zealous in making direct charges of cheating against a student. I would be mindful of those signs that arise and use those signals as evidence that the student falling under suspicion requires individual attention. That attention would be aimed not so much at catching the student as at removing the possibilities of cheating and thereby facing the student with the necessity of coming to grips with the subject.

Student Confrontations

Cheating can bring a teacher to one kind of awkward confrontation with students. But confrontations of many different kinds arise. I will not attempt to classify them, only to single out some that most teachers have to face.

First, there is the student who, to one degree or another, hates a teacher's guts. Often, the immediate reasons are not even apparent. Such situations may signal to teachers something about their manner or about the situations students are in. The truly disturbed or the dangerously hostile student is not the focus here. Teachers should not be reluctant to use the services a university community provides for such students. But in the case of the student who seems to find the teacher a particular target for resentment, hostility, and challenge, the teacher may have to make the first move. That is reason enough for teachers to sit down with individual students face to face as a regular teaching practice. Whether or not such occasions furnish the opportunity to ask a blunt question about a student's dislike or to indirectly reduce the hostility that is getting in both teacher's and student's way, they offer a shift in perspectives. Confrontation changes with setting. Given some skill in counseling, a teacher may be able to arrive at something other than a series of wearying encounters.

The aggressive, even hostile student will more than likely test the teacher's ways of handling a class. Confidence will enable a teacher to take a good deal of aggression short of actual disruption. A teacher should have the breadth and depth to accommodate aggression and hostility without losing force or integrity. It may be that the teacher must, in a real sense, win the hostile student over and establish respect. That is the basic challenge of teaching, as necessary for the passive students who give no one any trouble as for the hostile ones who do. That respect is not very likely to be established by doing any one thing; it may come only after an accumulation of experience and of repeated confrontations, some won and some lost. It may not come at all, if the confrontation becomes a test of egos or if the teacher uses his or her status to humiliate, ridicule, or demean the antagonist.

This is one situation where the faculty can be thankful for the limited term and the turnover of students. The next batch may be better, or at least that snotty character in the fourth row won't be around any more.

The Bad Class

There are plenty of ways individual students can make a teacher's day miserable. The right response involves luck as well as shrewdness. Which stance to take—between meddling and caring, useful involvement and purposeless worrying, coming down hard and exercising restraint—is never easy to decide. One can live with most situations involving individual students, and often doing nothing may be the best course.

But what does one do when an entire class goes bad? Every teacher experiences such classes, and it may be a comfort to the inexperienced teacher to realize that such bad classes don't entirely disappear with experience. Experience may provide more ways of dealing with them, even some chance of heading them off, and of establishing the necessary confidence between teacher and student that makes classes go. Lack of confidence is a major cause of the bad class, a problem hard to remedy because the teacher's insecurity grows as the class declines. False confidence is not likely to take the place of a real command of oneself and the situation. Perhaps the best general advice is to be honest and candid and to face the failure openly. Better to voice the doubts of all the class in acknowledging what everyone feels than to make matters worse by denying one's own doubts. The teacher's taking the lead in admitting that a class isn't going well may be a step toward a solution. Students may come forth with their sense of what is wrong. The teacher risks little more damage to his or her ego than the bad class is already inflicting.

Another general way of dealing with a bad class is to change procedures, routines, even directions radically. It may be better to make the change in concert with the class if possible, for part of the badness of a bad class is that the teacher and students are not pulling together. The expedient I mentioned earlier—dismissing a class altogether for a period of time—forces new relationships to be established when the class reconvenes. If a class involves an unusual amount of drill and recitation, a respite from these demands may create a climate in which something can be accomplished. A class adrift in discussions that never seem to go well could explore a good many alternative ways of dealing with the material. A class dominated by a series of lectures that seem to find no live connections can benefit from the lecturer's silence. All of these are home remedies, easy to voice now, hard to carry out when the teacher is locked into a bad class going badly.

This last fact leads me to advise teachers to make a general practice of interrupting a class at regular intervals to find out from the students how the class is going. Some instructors use written response sheets; others set aside a period of class time for discussion of specific aspects of the course; others let a particular assignment lead to an open discussion of how the students are working with class materials and responding to the instruction. However this information is gathered, focusing on specific matters is preferable to a general how's-it-going-this-morning approach. Asking students whether they are experiencing difficulties with a text, finding it useful, or using it at all is not a sign of a teacher's insecurity but of confidence in his or her students and a willingness to learn from them. The teacher who follows such practices has already established one useful way of dealing with a bad class: asking them what the problem is. The ordinary routine of such inquiry removes the self-consciousness of initiating a discussion that may worsen an already bad situation.

Faking and Getting Caught at It

The most embarrassing situations I have faced as a teacher are of my own making. I suspect that they are as embarrassing and maybe as frequent for other teachers. Fortunately, these situations have become less numerous with experience, though I am not yet confident enough to say that in a few years they will never occur again.

The situation is simply that a student asks a question that you almost know or should know or did know but which you don't know now, yet you find yourself giving an answer. The quickness and sureness of your reply are often quite the opposite of the doubts you inwardly hold. Often as not, the quick response is drawn out by a student who in some way has already challenged your competence. And why one doesn't simply say, "I don't know," "I'm not sure," "You can look it up in ———," is part of the mystery of teaching or a very unmysterious aspect of the thin grasp any of us have on exact fact at a given moment. In any event, the shame comes afterward, soon if we have time to look up the matter right after class, maybe not until late evening when the thought that the question might come up again sends us scurrying to the sources. Likely as not, we have missed by one century or several, confused sources or ideas, reversed the order, or forgotten a more recent theory. So we are wrong. We can admit it privately to the inquiring student, admit it to the class, wait until somebody brings it up, or hope that no one will ever refer to it again.

Obviously, the second course is the best, but oddly, all our powerful graduate training and most of our experience have not made it easy to admit our mistakes. In earlier days, my way of correcting mistakes took the form of overkill. The correction was wrapped in such an abundance of other information that the original question was made to seem altogether trickier and weightier than it was. In truth, I changed the misdemeanor of being wrong in a simple way into the felony of obfuscation on a grand scale. I may have even dazzled some students by my display; more likely I lost their attention after my first clarification of fact.

There are those occasions where circumstance or a clever student has placed a series of snares in our path. One shaky answer challenged, the teacher shores it up with another fabrication; a third challenge, another student chiming in, and fabrication turns to an elaboration of subtleties that neither student nor teacher comprehends. There is no way of digging yourself out from under these layers. Leave town with no forwarding address.

All of this anguish created from the simple difficulty of saying, "I don't know." But simple as it is, that difficulty is part of the complexity of being a teacher. A close friend of mine, a man of far more probity than myself, confessed to having faked often in his youth. Now an established scholar, he enjoyed the luxury of saying, "I don't know." We shared a belief that we had more occasions to say it, lived a cleaner life for doing so, and had not yet undermined the students' confidence by freely admitting our ignorance.

The lesson is clear, if one can but heed it. Start saying, "I don't know" early, and resist the natural tendency to fudge, waffle, or dissemble. If you admit ignorance and then find out and provide a right answer at the first opportunity, students will gain respect for the common ignorance and for ways of combatting it.

Questioning the Teacher's Authority

Less common than wrong answers to students' questions are the situations where the general authority of the teacher is questioned. The students may refuse to grant respect and trust to a new professor little older than they are. The situation can also crop up if the new professor comes on too strong, tries too hard to impress, and questions his or her own authority by asserting it too conspicuously. More pathetically, the situation may arise with an experienced teacher out of touch with the subject or with events and faced with students who find ways to ignore him or her at best or to mock and belittle him or her at worst.

When such situations arise, the most successful course is not to assert the authority of position too strongly nor to forget the power that resides in personal authority. That is, one confronts the student not from the authority invested in a superior position but from the authority of a person whose differences can be useful to the student's learning. In this situation, as in the others discussed thus far, the teacher does well to recognize how greatly the egos of both parties to a confrontation are involved. As the professional whose particular skill should include working with people, the teacher should be the one to keep differences from becoming ego confrontations. Teachers do not always have to be right, even when they are right; they certainly do not have to appear to be right when they are, as may be the case, wrong.

Obsequiousness, Flattery, and Other Defects of Character

Ian Watt, in discussing the way the authority of an autocratic teacher can cripple the student, cites a report of seminars given by A. S. Cook, professor of English at Yale (Pierson, 1952, pp. 284–286):

> His teaching was to the last degree exacting and remorseless. He did not lecture, but conducted his classes by Socratic questioning, never if he could help it divulging a fact himself but forcing each student to expose his ignorance, and then invariably examining him the next time to see if he had corrected it. There were no rules of fair play in his quest of truth. He even tried to correct faults of character . . . at least a third of every class hated this man who always hurt them.

Setting aside the exacting and remorseless side of Professor Cook's nature, I am drawn to consider the many ways teachers have of responding to manifestations of students' characters and personalities. In my earliest teaching days, I encountered a fellow teacher who didn't like students to smoke. "I always lower their grade one mark," she told me. Very recently, a colleague unburdened himself about a growing and almost ungovernable dislike for a student whose character defects mingled fawning with condescension. The brown-noser has a long lineage; he was preceded by the apple-polisher who was preceded by the syco-phant. Teachers are offended at, taken in by, or show tolerance and hope toward these and other irritating traits. I prefer to tol-erate and hope, if only because teachers and teaching contribute to the con games some students play. Since personal irritation at a fairly low level is often involved, I counsel a chastening of one's automatic responses to personality types that may clash with, or even mirror, one's own patterns. Character defects are not remedied on the spot. And though I do not deny the power of teachers to help shape students' lives, I prefer the slower work-ings of a teacher's integrity, candor, and discernment to con-frontations intended to adjust another's character. That prefer-ence does not set aside a teacher's responsibility not to be conned easily and not to impute bad motives on slender evidence.

Entanglements and Assignations

The situations just described involve confrontations of a disagreeable kind. But teachers have an undeniable power of at-traction, and confrontations of another kind may seem too in-viting to resist. A teacher should be able to detect infatuations and crushes and deal with them in ways other than by taking sexual advantage. He or she should be able to develop deep, even lasting affections without booking dual passages to roman-tic places or a double room at an inconspicuous motel. For the most part during one's teaching life, the teacher will be older, if not wiser, than the students. There is usually some wisdom in being older, even if as one gets much older there is probably more yearning.

In the seventies, this stand may have seemed drearily moral to those enjoying sexual freedom. But freedom also in-creases responsibility, and with the spread of AIDS greatly in-creases risk. The morality is not in the act itself; the laws cover-ing adultery, statutory rape, buggery, and the like suffice in these respects. The morality lies rather in the leverage the posi-tion of teacher gives one person over another and also in the fragility and ambiguity of love and the way love is intertwined with learning. Certainly I deplore incidents of sexual harassment, usually of women students by male professors, though I am not sure the "lecherous professor" (Dziech and Weiner, 1984) fairly characterizes the professoriate at large. But my concern is other than confronting such gross sex transactions over grades as are alleged by both student and faculty scuttlebutt. I am talking about the deep and genuine feelings of love that grow up between teacher and taught and about how to keep from damaging others because of them. I have no recipes and little heart to offer any more advice than to be guided by respect, caution, and love turned more toward *caritas* than Eros.

I have already mentioned, in talking about counseling and advising, the remote likelihood that a faculty member will have to deal with genuinely disturbed individuals. But there is a range of human behavior, best described as that of people in need, to which teachers are often exposed. A deliberate professional distance, helpful to teachers in many ways, may be a specific way of not inviting entanglements. Refusing to assume the position of priest or psychiatrist also helps, and that refusal is not a matter of prudence but of a recognition of the limits of one's own calling. In this, as in so many aspects of teaching, one finds one's own way.

Discrimination

The college campus, like the world outside, has become much more sensitive since 1960 to the presence and rights of minorities. Throughout this book, I have tried to speak as a teacher, without respect to my being one of the white male majority professors. I have been aware, almost from the time I began full-time teaching, that the campus climate was, as Hall and Sandler (1982) described it, "a chilly one for women," that women students had limited access to some fields of study, that women faculty stayed in rank longer than men, that they were paid less, and that some men professors had ways of treating women—students, faculty, staff, and probably their wives and mothers—that irritated me. I was aware, too, that race and family and money counted, particularly in the upper tier of colleges and universities. And having lived through the recent decades of struggle for civil rights, I still wonder how long it must be until American democracy acts by as well as expresses belief in the fundamentals of freedom and equality.

A true teacher should above all feel an obligation to those who come to learning by way of having to overcome all those obstacles put up by privilege and prejudice. Such a teacher should not need to be warned about slights based on differences of race or gender or age or preferences of many kinds. And yet, the situation of a teacher leaves one vulnerable. We do not, probably in any class, like all of our students in exact equal measure. At the same time, that should not prevent us from treating students fairly, making ourselves available to all, being sensitive to inadvertent slighting and favoring, and being receptive and understanding rather than defensive when a student, for whatever reasons, feels discriminated against.

As respects the classroom, any teacher need be sensitive to individuals who feel isolated by virtue of many causes, race and gender being large and important reasons for such feelings. Many older teachers have broken habits of address, of joking, of reference by which, often inadvertently, such singling out has been made manifest. Confrontations have sensitized other faculty members. Young teachers have inherited some of the freedom from prejudice which the civil rights disturbances were dedicated to eradicate.

But already in the late eighties clear signs have begun to appear that neither women nor minorities, students nor faculty, have reached a point of equality of access and treatment. So my advice in this respect is not only to maintain the openness and freedom from prejudice that befit a teacher, but to work against academic privilege and to help others gain recognition and acceptance within the world you may securely occupy.

Accusations

A teacher is likely to face a variety of accusations during his or her career. Some will come from students, some from colleagues and administrators, some from the public. It is not unusual to be charged on occasion with unfairness in conducting a class, in correcting tests, or in assigning grades. The repetition of such charges term after term, however, should raise serious questions about how the teacher so charged goes about his or her work.

Here again, the context in which such charges are brought is very important, for the teacher can affect that context in desirable ways before a crisis develops. I mean simply that the teacher should make sure that students understand that the teacher's judgments are not infallible and that specific avenues of appeal are open to those who feel they have not been treated fairly. College and university codes commonly spell out these avenues of appeal and redress, and the office of ombudsman was created in many institutions to make these avenues more accessible. Chairpersons should accept as an important part of their function the role of first level of appeal for students who feel that an individual professor has been unfair. Deans have a similar responsibility where the professor is the chair or where the chairperson does not recognize the legitimacy—not of the student's charge—but of the student's making such a charge. My interest is in getting the professor to offer such opportunities first. It is difficult, certainly, to listen objectively to a student's charge that you have been unfair. Nevertheless, the opportunity to express a felt grievance may be more important to the student than is obtaining redress. And the student's view of a situation may, in fact, reveal unintended unfairness to the teacher. A teacher should not bridle at the evidence the student brings forth. If teaching gives the students the impression that criticism and judgment are prized, teachers can not very well rebuff criticism nor turn back a student who questions their judgment.

This brief look at some common situations teachers face may not have turned up more than a set of homilies on how to get by. I underscore the general advisability of facing up to situations, of candor and honesty and self-awareness in dealing with them, of recognizing our own possibilities of error, and of not dwelling overmuch on those possibilities in everyone else. Openness, patience, consideration, courage, tolerance, and generosity are also good for dealing with vexing situations. If all else fails, avoid the occasion for sin.

15

Motivating
Students and Faculty

Like trying to get students to think, or to perceive or feel, motivating students to learn is an implicit concern throughout this book. The emphasis on interaction between teacher and student, the importance of a teacher's presence, the thoughtful consideration of what effect tests and grades have upon students' learning are all closely related to motivation.

Motivation, like other aspects of teaching and learning, has produced a large body of literature, much of it concerned with basic theories and problems of definition and measurement, which lie beyond most teachers' practical interest. I make specific reference to current scholarship in discussing the preparation of college teachers in Chapter Sixteen. Stanford Ericksen's *Motivation for Learning* (1974) may be more immediately useful in its setting forth "the main ideas about motivation and learning that are prerequisites for good teaching in most content-specific courses" (p. vii). The collection of essays, *Motivating Professors to Teach Effectively*, edited by James Bess (1982), has a similar utility for considering how to motivate professors.

Motivation is commonly perceived as being either *intrinsic* or *extrinsic*. The former, coming from within, is generally accorded greater worth; the latter recognizes how much we are driven by outside forces. These terms are closely related to the concepts of behavioral psychology, *rewards* and *punishments*, *positive* and *negative reinforcements,* as being basic to motivating behavior. However modern psychology (McKeachie, 1986, p. 222) has refined and gone beyond these basic categories, they still are useful to discussing motivation.

Motivating Students

Most teachers probably have some goal of moving their students beyond a dependency on extrinsic motivations to become more intrinsically motivated. This may be, after all, but another aspect of a human being's moving from dependency to independence, in which education plays a large part.

Indeed, in opting for a college education, the student is under strong extrinsic motivations to achieve a condition in which he or she can be more intrinsically motivated. Faculty members who deplore such common student aspirations as getting a secure job at high pay in an interesting line of work forget that such supposedly banal aspirations relate closely to fundamental human drives. Similarly, the preoccupation with grades and their singular motivating power may be an academic manifestation of the drive for self-preservation.

Thus, I counsel at the outset that a teacher need take advantage of such extrinsic motivations as exist and hope to provide an atmosphere in which, as time goes along, intrinsic motivation becomes more important. It seems, then, a proper concern in motivating students to find out, with respect to learning, what is motivating them and what is not.

For reasons of motivation alone, what I have already written about advising, tutoring, and mentoring deserves special emphasis. The condition of mass education too easily puts students in a real or imagined condition of "don't fold, mutilate, or spindle," in which much of their overt motivation may be that of hostility to the system. Conversely, finding out about a student's short- or long-term goals, even seeming to care, can be highly motivating.

It may be even more important to find out what lies behind a student's seeming lack of motivation. Students, in my experience, do not readily come forth with explanations of poor performance. Or the mixture of stock excuses and genuinely serious difficulties creates a climate in which candor in this respect is often absent. There are many forces that put a student in a given college—parental pressure, a lack of alternatives or information, convenience, athletic scholarships—which may not furnish much motivation for learning. Once in college, motivation waxes and wanes as do love affairs and often in concert with them. Without advocating a counselor's relationship with every student, I think a teacher sensitive to these and related matters is likely to have some success in motivating students.

What it amounts to in practice is getting away from an impersonal and inflexible attitude toward students. One must not only be approachable but actually do some approaching. One must give up the notion that all papers must always be in on time, that every exercise counts just as much as any other, and that grades are all that need be said about a student's performance. One must realize that using class time and office hours deliberately to find out how students are doing and responding to their difficulties and successes is not slighting the subject matter but raising the students' level of engagement with it.

Faculty behavior aside, departments vary widely in the extrinsic motivations they provide. Engineering, business, computers offer an outside job market that compensates for a lack of motivation of other kinds. Teachers of most liberal arts subjects have fewer of such incentives. Still, knowing something of opportunities that lie outside the college years, sharing with students one's own concerns for making a living, being able to offer advice about the world of work, can be motivating for students in any discipline. Moving closer to specific sources of extrinsic motivation, students often become aware of scholarships, part-time jobs, awards of various kinds through informed faculty. Faculty play a large part in the identifying and recommending that may keep students in school or channel them into extrinsically rewarding activities.

Teachers can easily forget that students themselves are an important source of motivation. Social approval is a desire in most students. Given the generally competitive air that prevails in American colleges, students are often caught. In some climates, high grades become a disincentive as the group looks askance at the students who raise the average. There may be more social approval, depending on the temper of the group, for middling or even low performance. These possibilities must be acknowledged, but what is of greater importance to motivation is how a class as a whole responds to class hours, assignments, tests, and other aspects of instruction and the learning environment. Bouton and Garth (1983) suggest many ways in which faculty can move from relying solely on motivating the individual's learning to motivating the group. Breaking away from the dominant competitive model with emphasis upon individual achievement is a major step for higher education if it is to realize the full potential of cooperative learning in which motivation comes from both the individual and the group.

In further considering what extrinsically motivates students, teachers also must think of those extrinsic motivations which on every campus compete with learning. There is a continual excess on college campuses that mirrors the excesses of society outside. The invasion of video games and big-screen TV are two of the latest additions, making the choices even greater between bowling or "Guiding Light" or going to class. It is not then only the difficulty of finding extrinsic motivation for an internal growth we hope might take place, but that of resisting outside forces. Some day the university may act as responsibly as civil communities in enacting some sensible zoning laws, of prohibiting, for example, rock music within several miles of classrooms.

The pervasiveness and seductive power of media have caused some professors to be more resentful of having to compete for the student's attention. The myth that the popular teacher is a poor one gains support from such a reaction. But a much more important recognition is the simple one that as a teacher gains and holds the attention of students, so does the level of motivation rise. The interest which precedes motivation often begins with the enthusiasm, the energy, the commitment that motivate the teacher. It comes across to students by the way a teacher enters the room, gets genuinely caught up in a class discussion, and elicits and answers questions in a lecture. It resides in such acts as getting tests back on time and offering useful feedback, in reading aloud or duplicating for the class parts of or whole papers and not just "best" papers. It often culminates in the class taking on its own identity, one in which the desire for everyone to share in, to do well with the experience is a strongly felt source of motivation.

Many teachers are wary of overtly providing extrinsic motivation, whether it be consciously heightening the impact of their own performance or thinking of ways to give actual rewards. I have never felt unprofessional in either respect. I would feel unprofessional if I did not work still to enhance the impact of my teaching, inside the classroom and out. I commonly award books—for they are my stock in trade—and other trifling prizes to students for a variety of achievements, and even non-achievements. In recent years I have gone back to a practice I remember as motivating me when I was in high school, that of excusing students who were doing very well from the final exam. I think, in general, we teachers are insufficiently ingenious in devising simple means of extrinsically motivating students.

Finally, grades constitute a prime source of extrinsic motivation. Students do work for grades, and while I, like many of my faculty peers, tend to deplore grade-grubbers, I try not to think too meanly of them. For in our deploring of students' job seeking, we often forget we do it from the security of having jobs, and in deploring grades, we forget we give rather than get them. Thus in giving fair grades, in linking them as tightly as possible with what has been or is to be learned, in seeing ourselves as assisting students in getting good grades rather than keeping them from them, we can use grades as a proper and important source of motivation.

The line between extrinsic and intrinsic motivations is not as distinct as the terms *inner* and *outer* may indicate. A high grade or a monetary award, for example, may be a source of increased self-esteem which lies at the base of intrinsic motivation. The goal of a teacher with respect to grades and tests may be to bring the student to a point where he or she is relatively independent of the need for them. Among education's highest

aspirations is the development of the self-motivating and continuing learner.

Perhaps the greatest source of intrinsic motivation is the
inner satisfaction that comes with doing a task well. That is
probably why students feel disappointed with getting back even
an excellent paper with no other mark than a letter grade. They
want the kind of confirmation that in specific ways can be identified with their own sense of what was well done and for the
general purpose of motivating them to do well along lines that
worked before. Teachers are terribly important to that inner
sense of being able to do it which precedes performance.

Recognizing achievement is the culminating act of establishing tasks and goals that the student can achieve. McClelland
(1985) identifies an achievement motive as one of three important motivation systems, the other being the drive for power
and the seeking of affiliation. He writes (p. 603), "There is no
lack of motives to be investigated, specifically, the need to nurture and be nurtured, curiosity, and the need to maintain consistency and avoid dissonance all cry out for investigation." His
and related research support the common-sense perception of
teachers that students learn best from tasks that are neither too
easy nor too difficult. Motivation is highest when there is a fair
chance but not a certain easy chance of success. Facing the
numbers of students we have in a class, often widely varying in
motivation as in aptitudes and experience, posing assignments
and making up tests take great care when we consider their impact on motivation. In general, failure in learning breeds failure,
perhaps even more than success breeds success. The teacher I
mentioned before who devised some tests that every student
could pass was not being soft; he was wisely recognizing the importance of individual achievement for motivation. If we eliminate as the only purpose for tests the sorting out and ranking of
students, then we are free to use them for motivating students
in a variety of ways.

There are two other aspects of intrinsic motivation I wish
to mention. The first grows out of an experience with a junior
in a writing class. She sent me a Christmas card thanking me for
respecting her writing, for being respected by any professor was
new to her college experience. I knew vaguely what she was

talking about, for she had told me when she enrolled that her journalism professor had told her she couldn't write. How a journalism professor could make that judgment puzzled me, but I suspect it went beyond her writing abilities. That school had become strongly professionalized and she probably hadn't come off as the kind of student that the professor found acceptable to his idea of the profession. But what that quarter's experience brought home to me is how much we teachers are conferrers of respect. College years are not nearly as carefree as they might seem. A student's self-esteem is on the line much of the time. If we want students to respect learning, we must respect their efforts, however ill-informed and unsophisticated they may seem. We must respect *them,* not for what they will be when we get through with them, but as they are now. Perhaps that is why it still seems possible to suggest Mr. and Miss or Ms. as a good choice in addressing students. As formal, even quaint, as it may be, it still confers a degree of respect.

The opposite side of conferring respect is taking it away. Teachers can do it in many ways—by not showing up for appointments, by being chronically late for class, by brushing off students after class, by calling on a student not prepared for class, or not calling on one who is. But stripping away respect may be done deliberately, the worse for being rationalized as a source of motivation residing in fear or anger or a desire for revenge.

What I am singling out is using fear, arousing anger, creating anxiety as sources of motivation. There is no question that fear motivates; in its most naked form it is closely linked with self-preservation. Students will find motivation to study if they fear the consequences of not doing so enough. A student may be highly motivated out of anger at being made to look stupid in front of his or her peers. Research evidence (McKeachie, 1986, p. 246) suggests that the relationship between anxiety and learning is more complex than the common assumption that anxiety is necessarily detrimental to learning. Common sense says that anxieties created by what may be required of a student in a class may motivate that student to keep up with readings and otherwise be engaged with the subject matter.

Every teacher has engaged in such practices. The very nature of teacher and student arouses these potentially motivational responses. Within the simpler behavioral framework of *rewards* and *punishments,* such behavior carries the motivational framework of the stick side of carrot-and-stick. I do not deny its utility, particularly for short-term gains, though I do not think learning within a free context in an atmosphere of fear and threat gains much in the long run.

Philosophically, I believe motivation is greater, more enduring, and above all, more likely to lead to a higher degree of intrinsic motivation if it grows out of positive rather than negative reinforcements, rewards rather than punishments. At the specific level of daily or term-by-term performance, a teacher can do much to provide positive reinforcements.

First, *making goals and objectives clear and attractive.* Beyond specifying the expectations placed upon the students, the teacher at the outset has opportunities to make clear the larger goals for the course and to declare in a variety of stimulating ways the desirability of achieving them.

Second, *setting achievable goals at definite stages of the term.* Thus, students will be motivated by a sense of partial achievements related to a larger goal. At each stage the teacher has opportunities to motivate individual students as well as the class. Good performance reinforces itself for those who do well. For those who don't do well, a teacher needs to provide motivations such as careful reviewing of tests, chances for individual or group tutoring, repeating of tests or assignments, and the like, acts which may help more students enjoy the motivation that goes with successful achievement.

Third, *increasing the possibilities for cooperation among students.* Teachers tend to let competition dominate by perceiving course work largely in terms of individual achievements, thus slighting the opportunities for mutual reinforcement and motivation among the students themselves.

Fourth, *throughout the term, being sensitive to the rhythms of the course, to the ups and downs in group and individual performance.* Much of motivating a class resides in knowing when to ease up and to bear down.

Finally, *within any subject matter exists what teachers may regard as the purest source of motivation.* A very strong believer in this source may object to much I have been saying about a teacher's responsibility to provide motivation. Students should find my subject interesting, such a teacher may say. If they don't, let them take up something else. There is an idealism in such statements I respect, but there is a blindness to reality that puzzles me.

Let me suggest some ways in which teachers may draw out the motivation that resides in a subject. Curiosity is certainly a strong source of motivation; the ways teachers help unfold a subject's mysteries is therefore important. Arousing and satisfying curiosity in the myriad ways any subject matter affords is also a technique worth developing. Personalizing a subject matter—"what it means to me"—is another way of providing motivation. Experiencing a subject matter, moving a student from understanding to doing, ultimately providing the student with empowerment, is another. Yet another is exemplifying and embodying. Humans are strongly motivated by other humans. Seeing someone doing something well is often the first step to wanting to do that thing well oneself. Thus the teacher's very self is a source of motivation, just as are the individual acts by which a teacher exemplifies, carries out before the students' eyes, aspects of a subject.

Research into motivating students has also been extensive within elementary and secondary education. Madeline Hunter (1985) has developed specific motivational programs used widely in school districts throughout the country. Raymond Wlodkowski (1984, 1985) has suggested that teachers who wish to motivate students devise classroom activities that develop positive attitudes, meet needs, stimulate, create a favorable emotional climate, increase or affirm competence, and provide reinforcement. The work of these and other educators is consistent with what I have been discussing here within college and university settings.

Motivating Faculty

Motivating students is closely related to motivating ourselves. The attitude that may damn teachers most in students' eyes is that of not seeming to care. Joseph Katz's collection of essays, *Teaching as Though Students Mattered* (1985), specifically confronts that attitude. Not caring has many ways of revealing itself as well as many causes. A clever cynicism has a superficial appeal to some students, and is a mark of intellectual sophistication for some professors. But long maintained it may mask an erosion of respect for what one is doing that marks not being motivated to do it.

To begin with, then, for professors to be motivated they must believe in what they are doing. Probably what motivates a professor in the first place is some love of learning, whether it take the form of sharing with others what one knows or of a driving urge to find out something that no one has known before. In simple terms our motivation comes from our students, our commitment to a subject matter, and in time a sense of identity with an institution.

All these are subject to change and decay. At one time our students may be the driving force, at another the book we must write, at another our need to play a large part in shaping a department or college. Too many students, too many papers, too much going over the same ground, a growing distance between ever-young students and ever-growing-old professors may erode satisfactions from teaching. The glut of scholarship may in itself diminish the small significance of what one publishes, and beyond that are the pressures, the details, the small audience response, the frustrations of finishing a complex piece of work, the futility of starting another.

But the fact that one can go stale in all aspects of professing also emphasizes the variety of expectations which characterize college professing. The many demands which we are worn out by are also that many sources of motivation.

All young teachers must come to terms with the multiple demands placed on them. To the energetic and pluralistic, this very variety affords motivation. The kind of motivation students provide is different from that provided by a library or laboratory. And the act of searching, motivated greatly by an occasional finding, is different from the reward of seeing one's name in print. Different, too, from taking part in professional activities, from being led on by the chance to meet colleagues from afar to gaining a position of national importance.

Through much of an assistant and associate professor's career, there is likely to be an excess of motivation rather than a dearth, and a mixture of negative as well as positive forces. "A wealth of research studies," Deci and Ryan write (1982, p. 28), "has enumerated the conditions within which intrinsic motivation is likely to be diminished and enhanced." The young professor could best be advised to select out a course to follow, one consistent with an institution's demands but compatible with one's own desires and talents. I have long argued for reward systems which recognize diversity, but faculty will always have to reconcile to some degree the facts of institutional support and demands with the needs and desires of the independent practitioner.

The move to accommodation begins with the choice of positions. A recent study (Fact-File, 1985) reveals a higher degree of satisfaction among professors at the research university and the private liberal arts college. The reason is probably both a self-selecting and winnowing process that places the faculty in the first place and the clearer definition of goals that prevails at both kinds of institutions. Where goals are less defined, where the faculty may have ambitions for a different kind of institution, satisfactions are less.

But given a position with which a faculty member is reasonably compatible, what courses then lie open? I think these are not difficult to define. One is that of giving primary emphasis to scholarship of the kind most respected in a discipline, teaching responsibly but with as much economy as possible, and accepting such service responsibilities as can't be escaped. Another is to throw one's greatest energies into teaching, keeping in motion some active and visible scholarship or writing or performance, and accepting the fact that energetic teaching will probably result in more demands for service. A third is to try to do everything well and abundantly.

Given the usual pretenure period, it is also possible to adopt specific strategies compatible with one's immediate goal of gaining tenure. Some faculty can find a reasonable fit between what they are teaching and what they are pursuing and publishing. Others must accept a going back and forth, periods when teaching has top priority and other periods when finishing a piece of scholarly work has top priority. Still others gain institutional respect by a larger commitment to departmental and institutional functioning.

In most settings, none of this is easy. On the other hand, there is probably more assistance at hand than young professors realize and take advantage of. One of the neglected aspects of institutional life is how closely faculty members identify with the age and rank cohorts that marked their coming to a university. Wise administrations would seek to bridge these age cohort differences, but commonly it is the faculty member who must seek a larger and ultimately more motivating identity.

A second identifiable aspect of motivating faculty can be found in the years following tenure and before reaching the highest rank. Tenure is commonly defended as necessary to academic freedom, but it might be emphasized that freedom of another kind may be quite as important. Those who gain tenure easily may not be sufficiently aware of how gaining tenure after considerable struggle is a gaining of freedom itself. Not the freedom to express one's opinions—the Constitution of the United States gives greater guarantees than most universities offer—but the freedom from constraints, from channeling one's energies, from keeping all the balls in the air for most of the time.

In saying that, I am emphasizing that achieving tenure removes a prime source of extrinsic motivation and may mark the real beginning of intrinsic motivation. Scholarly productivity may be the best indication of how necessity drives published scholarship. Blackburn's (1982, p. 97) study and others indicate a falling-off of published scholarship, at least in the natural and social sciences, in the posttenure years with some resurgence in the years just preceding the promotion to full professor. Even these studies must be viewed with some caution. We have some few studies that show that the commitment to teaching or service does vary throughout a career but without clearly identifiable phases. It is a reasonable conjecture that tenure brings more freedom of choice about where a faculty member wishes to place his or her emphasis.

Thus there is the shift in emphasis to intrinsic motivation. This is not to say that associate professors are not salary conscious, or unaware of the prestige of institutional and disciplinary recognition. In fact, the motivation that comes from seeking a better position on the national market or of building the reputation that will attract offers or of moving into administrative positions will drive many faculty members. In these respects, a commitment to teaching probably suffers. Those who retain that commitment will draw their motivation from the students and the kind of local rewards and recognition that a college may provide. Somewhere in these years, I suspect, the erosion of motivating forces may begin. That group of faculty who are somewhat outside the groups identified may find it hard to break out of routinely performing what have become routine chores. Many of this number will never achieve full professor rank or only after a prolonged struggle. Despite institutional pieties about the essential dignity of all ranks, not gaining the highest rank is likely to have adverse effects. Rarely do institutions provide any compensatory motivations for faculty caught in that position. Thirty or more years lie ahead with no formal mark of growth or advancement. Women faculty members are made to suffer these conditions more than men, somewhat as newly acquired minority faculty will be excessively motivated by the many obligations placed upon them.

Even for those who gain the full professorship, a period of twenty or more years can be expected in this terminal rank (Blackburn and Lawrence, 1986). In either case, any faculty is likely to have a majority of members for whom staying within the ordinary framework of university responsibilities provides little to differentiate year from year. The often harassing fact of a multiplicity of expectations may function in a positive way for some of this faculty for which extrinsic motivations have been much reduced. That is, faculty members can, if they will, tackle new courses, can channel or vary their scholarly efforts, can seek out visiting positions, move in and out of administrative positions. There is a catch even here: the more successful a faculty member has been, the more opportunities lie open. For those less successful and yet fully committed, something like burnout may occur. Seldin's volume, *Coping with Faculty Stress* (1987), contains articles examining the condition and proposing ways of dealing with it.

In all I have been saying here, administrations bear a large responsibility. As in any effectively functioning organization, administrators should be good motivators, as good in their way as teachers for their students. The argument follows that teachers who motivate students are good choices for department chairs and deans. The counter argument is that such persons should not be taken out of the classroom.

Given the nature and structure of university administration, it is probably only the exceptional administrators who are prime motivators for the faculty. Students and colleagues are probably more important sources of motivation. Much faculty motivation must come from within, and insofar as faculty members possess some professional skills in motivating others, they may be expected to use these in their own behalf. In truth, my experience with faculty development is a heartening one in that much of its vigor and effectiveness come from established faculty members who see in it not only motivation for themselves but opportunities to provide motivation for others.

PART FOUR

Learning to Teach

16

Preparing College Teachers

The entire subject of how best to prepare college teachers is clouded over with unproved and perhaps unprovable hypotheses about knowledge and its impact. My own (Eble, 1983) are at odds with those accepted by many of my colleagues. None of us can offer other than anecdotal evidence that the benefits deriving from academic research, either in the developed capabilities of the scholars or in the fruits of their work, justify the imposition of common patterns and aims over the number and variety of human beings now undertaking advanced study. Events of the world as distinguished from practices of the academy suggest, at the least, that *capabilities* and *fruits* applied to what comes from pure and applied research are ambiguous terms. On the other hand, who is to say of teaching other than that it is, like research, an assumed good whose effects are describable in terms like Henry Adams', that the teacher affects eternity. And if I choose to argue that four more years in the undergraduate college would be better schooling for college and university teachers than a comparable time in the graduate school, no empirical data will prove me right or wrong.

What does graduate education contribute to the development of college and university teachers? Principally, graduate education aims to give a student a competence in a subject matter. From my point of view, that competence is too narrow, but students being what they are, graduate programs may be broader than they appear. That is, the real world is hard to shut out, and however esoteric the final dissertation research, a range of subjects, teachers, and experience is included within the four to ten years of graduate work. Still, in most disciplines, the training for men and women whose lifetimes will be engaged largely in undergraduate teaching is unnecessarily narrow.

As regards subject matter, most graduate programs respond to the dilemma of too much knowledge and too little time by narrowing the focus of the student's work. For the student, there will never be less knowledge or more time. The choice between depth and breadth, concentration and diffusion, disciplinary and interdisciplinary work will remain throughout one's career.

The argument over depth and breadth is not solely the concern of education; it is a personal, internal argument about how the individual chooses to seek and shape experience. Wise counsel comes from both sides, from F. Scott Fitzgerald, "Life is best looked at from a single window after all," and Henry James, "You must live all you can. It's a mistake not to." As specifically regards education, Whitehead writes: "Nothing but a special study can give any appreciation for the exact formulation of general ideas, for their relations when formulated, for their service in the comprehension of life" (1949, p. 23). But as specifically regards university education, Whitehead also says, "A well-planned university course is a study of the wide sweep of generality," and "Education is the guidance of the individual towards a comprehension of the art of life; and by the art of life I mean the most complete achievement of varied activity expressing the potentialities of that living creature in the face of its actual environment" (pp. 37, 48). Breadth and depth, like Whitehead's freedom and discipline, are not mutually exclusive, though one will incline more toward one at one time, and toward the other at another. The period of graduate study is long enough for programs to follow a student's bent in moving from one to the other; the aims of teaching are sufficiently broad that the teacher's course of study would not be harmed by emphasizing breadth.

Given human limitations in the face of the vastness of knowledge, mastery of any one competence or subject matter is probably a delusion. Kenneth Cooper, a professor of history, has put the matter well: "We do not like to admit that our knowledge is superficial, yet in a world of explosively expanding knowledge we cannot have anything but superficial knowledge of most subjects. We do not choose between superficial and deep knowledge of most subjects; we choose between superficial knowledge and no knowledge" (1975, pp. 90-91). If something less than mastery is accepted, then continued learning about a wide range of things may be a better posture for the teacher than the stock preference for "keeping up in one's field." Few fields worth pursuing reward—except by academic measures—the isolated pursuit that phrase implies. The teacher who keeps up in his or her field may find that students are the only ones on campus who are reasonably current in other important fields. Examples continue to arise of truly eminent scholars who move from one field to another or whose work does embrace many fields. The difficulty is, in part, that scholars of modest competence—most of us—take the course most open: exacting work within a narrow range. That same degree of exacting competence applied to a broader range would better serve the effective undergraduate teacher.

But the most crucial arguments for breadth have to do with teaching as an act. Learning theory supports the fundamental importance of learning in a context. The diversity of students in undergraduate courses argues for the teacher who can provide most in the way of relevant contexts. Whether those contexts come from richness of experience, a restless curiosity, opportunities for leisure and study, or an education aimed at breadth, they are necessities for affecting the learning of diverse students. Professors gravitate to the bright, well-prepared students. They are easier to teach, and they appear to profit most from instruction, which may simply mean they are most like the professors. But in the increasingly pluralistic colleges and universities of the next decades, the master teacher is likely to be the one who can provide contexts for many kinds of students.

I am not hopeful that the arguments just made, familiar arguments in at least three decades of reports calling for reform in graduate education, will result in changes in graduate study.

The recent report of the Association of American Colleges (1985) bluntly cites "the failure of graduate schools to prepare holders of the doctorate degree for careers in teaching" (p. 29). The report's section on college teaching describes the basic situation: "The emphasis of the graduate school years is almost exclusively on the development of substantive knowledge and research skills. Any introduction to teaching comes only incidentally through service as a teaching assistant, with only occasional supervision by experienced senior faculty. During the long years of work toward the doctoral degree, the candidate is rarely, if ever, introduced to any of the ingredients that make up the art, the science, and the special responsibilities of teaching" (p. 29). The Bennett report on the humanities in education (1984, p. 19) describes the effects of graduate education on teaching in a similar way: "Instead of aiming at turning out men and women of broad knowledge and lively intellect, our graduate schools produce too many narrow specialists, whose teaching is often lifeless, stilted, and pedestrian."

The views recently expressed by Jules LaPidus, president of the Council of Graduate Schools (1987, pp. 3-6) admit that some doctorate recipients do become college teachers but deny almost any responsibility for the teaching part of their future careers. It is true that a smaller percentage of Ph.D.'s are entering college teaching, but it is also true that outside some of the sciences and engineering, the majority of Ph.D.'s still assume college and university teaching positions. Graduate study may develop competences in subject matters, but it produces large numbers of highly trained but uneducated college teachers. Insofar as doctoral programs prepare research specialists who do, in fact, become researchers within their specialized disciplines, I have no wish to question their emphasis. But the obvious fact is that graduate programs do not solely or even primarily train research specialists. The training for research scholarship includes some things useful to the future teacher, leaves some things out. Traditions and conventions stand in the way of recognizing divided purposes in graduate education, and institutional patterns are hard to change even when those purposes have been recognized. Since my concern is for teaching, I confine my suggestions to that aspect of advanced education. I do not propose exclusive paths for researchers and for teachers or imply that useful alternatives for some students in some disciplines should be made requirements for all. Where the person's goals, priorities, and competence tend clearly toward teaching, then these considerations should loom large. There is certainly, by now, room for an emphasis upon either teaching or research, and each might be helped by an examination of the particular needs and aims of the other.

The reader may suspect that my intent is to argue for the inclusion of specific pedagogical training in advanced degree programs. I intend much more to argue against the exclusion of many kinds of satisfying and useful learning, including that which concerns learning itself. As it is, almost anything that smacks of pedagogy has been excluded from graduate programs. Apprentice teaching is a part of many of those programs, not because it is useful in developing the student's competence, but because it supports graduate students financially and provides a source of cheap instruction in the undergraduate college. Thus, a suspicion toward pedagogy stands in the way of giving attention within the graduate program itself to developing teaching skills. And the use of assistants as low-cost instructors gets in the way of developing apprentice teaching as an integral part of the graduate student's professional development.

If, as I suspect, the prejudice against pedagogy is too great to overcome, then it is unwise to suggest a general curriculum in pedagogical subjects for the prospective college teacher and to be wary of even appearing to emulate successful practices within colleges of education. Rather, I suggest serious consideration of what beginning college and university teachers might most need to know beyond their training in a subject matter. Certainly this will include some knowledge about, and experience in, teaching. As minimal as this claim is, it is not satisfied by the present practice of meeting the need for knowledge and experience outside or in addition to the "serious" work for the degree. Meeting this need must be an integral part of the program, as highly respected, as subject to the involvement of mentors, as capable of supervision and examination, and as favorable to shows of individual initiative and imagination as any other part of the program.

Well, then, what should the beginning teacher know? Certainly an acquaintance with how humans learn, the subject of extensive research within education and psychology, but one whose findings are difficult to translate into the practicalities of teaching. "The poverty of application of learning theory to education cannot be denied," B. R. Bugelski writes in his book *The Psychology of Learning Applied to Teaching* (1971, p. 39). He cites Hilgard's fourteen broad applications (Bower and Hilgard, [1956] 1981) and his own review of the literature to arrive at a brief list as "rather slim pickings from the vast learning-theory literature."

In my own conduct of courses in teaching for graduate students, learning theory has been the most difficult topic. I will attempt here merely to list some of the main principles that seem to have substantial empirical support and useful applications. They are gleaned from Bugelski's book and the other books listed below; the phrasing is my own, as is the loss of accuracy in trying to be brief. I regard the list as notations to encourage teachers to review familiar points and to find out more about unfamiliar ones.

- Learning is an active, continuous process. Purposive action is better than mere repeated motions. Humans learn many things they don't need to know.
- Learning takes place in terms of stimulus and response; conditioning is a common term to describe the process. Catching and maintaining a learner's attention provides the necessary condition for a desired stimulus to evoke a response.
- Learning is affected by the learner's set—that is, a predisposition to react to some stimuli in a particular way.
- Learners can be motivated in many ways to learn specific things. Conflicting motivations may get in the way of learning.
- Time and conditions affect learning greatly. Individuals vary greatly in the time they take to learn something.
- Association is an important aspect of learning. Identifying, grouping, and sequencing assist learning.

- Reinforcement is the general term for stimuli introduced to reinforce behavior that stimulates further learning.
- Rewards seem to affect a wider range of learning more favorably than does punishment.
- Relearning is much easier than original learning. Recall is different from retention; given the right stimulus, learners can recall more than they commonly suspect.
- Progress in learning is not uniform, but frequently reaches plateaus where the rate of learning slows appreciably.
- Interference is a common cause of forgetting. New and similar learning can interfere with the old. Learning a thing well helps to counteract interference.
- Interfering responses may inhibit learning; therefore, they may have to be removed to foster learning.
- Transfer of learning has been too uncritically accepted in the past. Success in learning some things may make it easier to learn others. It is possible to learn how to learn.

Some useful sources which are aware of the complexity of learning theory but capable of describing some of that complexity in terms applicable to teaching are Bruner (1968), Cole (1982), Howe (1984), Keller (1969), Kuethe (1968), Marton, Hounsell, and Entwistle (1984), Skinner (1968), and Travers (1982).

Another body of materials has to do with some of the rudiments of instructional practices; testing, grading, fashioning readings and assignments, creating a course, are subjects taken up at length earlier in this book. Wilbert McKeachie's *Teaching Tips* (eighth edition, 1986) has existed virtually alone since 1951 as an attempt by a college professor to provide a handbook for beginning teachers. Many of his observations come from his practical experience, the common-sense wisdom that defines an experienced teacher's practices. But more important, McKeachie's advice is authenticated by careful attention to theory and research that bear upon the particulars of teaching. Other useful books of this kind, not previously mentioned, are Beard (1972), Ellner and Barnes (1983), Fuhrmann and Grasha (1983), and Gullette (1982).

Closely related to literature dealing with instructional practices is the material that looks at broader patterns of instruction, examining such traditional modes as lecture, laboratory, discussion, the large class, the seminar, the colloquium, and the workshop and that also proposes refinements of, or innovations in, these standard practices. Of great current interest are those means of instruction, most depending heavily on educational technology, that diminish or alter the role of the teacher.

So there is a content, diverse, interesting, and useful. How best to draw on it? One of the most effective ways is also one of the most common means of graduate instruction: the graduate seminar. Teaching as a subject, among graduate students who have teaching responsibilities, meets most of the general specifications for a good seminar—a place for exchanging information, for examining research critically, for discussing experiences in teaching, and for fostering continuing study. Students will have common experiences and interests and can examine in common the knowledge useful to the topic at hand. The professor cannot so easily slip into the role of expert and become the lecturer, nor need the many topics useful to teaching be put off until the students have prepared seminar papers. The very conduct of the seminar—how students learn in this setting —is in itself part of the substance of the course. In addition, the faculty needs this kind of exposure. The teaching seminars are not the property of the "teaching" specialist; rather they are the common enterprise of faculty and students in a relationship as colleagues. Seminars in teaching should be a routine part of graduate study for all students planning to teach. They should carry credit and be as demanding as any graduate work. Models for such seminars exist in various disciplines in a good many universities, though not by any means in a majority of programs or institutions.

The teaching seminar I am supporting is not the weekly gathering of teaching assistants to discuss the how-to's of a specific course, usually the many-sectioned course in which the graduate students are poorly paid and the undergraduates poorly taught. Such training sessions, used as much to relieve the department's conscience and anticipate student complaints about apprentice teachers as to ensure effective teaching, have a place.

But they commonly lack commitment from the faculty, focus on a narrow range of concerns, and are seen as a necessity arising from the use of teaching assistants rather than as a vital subject matter component of the graduate program. The teaching seminar is dependent upon its students being engaged in teaching, but the seminar has wider objectives than deciding which text is best for course A or how one deals with cheating in that particular course. Graduate students, left to their own devices and grouped together in the small spaces universities commonly provide, conduct such practical discussions and exchanges anyway. Formalizing shop talk may not be an improvement; respecting it, adding to it, and reinforcing it are more the goals. Technology has a use here. The availability of television equipment, particularly the portable camera and VCR, makes it possible for all prospective teachers to see themselves in action. Further, playing back a tape provides a way, not merely of reflecting right after a class about how the class has gone, but of identifying and puzzling over the particulars that affect results.

"Practice teaching," as it was once called in colleges of education, is still the most accepted and effective part of the teacher-training program. The teaching assistant is learning by doing in much the same way in the graduate program. Such actual teaching, not so much under supervision as in concert with peers and faculty, is the heart of learning to teach, and the matters I have discussed here should not obscure that fact. Koen's and Ericksen's survey of TA-training programs among the fifty universities that produce the most Ph.D.'s concluded "that in the middle 1960s, the universities had made relatively few administrative adjustments and even fewer time commitments toward assuming formal responsibility for training the apprentice teacher" (Ericksen, 1974, p. 221). My reading and consulting during the seventies has not uncovered any great change. " 'Methods' courses," Ericksen observed, "appeared to be a universal anathema, and almost one-third of the departments implicitly took the position that the apprentice teacher learns to structure the pedagogical issues for himself and to work out his own solutions" (1974, p. 221).

There are some indications that in the past thirty years, teaching assistants and part-time teachers have become responsible for an ever-larger share of undergraduate teaching (Eble, 1987, p. 8). One of the few beneficial consequences may be an increase in support programs for preparing future teachers. Diamond and Gray's (1987) national survey of teaching assistants shows a great variety in what is expected of TAs and at least as much variety in the kinds of support programs offered. Overall, three-fourths of the respondents noted the existence of a support program, but fewer than half included the kind of preparation advocated here. A national conference on teaching assistants (Chism, 1987) has drawn attention to these and other important issues.

The conclusion I am moving toward—one implicit throughout this book—is that teaching skill is not so much taught as it is nurtured into existence. The faculty should know as much as gardeners about necessary nurture and take as much pride in the eventual flowering. Left wholly unattended, as is commonly the case, students risk getting less than they have a right to expect from mentors who know and care about learning. Constrained to give teaching secondary attention, students may miss the central lesson of developing as a teacher: identifying one's strengths and weaknesses, following one's bent, making the most of what one has. Koen's conclusion about the best kind of training program for assistants placed primary importance on the stance of the department leadership and senior faculty in recognizing the importance of teaching.

An added objective of a graduate program that seriously aims at preparing excellent college teachers should be to offset some of the adverse effects of graduate study itself. Graduate school education has been described as "learning on one's knees"; surely a better education is learning on one's feet. The inability to shake off graduate-student servility may cause new teachers to begin teaching with presumptions shaped by their most recent experience—for example, that passive verbal transfer is an effective mode of instruction; that college students have long attention spans; that if teachers prepare well and keep talking nothing bad can happen; and that authority and truth reside in the figure behind the lectern. All of these presumptions are bad for teaching.

Rather than accepting models of teaching drawn from graduate-school practices, prospective teachers should have the opportunity to examine analytically a variety of teaching situations and acts. Very interesting attempts have been made to capture specific teaching behaviors on film (see Burdin and Cruickshank, 1974). The Center for the Teaching Professions at Northwestern University has produced some very interesting videotaped vignettes of teachers in action useful to stimulating discussions of teaching practices. These and other films I have seen isolate teaching acts so that the observer becomes aware, among other things, of the complex ways in which teachers project themselves and make or fail to make an impact on students. One cannot come away from watching teachers in action, alive or on tape or film, without recognizing the importance of physical presence. Accepting that importance, teachers have a chance of putting close observations of themselves and others to work.

In the long run, the attitudes toward teaching shaped in graduate school are as important as subjects encountered and skills acquired. But many of the attitudes I prize—respect for teaching, curiosity about the process, humility toward finding out, willingness to work at being a good teacher—grow out of acknowledging that teaching has substance. If the development of teachers went right in the years of formal study, these attitudes might be more apparent thereafter.

Let me address myself directly to some of the attitudes I hope beginning teachers will bring to teaching, whatever the content and quality of their graduate work. The first is generosity. Aristotle made much of what is commonly translated as *magnanimity*, the sufficiency of person or possessions that makes generosity possible. I suspect that generosity is not a common strength among young teachers and that it may develop among older teachers as they lose their view of the specialness of their own learning and become less protective of the hard-won knowledge they have just acquired. The young teacher also operates under institutional regulations that do not often support generous impulses. Someone in the system is watching, and one must be rigorous, exacting, and sparing of praise and reward. There may be a healthy balance in the fierceness of the young and the relinquishing of the old. But setting aside these possible tendencies, I encourage generosity at the outset. The right attitude toward knowledge is surely a generous one, an attitude powerfully urged from the fact that knowledge, while permitting feelings of acquisition and ownership, suffers no loss when it is shared with and given to someone else. Teaching, by this basic attitude, is always a giving out, always a chance for benefaction. And as to generosity to students, few people are ever hurt by being regarded too generously. The shaky confidence about what one can learn, about how much one knows compared with someone else, needs constant shoring up.

Shucking off feelings of superiority, ridding ourselves of the arrogance we may have acquired in our special pursuits, is another side of generosity. One of the folk figures of teaching is the supremely arrogant professor, who has the overpowering strength of study and learning to justify that arrogance. Acts of arrogance attract the teachers, if only because power and the opportunity to display it in diverse ways are so much a part of teaching. And arrogance does work at times, though usually only in the long run as the fuel for resentments that drive a humbled student to exceed the arrogant master. Indeed, arrogance in folk tales may be valued most for the satisfaction of seeing the arrogant toppled from their perches. Arrogant teachers are similarly prized for the time when someone will give them their comeuppance.

A willingness to take risks is another attitude worth courting. Teaching is not a safe occupation, either for teacher or student. That statement, of course, is metaphorical, for on the face of it, college teaching is a safe occupation, clean and undemanding. But here as elsewhere, I am not merely concerned with what teaching is. Teaching that gains my respect is risky in the consequences it may have for the learner and in the chances teachers take in their practices.

In just my last few years of teaching, I have come to prize risks more, for incidents have accumulated in which taking a risk has led to extraordinary experiences. Many of these risks involved the teacher relinquishing control in order to let students go where they will. Some involved choices of materials outside the safe boundaries of long-time acceptance. Some involved what Thoreau called "extra-vagance" in direction or manner of inquiry. All were risks guided by experience and a sense of responsibility. All involved choices that created anxieties, left results in doubt, courted failure. Almost all were calculated risks, though a number developed quite unexpectedly. Most appeared to me to be justified by the extraordinary outcomes of individual learning. In the most remarkable instance, that outcome was a roomful of students discovering affection for each other in the act of learning, a case where cognition gave way to illumination.

For young teachers, an earthbound aspect of risk is honesty. I do not know whether people grow more or less honest with age. Innocence is rightly attributed to youth, but whether that innocence implies greater honesty, I do not know. And though competence in not being honest grows with experience, I think I have become more honest through the years, probably not because my virtue has become greater but because I can now afford to be.

The most common and vexing dishonesty is pretending to know more than one knows, which can be blamed either on vanity or a lack of confidence. Showing off and defensiveness always give one away. In mastering most skills, confidence is the key. To me, the saddest images of teaching are those of teachers who have lost confidence, for whom the prospect of facing students has become a chore, a dread, ultimately an impossibility. Building confidence is a little like acquiring virtue. You acquire confidence by being confident. The next best thing is acting confident or, at the least, not acting defensively, resisting the tendency to show off and being grateful to whatever and whoever lends you support.

Perhaps a teacher's confidence grows most by minding the rivets, by mastering the simple, identifiable particulars of a teacher's preparation and performance. Having one's stuff in hand, timed to fit the hour, focused on limited objectives, thought over in respect to possible questions, and directed toward an end is the kind of basic preparation I have in mind. Taping some presentations offers a way of examining in private the hesitations, confusions, and circumlocutions that destroy confi-

dence in public. Talking with others about details of the craft
can resolve indecisions that get directly in the way of gaining
confidence. Admitting one's fears, doubts, and imperfections is
a commonplace way of gaining a basic understanding of one's
strengths and weaknesses. Having a good day in class or—the
Lord willing—a succession of good days helps most of all.

Though I would have teachers systematically pursue
teaching skills, I would also have them recognize an essential
looseness in their craft. Teaching, like writing, is a craft that
finds its exact way each time out. I once had an intense argument with an English teacher who took me to task for saying
offhandedly that a teacher could be too well organized. That
seemed to me a simple truth, but to her my statement assailed
revealed truth. Organization was on an ascending scale, the highest organization, I presume, approximating or being heaven.
What I have in mind is the organization that, whether by advance design or extemporaneous skill, leaves room for organiz-
ing as it goes. The teacher provides the sketch, but the structure
creates itself not only from design but from second thoughts,
diversions, impasses, and lucky accidents. It proves itself not as
it meets formal criteria but as it successfully brings things together in the understanding of the student.

The contest between formal organization and student
understanding is clear in the following student complaint (*Ad
Hoc* Committee on Quality of Teaching, 1970, p. 23):

> Take someone who's been teaching a course
> for a few years and has it all planned, and the lec-
> tures are written and everything; but perhaps some-
> thing that's particularly interesting to a particular
> class sparks some questions and the guy just panics,
> "Oh, oh, we're running out of time here." And you
> can tell that he's thinking that he's not going to be
> able to make the last lecture of the series if he gets
> thrown off by more than ten minutes in any one
> session. And that is to me destructive because a lot
> of really valuable learning could be going on right

there if he'd listen to the questions and answer them. Maybe we wouldn't get quite as far in this whole long chain that he has planned out for us but we might get a richer experience and learn more about what we actually do cover. All I think of is certain post-office clerks—you go in and if you want to vary one inch from any step of procedure at all they just fall to shreds.

I'm drawn to a likeness between good organization and one aspect of music. Jazz improvisation succeeds as it moves somewhere within a zone of organized sound, with chaos at one extreme and cliché at the other. The musician's satisfaction derives from the attempt as well as from the achievement. And what is attempted and achieved is not wholly in the improviser's control, but is dependent on the other musicians and affected by the audience.

What is most worth reflecting upon is the way learning seems to grow, not just from slavish adherence to a precise set of directions or from exact imitation of a demonstrated skill, but from some freedom in following hints and inclinations. Perhaps exactness is impossible for the learner, and in the process of backing off from a task and coming back to it, the learner not only comes closer but also internalizes the learning and makes it a part of him- or herself. With a roomful of students, an idea not completely filled out in advance may have more impact, more chance of inviting participation, and more possibility of carrying conviction as it fills itself out. Proceeding in a direction an excited student has suggested may also generate more enthusiasm than following the well-plotted direction posed by the teacher. The many and varied possibilities that open up when teachers expose themselves and a class to the leads provided by a roomful of students are reason enough for developing skill at improvisation.

The final attitude for teachers to develop is some suspension of judgment about students and their capabilities. This advice arises from many experiences with teachers who go down their class rosters ticking off the abilities of every student. Donald Barthelme has captured what I mean once and for all (1964, pp. 5-6):

> Baskerville's difficulty not only at the Famous Writers School in Westport, Connecticut, but in every part of the world, is that he is slow. "That's a slow boy, that one," his first teacher said. "That boy is what you call *real slow,*" his second teacher said. . . . "That's a *slow son of a bitch,*" his third teacher remarked of him, at a meeting called to discuss the formation of a special program for Inferior Students, in which Baskerville's name had so to speak rushed to the fore.

We all make such judgments; one quarter's work may be sufficient to label a student an A or B or C for the rest of his or her college work. Classes can also be judged in such ways, either the ones we teach or that others teach, the survey courses impossible to teach, the early periods anathema to the students, the general education offerings beneath our attention. Much of this is not prejudgment so much as a lack of judgment. Nor is reserving judgment to be confused with an unwillingness to exercise judgment. In teaching, judgments constantly must be made, many of them in the reality of the moment. So I am not asking for the development of a virtue here. Rather, I'd settle for trying to know what we're talking about and for being modest and hopeful about what we don't know. For there are few things we learn for certain, and when this learning involves the capacities or inclinations of others to learn, our basis for judgment is very uncertain indeed.

Good teachers I know are not all exemplars of even those virtues I choose to emphasize. Nevertheless, developing as a teacher can be described as becoming wiser and less judgmental, more generous, less arrogant and yet more confident; being more honest with oneself and students and subject matter; taking more risks; showing forth without showing off; being impatient with ignorance but not appalled by it. All these attributes are partly matters of personal development, but they are not unrelated to learning teaching techniques, acquiring knowledge, and expanding one's professional range.

What affects teachers most when they start out has not even been mentioned here. That is the visible and invisible hand of the institution which employs them. That hand does its work with induction rites and welcoming ceremonies, forms and schedules, course planning, memos, and meetings—all those details that are a part of institutionalized education. Generosity, honesty, reserving judgment, willingness to take risks are about as important to living within an institution as they are to teaching. The actual details of how a bureaucracy functions and how an individual might best function within a bureaucracy are subjects worth studying but not studying too much. What I have to say on these matters will follow in the concluding chapter.

17

Being a Teacher

Coming to the end of this book, I am struck again by the fact that teaching is so much more than can be put down in words. Teaching may be irrevocably anecdotal, the truth of it most approached in that inexhaustible exchange among teachers and students about this student and this teacher and this situation. From this perspective, teaching is most satisfying in what happens day by day and in some glimmerings that suggest the impact of teaching upon learning over the long span.

But no college teacher is free to teach and enjoy teaching in this way. The price of committing oneself to teaching as a profession is to commit oneself to an institution. There are gains and losses. One's income is not directly dependent on either students taught or results achieved, but one's professional life is no longer free from the realities of institutional life.

Every teacher must accept professional responsibilities that go beyond teaching classes and remaining alive as a scholar: the duties of a citizen in an academic polity. University politics are so vicious, someone has said, because they involve such small stakes. The truth there may be in that remark makes me cut short my discussion of a teacher's political life, however much politics may preoccupy a teacher. Committee work and administrative assignments and dealing with the bureaucracy are not the inspiring aspects of college teaching. University senates are not inspiring bodies; their presence is justified as democracy is justified by its being better than all the other alternatives. Either the individual serves as a responsible citizen and takes a hand, or someone else does it worse. There is an illusion that governing bodies—faculty senates, college and departmental faculties, faculty associations—and the officials who run them can always be concerned only with the vital matters. Disillusionment with the actual level of operation is, therefore, common and severe. It may be possible to reduce the trivia that exhaust department chairs and demean the operations of senates. But it is simply not possible to always breathe the air of high policy without confronting some low-altitude details.

So I counsel teachers to avoid expecting too much or too little. Teaching is affected by committee debate, department actions, university regulations. Not expecting too much may be a matter of widening one's perspective to include the beliefs others hold about teaching and narrowing one's belief that consensus is easy to achieve. Not expecting too little involves, most importantly of all, respecting political involvement and checking the automatic reflex of avoiding committee work or belittling it when one is caught.

The common sympathy expressed when a colleague becomes an administrator is cant at the best, ill-concealed envy or fear at the worst. Disdain for university politicians falls on too many individuals who invest their time in the necessary and useful work that goes with self-governance. If committees set reasonable aims and firm deadlines for achieving those aims, they can accomplish satisfying tasks. In those complex and changing and important matters like the substance, integrity, and emphasis of the curriculum, I see no better way than group deliberation and action. If administrators opt for limited terms and are charged with responsibility for full commitment during that period and are visibly respected by faculty for carrying out their aims and tending to the details, then it might happen less often that some "good ol' boy" is stuck with these jobs or that they are turned over to administrative mediocrities. And if senates and similar groups recognized the price of running a legislative body well, they might transact more important business and raise their own morale. Running a legislative body well entails a

minimum attention paid to seeing that committee work, for the
most part, does not fall to a comparatively few individuals and
that those who from time to time are charged with heavy responsibilities are relieved from other duties during that time and
rewarded for the additional burden.

The reluctance with which many faculty members take
on professional responsibilities seems to be even greater among
young professors and with respect to outside professional affil-
iations useful to developing as a teacher. The decline in mem-
bership of the American Association of University Professors
(AAUP), whatever other causes it may have, reflects adversely
on those entering the profession who should have kept it alive
and vital. Collective bargaining, with its basic emphasis on pay
and working conditions, has provided little in the way of making new teachers aware of what it should mean to be a college
or university professor.

Every generation, it can be said, has to relearn much of
what was known by a previous one. But that relearning is the
more difficult if a new generation remains unexposed, either
through the written record or through personal acquaintance, to
that knowledge. Through the years, affiliation with the AAUP
has been for many the means of ongoing discourse about a wide
range of matters directly affecting teaching in all fields.

As the extent of ignorance about these professional matters has risen, so has the level of anarchy. The decline in a common curriculum, in the late eighties an object of belated concern, is not just a matter of faculties never being able to agree
on a curriculum. It also reflects a general indisposition, marked
among the younger faculty, to work with others or to come to
agreement about principles, values, and practices in scholarship
as well as teaching. Team teaching and interdisciplinary work,
for example, have hard going in all times, even harder going at
present. The rise of litigation, as another example, indicates not
so much the intransigence of an institution, but the failure of a
community to recognize and be. guided by commonly accepted
customs not needing the intervention of law. Mentoring, discussed previously as a highly regarded but seldom achieved aspect of teaching, might be expected to arise among college fac-

ulties where the young and inexperienced could well learn much about teaching from their faculty mentors. Its almost total absence in the development of young college teachers is another indication of the condition I am describing.

Being a teacher involves all these things: cooperating in many ways and at many points of affecting learning; affiliating with the profession outside one's institutional and subject matter domains; and learning from one another.

During my years as an official improver of teaching, I was told repeatedly that the best way to improve teaching was to improve the reward system. For, the argument goes, teaching is given lip service but not rewarded. Salary and prestige go to the publishing scholar, the recognized authority in a field, and what's left is spread out among the rest. I have little patience with the reward system, with the hypocrisies it encourages, the inequities it maintains, the chronic irritations it causes, and the values it supports. But such an obvious ill as "publish or perish" is not imposed from the outside. Outsiders are not spawning the journals and writing the articles and voting on the promotions. A better reward system rests upon a responsible and enlightened faculty, one in which being a professional teacher requires a continuing breadth of exposure and outlook beyond that which arises from solely concentrating on one's subject matter. Improving teaching has been a chronic concern of higher education as well as of individual institutions. A review of such research is that of Levinson-Rose and Menges (1981).

Would-be teachers joining college and university faculties probably face more scrutiny of their teaching today than in the past, but they may also get more support in developing as teachers. Student evaluation is the most common form of scrutiny; faculty development the major source of support.

Since the 1960s, student evaluation has become a formalized part of the reward system in a majority of collegiate institutions (Seldin, 1984). I was much involved during the seventies in trying to explain what is actually known about student evaluation, often to hostile faculties. My sympathies were with students who have too little to say about the quality of teaching. But more important to me was the possibility that finding a means of recognizing the quality of teaching would make the reward system more favorable to teaching.

At the present time my hopes are strongly qualified and for a number of reasons. First, though student evaluations are used widely, they are often done poorly, and despite the relative simplicity of administering such evaluations well. Second, evaluations that might improve teaching directly need competent interpretation. Very little has been done to provide a framework whereby the specifics of student evaluation might be made more useful to faculty. As a corollary, administrations too often seize upon them for their use in the reward system and forget their better use in helping a teacher gain insight into teaching. Third, when used in the reward system, they are easily subverted. That is, a prevailing judgment favorable to an assistant professor can marshal both favorable and unfavorable student evaluations to support the case. The reverse is even more common. Yes, the student evaluations are favorable but can they be trusted, and aren't those high ratings attributable to meretricious popularity, and besides, the scanty publications record shows an escape into teaching. Finally, ranking teachers largely on the basis of student evaluations has added "teach or perish" to "publish or perish." The general ineptness of administrators with respect to stimulating good teaching and the power of peer review makes me skeptical that student evaluations have contributed what it seemed they might.

Despite these reservations, evaluating teaching continues to receive careful study (Aleamoni, 1987; Centra, 1979; Costin, Greenough, and Menges, 1971; Eble, 1972b; French-Lazovik, 1982, among others). Very recently, and from outside the university, special state commissions on higher education in California reviewing the Master Plan (Jaschik, 1987, p. 18) have recommended that "tenure review should be changed so that teaching ability is given equal standing with research for University of California faculty members and so that service in the public schools is a consideration in tenure and promotion decisions for all public-university faculty members." For Ph.D. candidates preparing to become faculty members, the commission recommends that "the learning of teaching skills . . . be a formal part of the curriculum."

Faculty development, now a recognizable activity on many campuses (Eble and McKeachie, 1986; Nelsen and Siegel, 1980), also offers support for faculty members aspiring to be excellent teachers. In an important way, faculty development is linked with evaluation of teaching. If weaknesses and strengths of teaching can be identified, then it is the responsibility of faculty development to remedy one and reward the other. An interesting fusion of student evaluation and faculty development is a program of "personal teaching improvement" developed by Wilson (1986) at the University of California, Berkeley. One part of the program uses student evaluations to give teachers a descriptive profile of their teaching. The other part consists of Teaching Improvement Packets offering specific help to improve identified weaknesses. Emeritus professors have also been successfully used to work with cooperating younger teachers.

Often supported by outside money, faculty development usually is broadly identified with improving undergraduate education in various ways. This emphasis probably arose from the obvious disparity between support for faculty research and support for teaching. The general result has been an emphasis upon teaching within faculty development efforts.

Where faculty development exists as a center or a committee dispensing foundation or institutional funds, faculty can get direct support for many necessities connected with teaching. Most programs have a small grants procedure supporting faculty travel, purchase of equipment, released time, convening of groups, and the like. What emerges on almost every campus where such funds become available is an identification of needs, often modest, but deemed important to teaching. Faculty discover that a conference on teaching offers as much of value as one on a research subject. The preparation of a manual or a set of slides or a self-pacing booklet, given modest support, gets accomplished rather than remains as something that might be done when one gets time. Similarly, revisions of the curriculum and of existing courses and working up of new courses profit from this kind of support. Development of new competencies necessitated by a shortage of staff, by expansion of fields of study, or by the advent of computers also gets useful support from faculty development programs.

The other large aspect of a successful faculty development program is the formalizing or simply greater identification and recognition of that core of faculty that constitutes on many campuses the teaching faculty. The officially unacknowledged separation, particularly in the research universities, of a research faculty from a teaching faculty offers opportunities for the faculty member wanting to give teaching first attention. The teaching faculty may well suffer unfairly from being regarded as second-class, but its presence gives the new faculty member a chance to mix with and talk to and learn from other like-minded faculty.

An interesting consequence of this separation, not necessarily desirable, is that the core program in undergraduate education becomes largely the responsibility of this teaching faculty. If these speculations are accurate, what I have been saying about the need for breadth in graduate programs and for broad professional commitments by the young professor becomes even more important. Every professor owes some of his or her time and expertise to that core of general or liberal studies, which the collective judgment of the faculty requires of every student. Within that obligation resides many opportunities for the young scholar with a gift for teaching. For being a teacher is an act of committing oneself to expanding the world for both oneself and others, of resisting the security and convenience of seeing the world narrowly.

I am sympathetic with the young professor who comes into a world already made. How does such a person, reasonably gifted and inclined toward teaching, operate within these realities? My advice comes from the secure position of a full professor who, whatever other anxieties he may have, no longer has to worry about promotion and tenure. Nevertheless, I encourage young professors to pursue their bent, not necessarily with both eyes on the main chance, but mindful of ways in which one can grow in personal accomplishments and satisfactions and serve others at the same time.

For the root condition of college professing is that it is a service profession, whether one thinks of serving humankind by advancing truth or by serving students. One need not get into the posture that service is its own reward, yet even the irritations that arise from feeling underpaid and underappreciated may be kept from becoming enfeebling if one gains genuine satisfactions from serving. In this respect, teaching may get as good a break as scholarship. That is, posterity has a hard time indicating its appreciation for one's valuable contribution to knowledge, while students are close at hand, ask much less, and respond more. True, a student's occasional thanks for a good class, under the reward system we have, may not match an acceptance of a minor piece by a major publication. But I am not offering remedies here, only comforts. I am also threading a fairly narrow way. I would certainly not have teachers fall into the Elbert Hubbard posture that greeted me in my very first college teaching job. It was on the department bulletin board in 1948, as it had earlier in the century been spread across the land (1927, p. 42):

> If you work for a man, in heaven's name work for him! If he pays you wages that supply you your bread and butter, work for him—speak well of him, think well of him, stand by him, and stand by the institution he represents. If put to the pinch, an ounce of loyalty is worth a pound of cleverness.

Service does not mean servility; it is not a matter of servant and master. I think I have served a great deal; I have never consciously been a servant. So young teachers are not forced to accept the conditions they find at their colleges. Some conditions are plainly bad, attributable in large part to faculty acceptance. Others remain bad despite years of attempts to better them. Bad or good, the conditions that affect teaching become a part of the new faculty member's responsibility, and part of that responsibility is to assert one's efforts toward the common good. That common good is ill served by guises of loyalty, gentility, or indifference that protect institutions from their own mediocrity.

At the same time, I am not very sympathetic to the in-

transigent, the bullheaded, the inflexible, and the self-righteous.
I have too much sense of my own superiorities not to be suspi-
cious of superiorities held too firmly by others. Thus, I would
not have utter confidence that my own defects are not the reason why I perceive defects in the system. Service is, to me, an
essential part of any work I would tolerate for long; it is also, as
I have said, a root condition of the teaching profession. I have
spent my life quarreling with my profession, an impossible way
to live, I think, except that I have won some and lost some and
moved the immovable even as I am dismayed at how little that
movement was. There are also some great satisfactions in sub-
verting the system, almost as great as those that come from sub-
verting ourselves. That system, short of its worst manifestations,
has respected a variety of services and fostered a variety of ways
to perform them. It is in enlightening the system itself, more
even than in protecting the individual, that I find freedom so
essential to teaching. For, without that freedom in the profession, the system itself might not provide enough scope to serve
in ways consonant with one's individual satisfactions, much less
sanction individual attempts to work by one's own measure.

Early in my teaching career, I asked an eminent Harvard
scholar, following his formal talk to an English department faculty, how one might reconcile the conflicting demands of teaching, publishing, committee work, and professional activities. He
answered that these demands posed no conflicts for a person set
in the right path. He was putting me down, though he was not
discourteous, impatient, or even unkind. He had never felt such
conflicts or thought them important if he had. His answer was a
bad answer, nevertheless. The question has been asked of me
too many times in too many guises for me to be deceived into
thinking that it is no question. And I have had too many years
of finding my way among conflicting demands not to regard the
issue as an essential fact of academic existence.

For the teachers and scholars I prize, there will always be
conflicting demands. Early in our careers, I think, we do some
things—formal scholarship, for example—so that we might gain
the freedom and respectability to do others—raise our voices
about teaching, for example. We give up some things to some

degree for some period of time—teaching and formal scholarship—to engage in the necessary work of, say, setting new directions for a department or college, to disappear into an administrative position, or to give top priority to committee work. My own path has been to refuse to relinquish for long my hold on any of those three obligations that loosely define the college professor's task: teaching, scholarship, service. But I do not regard my path as necessarily the best to take. I might have directed my efforts more toward one or the other obligation, with no less sense of responsibility and purpose. However, I could not have altogether neglected any one of them without feeling that I was somehow falling short. The important thing is to recognize the choices we have in directing our efforts and in following our strengths and inclinations without abandoning our obligations.

As this advice falls upon those teachers with a high regard for teaching, I would ask that they measure themselves neither too harshly nor benevolently. I find teaching uncommonly interesting and satisfying, and the attention I give it is probably uncommon, too. In a general way, I would like to increase the attention given to teaching by individual professors and the profession itself. But that desire does not diminish my respect for those whose aims and application and satisfactions do not match mine. Teaching at the top of one's abilities is exhausting. One cannot operate at that pitch all the time, and recognizing that fact is not a sign that one is falling short. Nor can teachers always be scrutinizing their practices as a first order of business or even keep up with new and useful developments. Since teaching is not any one thing, pursuing one's own individual way, even as it may stray from a focus on teaching, is not necessarily a sign of incompetence. In short, I am not asking for virtuosity in all teachers, though I am not reluctant to urge that the climate for teaching encourage more teachers to aspire to virtuosity. My counsel is not toward perfection, but toward recognition of the possibilities of embracing an honest craft and of giving generously to developing and maintaining skill in that craft.

If craftsmanship is to be honored, however, teachers cannot be too easy on themselves. Perhaps what teachers need, as much as attention to the craft of teaching, is more meditation on those character defects to which the academic person is prone. Blindness of one's own making describes many defects: blindness to the personal needs of individual students, blindness to a discipline's place in the whole of inquiry and learning, blindness to the university's place in the world, blindness to the necessity of being scholar and teacher and citizen of a community, blindness toward our ignorance and our vanities, blindness to the importance of vision in teaching. I would have teachers measured and rewarded by students who can honestly say, "I see," and not by professors who see all too little.

Defensiveness often accompanies blindness. In a comparatively benevolent form, defensiveness is the characteristic gesture of a collective faculty when faced with almost any criticism or proposal for change. This group reaction is one with the individual teacher's response to a challenge from a student. Defensiveness is the underlying cause of tabled motions, returns to committee, and tardy actions outdated by events. It is found in delaying tactics, in failure to implement, and reluctance to acknowledge. It is behind the pettifogging that characterizes faculty debate, the quibbling over trifles when important matters are at stake. It is a cover-up for shortcomings often worse than the shortcomings themselves. It has in no way been more evident than in the faculty's response to the evaluation of teaching. Prior to the revolt of the sixties, the professoriate was adamantly opposed to most proposals for seriously evaluating teaching; since that time, defensiveness has characterized a gradual acceptance.

Defensiveness is probably not as bad a trait as paranoia, so prevalent among academics that it can be described clinically: a systematized delusion that powerful forces among the students, peers, administration, trustees, and public are out to get the faculty. Feelings of personal persecution are one thing, but the general feeling that even the simplest of proposals proceeds from sinister motives is more distressing. Almost any overt action taken in behalf of teaching arouses the questions: Why is someone doing this? Who suggested it? What are they really after? Paranoia and conspiracy theory go hand in hand, and strenuous efforts to improve teaching have to face the sorting out of good guys and bad guys, the scrutiny of motives, and the identification of the collective forces arrayed against the faculty.

Hypocrisy may be less prevalent among college professors than among other licensed preachers, for there is often a cynicism about teaching that rules out hypocrisy. In its mildest form, this cynicism is a disbelief that teachers really do very much for most students. Thus, instead of making pronouncements that are violated in practice, the teacher makes few pronouncements that invite violation. Occasionally, a professor will lose credibility with students by falsely purporting to accept their style, manner, or values. And there is the common hypocrisy of taking one side in debates about learning and teaching but continuing to embrace opposing teaching practices. The fact that faculties tend to be politically liberal and academically conservative may show itself in various hypocrisies involving academic and community behavior.

The one such hypocrisy that bothers me most is fidelity to the rules for careful investigation in one's discipline but disregard for those same rules in many important academic matters outside the discipline. In people who set less store by fact, reason, and critical judgment, such behavior can be excused as a human weakness, reasonably consistent with the conduct of their personal and professional lives. But it is hard to excuse the tendency of faculty members to argue heatedly about matters relating to teaching and learning without bothering to become informed or even acknowledging that they might become informed. In the work I was doing toward improving teaching, it was easy to confront such professors publicly with sources they hadn't read or didn't know existed. But there was little lasting sense of achievement in this. Though I could for the moment end uninformed debate, I had no sense that I sent many professors off to the library or made them more respectful of learning outside their special domains.

Early in my academic career, I observed that faculties have a marked capacity to live with and even cherish their own deficiencies. That tendency may spring from a belief carried over from an earlier day that, having forsworn worldly ambitions, college professors have a right to be easy on themselves. The academic profession provided a haven for certain types, curious by nature and permitted by private means or institutional support to indulge their whims. College professing has moved well away from the traditions of gentility, yet an attraction to privilege, a liking for setting one's own terms, still characterizes the profession. As it affects teaching, the jealousy with which professors guard the prime hours for their own work is a nearly universal mark of self-indulgence.

I am not saying that polishing our virtues and curbing our sins is the way to develop into skillful teachers. But surely virtue is necessary to great teaching. Even a lesser art, an honest craft of teaching, cannot be achieved without it.

For the teaching I admire moves toward the most complete attainments of its highest ends, and it deals in virtue as much as in anything else. It is not just knowing or doing to which we aspire in learning. Our knowing is seldom free from doubt, our doing rarely pursues its way in certitude. If we learn anything by teaching, it may be that we all seem to fall short of some ultimate necessary learning. The formal postures of teacher and student are only systematic and partial ways of seeking illumination. As both Montaigne and Thoreau avowed, the lessons one teaches are not for someone else; they are those we teach ourselves.

Much of what I believe about teaching can be found in the story the pianist Claudio Arrau tells about his early years. "The first two teachers in Berlin were boring," he told an interviewer. "I wanted only to read more music, to perform more music. At 8, I loved the piano so, I would take my meals at the keyboard. By 10, dull teaching had turned me against music and myself."

"But you were rescued," the interviewer said.

"Desperate at 10," Arrau continued, "I was taken to play for Martin Krause. He was a severe old man, but children feel reality and behind this harsh mask was an incredible gift for opening up worlds" (Kahn, 1972, pp. 52, 54).

Few teachers can have pupils like Arrau, but all teachers can have the opportunity for opening up worlds.

References

Ad Hoc Committee on Quality of Teaching. *President's Scholars: Teaching and Learning at San Jose State College.* San Jose, Calif.: San Jose State College, 1970.

Aleamoni, L. (ed.). *Techniques for Evaluating and Improving Instruction.* New Directions for Teaching and Learning, no. 31. San Francisco: Jossey-Bass, 1987.

Anderson, C. *Technology in American Education, 1650–1900.* Washington, D.C.: U.S. Government Printing Office, 1952.

Ashby, E. *Adapting Universities to a Technological Society.* San Francisco: Jossey-Bass, 1974.

Association of American Colleges. "Integrity in the College Curriculum." *Chronicle of Higher Education,* Feb. 13, 1985, pp. 12–13.

Axelrod, J. *The University Teacher as Artist: Toward an Aesthetics of Teaching with Emphasis on the Humanities.* San Francisco: Jossey-Bass, 1973.

Baird, L. L. "Do Grades and Tests Predict Adult Accomplishments?" *Research in Higher Education,* 1985, *23,* 3–85.

Barthelme, D. "Florence Green Is 81." In *Come Back, Dr. Caligari.* Boston: Little, Brown, 1964.

Barzun, J. "Scholarship Versus Culture." *Atlantic,* Nov. 1984, *254* (5), 93–104.

Barzun, J. "Doing Research—Should the Sport Be Regulated?" *The Magazine of Columbia University,* 1987, *12* (4), 18–22.

227

Beard, R. M. *Teaching and Learning in Higher Education.* Harmondsworth, Eng.: Penguin, 1972.

Bennett, W. J. *To Reclaim a Legacy: Text of Report on Humanities in Education.* Washington, D.C.: National Endowment for the Humanities, 1984.

Bess, J. L. (ed.). *Motivating Professors to Teach Effectively.* New Directions for Teaching and Learning, no. 10. San Francisco: Jossey-Bass, 1982.

Blackburn, R. T. "Career Phases and Their Influence on Faculty Motivation." In J. L. Bess (ed.), *Motivating Professors to Teach Effectively.* New Directions for Teaching and Learning, no. 10. San Francisco: Jossey-Bass, 1982.

Blackburn, R. T., and Lawrence, J. H. "Aging and the Quality of Faculty Job Performance." *Review of Educational Research,* 1986, *56,* 265–290.

Bloom, A. *The Closing of the American Mind: How Higher Education Has Failed Democracy and Impoverished the Souls of Today's Students.* New York: Simon & Schuster, 1987.

Bok, D. *Higher Learning.* Cambridge, Mass.: Harvard University Press, 1986.

Bork, A. *Learning with Computers.* Bedford, Mass.: Digital Press, 1981.

Bork, A. *Personal Computers for Education.* New York: Harper & Row, 1985.

Bouton, C., and Garth, R. Y. (eds.). *Learning in Groups.* New Directions for Teaching and Learning, no. 14. San Francisco: Jossey-Bass, 1983.

Bowen, H. R., and Schuster, J. H. *American Professors: A National Resource Imperiled.* New York: Oxford University Press, 1986.

Bower, G. H., and Hilgard, E. R. *Theories of Learning.* (5th ed.) New York: Prentice-Hall, 1981. (Originally published 1956.)

Bradley, A. P., Jr. "Mentors in Individual Education." *Improving College and University Teaching,* 1981, *29* (3), 136–140.

Bransford, J. D., and Stein, B. S. *The Ideal Problem Solver.* New York: W. H. Freeman, 1984.

Brookfield, S. D. *Developing Critical Thinkers: Challenging Adults to Explore Alternative Ways of Thinking and Acting.* San Francisco: Jossey-Bass, 1987.

Brown, R. W. *Harvard Yard in the Golden Age.* New York: Current Books, 1948.

Bruner, J. S. *Toward a Theory of Instruction.* Cambridge, Mass.: Harvard University Press, 1968.

Bugelski, B. R. *The Psychology of Learning Applied to Teaching.* Indianapolis: Bobbs-Merrill, 1971.

Burdin, J. L., and Cruickshank, D. R. *Protocol Materials: Training Materials for Uniting Theory and Practice.* Washington, D.C.: ERIC Clearinghouse on Teacher Education, 1974.

Cahn, S. M. "The Uses and Abuses of Grades and Examinations." In S. M. Cahn (ed.), *Scholars Who Teach: The Art of College Teaching.* Chicago: Nelson-Hall, 1978.

Carnegie Commission on Higher Education. *The Fourth Revolution: Instructional Technology in Higher Education.* New York: McGraw-Hill, 1972.

Carnegie Commission on Higher Education. *Computers and the Learning Process in Higher Education.* Edited by J. F. Rockart and M. S. Morton. New York: McGraw-Hill, 1975.

Castelucci, M. F., and Miller, P. *Practicing Collaborative Learning.* New York: Department of English, Speech and World Literature, College of Staten Island (CUNY), 1986.

Center for Research on Learning and Teaching. *Development and Experiment in College Teaching.* Annual Reports. Ann Arbor: Center for Research on Learning and Teaching, University of Michigan, 1966-.

Centra, J. *Determining Faculty Effectiveness: Assessing Teaching, Research, and Service for Personnel Decisions and Improvement.* San Francisco: Jossey-Bass, 1979.

Chambers, J. A., and Sprecher, J. W. *Computer-Assisted Instruction: Its Uses in the Classroom.* Englewood Cliffs, N.J.: Prentice-Hall, 1983.

Chickering, A. W., and Gamson, Z. F. "Seven Principles for Good Practice in Undergraduate Education." *American Association for Higher Education Bulletin,* 1987, *39* (7), 3-7.

Chism, N.V.N. (ed.). *Institutional Responsibilities and Responses in the Employment and Education of Teaching Assistants.* Columbus: Center for Teaching Excellence, Ohio State University, 1987.

Civikly, J. M. (ed.). *Communicating in College Classrooms.* New

Directions for Teaching and Learning, no. 26. San Francisco: Jossey-Bass, 1986a.

Civikly, J. M. "Humor and the Enjoyment of College Teaching." In J. M. Civikly (ed.), *Communicating in College Classrooms.* New Directions for Teaching and Learning, no. 26. San Francisco: Jossey-Bass, 1986b.

Clark, S. M., and Lewis, D. R. (eds.). *Faculty Vitality and Institutional Productivity.* New York: Teachers College Press, 1985.

Cole, C. C. *Implications of Recent Learning Theories.* Washington, D.C.: American Association for Higher Education, 1982.

"A 'Concerned Father' and His Bout with Academe." *Chronicle of Higher Education,* May 28, 1974, p. 8.

Cooper, K. "Did You Ever Think of Aristotle as a College Freshman?" In T. H. Buxton and K. W. Prichard (eds.), *Excellence in University Teaching.* Columbia, S.C.: University of South Carolina Press, 1975.

Copperud, C. *The Test Design Handbook.* Englewood Cliffs, N.J.: Educational Technology Publications, 1979.

Costin, F., Greenough, W. T., and Menges, R. J. "Student Rating of College Teaching: Reliability, Validity, and Usefulness." *Review of Educational Research,* 1971, *41,* 511-535.

Cross, K. P. "A Proposal to Improve Teaching—or—What 'Taking Teaching Seriously' Should Mean." *American Association for Higher Education Bulletin,* 1986, *39* (1), 9-14.

Daloz, L. A. *Effective Teaching and Mentoring: Realizing the Transformational Power of Adult Learning Experiences.* San Francisco: Jossey-Bass, 1986.

Daly, W. T. (ed.). *College-School Collaboration: Appraising the Major Approaches.* New Directions for Teaching and Learning, no. 24. San Francisco: Jossey-Bass, 1985.

D'Angelo, E. *The Teaching of Critical Thinking.* Amsterdam: B R Grüner BV, 1971.

de Bono, E. *De Bono's Thinking Course.* London: British Broadcasting Corporation, 1983.

Deci, E. L., and Ryan, R. M. "Intrinsic Motivation to Teach: Possibilities and Obstacles in American Colleges and Universities." In J. L. Bess (ed.), *Motivating Professors to Teach Ef-*

fectively. New Directions for Teaching and Learning, no. 10. San Francisco: Jossey-Bass, 1982.

Dewey, J. *How We Think.* Boston: D. C. Heath, 1910.

Diamond, R. M., and Gray, P. J. *A National Study of Teaching Assistants.* Syracuse, N.Y.: Center for Instructional Development, Syracuse University, 1987.

Dillon, J. T. "Research on Questioning and Discussion." *Educational Leadership,* 1984, *42* (3), 50–56.

Drake, S. *Galileo Studies: Personality, Tradition, and Revolution.* Ann Arbor: University of Michigan Press, 1970.

Dressel, P. L., and Marcus, D. *On Teaching and Learning in College: Reemphasizing the Roles of Learners and the Disciplines in Liberal Education.* San Francisco: Jossey-Bass, 1982.

Dziech, B. W., and Weiner, L. *The Lecherous Professor.* Boston: Beacon Press, 1984.

Ebel, R. L., and Frisbie, D. A. *Essentials in Educational Measurement.* (4th ed.) Englewood Cliffs, N.J.: Prentice-Hall, 1986.

Eble, K. E. *A Perfect Education.* New York: Macmillan, 1966.

Eble, K. E. *Professors as Teachers.* San Francisco: Jossey-Bass, 1972a.

Eble, K. E. *The Recognition and Evaluation of Teaching.* Washington, D.C.: American Association of University Professors, 1972b.

Eble, K. E. (ed.). *Improving Teaching Styles.* New Directions for Teaching and Learning, no. 1. San Francisco: Jossey-Bass, 1980.

Eble, K. E. *The Aims of College Teaching.* San Francisco: Jossey-Bass, 1983.

Eble, K. E. "Defending the Indefensible." In N.V.N. Chism (ed.), *Institutional Responsibilities and Responses in the Employment and Education of Teaching Assistants.* Columbus: Center for Teaching Excellence, Ohio State University, 1987.

Eble, K. E., and McKeachie, W. J. *Improving Undergraduate Education Through Faculty Development: An Analysis of Effective Programs and Practices.* San Francisco: Jossey-Bass, 1986.

Ellner, C. L., and Barnes, C. P. *Studies of College Teaching.* Lexington, Mass.: D. C. Heath, 1983.

Ericksen, S. C. *Motivation for Learning.* Ann Arbor: University of Michigan Press, 1974.

Ericksen, S. C. "Counselor, Advisor, Friend." Memo to the Faculty, no. 69. Ann Arbor: Center for Research on Learning and Teaching, University of Michigan, 1981.

Ericksen, S. C. *The Essence of Good Teaching: Helping Students Learn and Remember What They Learn.* San Francisco: Jossey-Bass, 1984.

Fact-File. *Chronicle of Higher Education,* Dec. 18, 1985, pp. 25–28.

Fader, D. N., and McNeil, E. B. *Hooked on Books: Program and Proof.* New York: Berkeley, 1968.

Fishman, E. M. "Counteracting Misconceptions About the Socratic Method." *College Teaching,* 1985, *33* (4), 185–188.

Fitch, J. G. *The Art of Questioning.* (9th ed.) Syracuse, N.Y.: C. W. Bardeen, 1879.

Fleit, L. H. "Overselling Technology: Suppose You Gave a Computer Revolution and Nobody Came?" *Chronicle of Higher Education,* Apr. 22, 1987, p. 96.

Flesch, R. *Why Johnny Can't Read—and What You Can Do About It.* New York: Harper & Row, 1955 (1986).

Ford, G. S. "Teacher and Taught." *AAUP Bulletin,* 1955, *41,* 467–488.

French-Lazovik, G. (ed.). *Practices that Improve Teaching Evaluation.* New Directions for Teaching and Learning, no. 11. San Francisco: Jossey-Bass, 1982.

Fuhrmann, B., and Grasha, A. *A Practical Handbook for College Teachers.* Boston: Little, Brown, 1983.

Gagné, R. M. (ed.). *Instructional Technology: Foundations.* Hillsdale, N.J.: Erlbaum, 1987.

Galilei, G. *Dialogues Concerning Two New Sciences.* Translated by H. Crew and A. deSalvio. New York: Macmillan, 1914. (Originally published 1638.)

Galilei, G. *Dialogue Concerning the Two Chief World Systems—Ptolemaic and Copernican.* Translated by S. Drake. Berkeley: University of California Press, 1953. (Originally published 1632.)

Gaudiani, C. L., and Burnett, D. G. *Academic Alliances: A New*

Approach to High School/College Collaboration. Washington, D.C.: American Association for Higher Education, 1985/86.

Gerschenkron, A. "Getting off the Bullock Cart: Thoughts on Educational Reform." *American Scholar,* Spring 1976, *45,* 218-233.

Gold, M. "A Letter from Professor Martin Gold." Memo to the Faculty, no. 18. Ann Arbor: Center for Research on Learning and Teaching, University of Michigan, 1966.

Graber, G. C., and Jones, L. F. "Transformative Education: The University Learning Community at UTK." *Teaching-Learning Issues,* no. 59. Knoxville: Learning Resource Center, University of Tennessee, 1987.

Granrose, J. T. "Conscious Teaching: Helping Graduate Assistants Develop Teaching Styles." In K. E. Eble (ed.), *Improving Teaching Styles.* New Directions for Teaching and Learning, no. 1. San Francisco: Jossey-Bass, 1980.

Gronlund, N. E. *Constructing Achievement Tests.* (3rd ed.) Englewood Cliffs, N.J.: Prentice-Hall, 1982.

Gross, T. L. *Partners in Education: How Colleges Can Work with Schools to Improve Teaching and Learning.* San Francisco: Jossey-Bass, 1988.

Gullette, M. M. (ed.). *The Art and Craft of Teaching.* Cambridge, Mass.: Harvard-Danforth Center for Teaching and Learning, Harvard University, 1982.

Hall, R. M., and Sandler, B. R. *The Classroom Climate: A Chilly One for Women?* Project on the Status and Education of Women. Washington, D.C.: Association of American Colleges, 1982.

Hawkridge, D. *New Information Technology in Education.* Baltimore, Md.: Johns Hopkins University Press, 1983.

Heller, S. "Collaboration in the Classroom Crucial if Teaching Is to Improve, Educators Say." *Chronicle of Higher Education,* Mar. 11, 1987, pp. 17-18.

Herman, A. L. "The Ugly Classroom." *Journal of Higher Education,* Oct. 1968, *39,* 376-387.

Highet, G. *The Art of Teaching.* New York: Knopf, 1950.

Hill, W. F. *Learning Through Discussion.* Newbury Park, Calif.: Sage, 1977.

Hirsch, E. D., Jr. *Cultural Literacy.* Boston: Houghton Mifflin, 1987.

Howe, M.J.A. *A Teacher's Guide to the Psychology of Learning.* Oxford, England: Basil Blackwell, 1984.

Hoyt, D. P. "The Relationship Between College Grades and Adult Achievement: A Review of the Literature." Memo to the Faculty, no. 18. Ann Arbor: Center for Research on Learning and Teaching, University of Michigan, 1966.

Hubbard, E., II (ed.). *The Note Book of Elbert Hubbard.* New York: Wise, 1927.

Hungiville, M. "The Passionate Poets in the Classroom." *Chronicle of Higher Education,* Nov. 4, 1974, p. 9.

Hunter, M. *Motivation Theory for Teachers: A Programmed Book.* El Segundo, Calif.: TIP Publications, 1985.

Jacob, P. E. *Changing Values in College.* New York: Harper & Row, 1957.

Jaschik, S. "Broad Changes Proposed for Higher Education in California; Could Have a Nationwide Impact." *Chronicle of Higher Education,* July 29, 1987, pp. 15-18.

Kahn, R. "The Fragile Genius of a Virtuoso." *Life,* Aug. 25, 1972, pp. 52, 54.

Kasten, K. L. "Tenure and Merit Pay as Rewards for Research, Teaching and Service at a Research University." *Journal of Higher Education,* 1984, *55,* 500-514.

Katz, J. (ed.). *Teaching as Though Students Mattered.* New Directions for Teaching and Learning, no. 21. San Francisco: Jossey-Bass, 1985.

Keller, F. S. *Learning: Reinforcement Theory.* (2nd ed.) New York: Random House, 1969.

Kepner, H. S., Jr. (ed.). *Computers in the Classroom.* (2nd ed.) Washington, D.C.: National Education Association, 1986.

Knapper, C. K. (ed.). *Expanding Learning Through New Communications Technologies.* New Directions for Teaching and Learning, no. 9. San Francisco: Jossey-Bass, 1982.

Koen, F. M., and Ericksen, S. C. *An Analysis of the Specific Features Which Characterize the More Successful Programs for the Recruitment and Training of College Teachers.* Ann Arbor: Center for Research on Learning and Teaching, University of Michigan, 1967.

Kraft, R. G. "Group-Inquiry Turns Passive Students Active." *College Teaching,* 1985, *33* (4), 149-154.

Kuethe, J. L. *The Teaching-Learning Process.* Glenview, Ill.: Scott, Foresman, 1968.

Kulik, J. A., Kulik, C., and Cohen, P. "Effectiveness of Computer-Based College Teaching: A Meta-Analysis of Findings." *Review of Educational Research,* 1980, *50,* 525-544.

LaPidus, J. B. "Preparing Faculty: Graduate Education's Role." *American Association for Higher Education Bulletin,* 1987, *39* (9 and 10), 3-6.

Levinson-Rose, J., and Menges, R. "Improving College Teaching: A Critical Review of Research." *Review of Educational Research,* 1981, *51,* 403-434.

Levy, P. *Tests in Education: A Book of Critical Reviews.* London: Academic Press, 1984.

Lowman, J. *Mastering the Techniques of Teaching.* San Francisco: Jossey-Bass, 1984.

Maas, J. B. *The Yellow Pages of Undergraduate Innovation.* New Rochelle, N.Y.: *Change* Magazine and Educational Change, 1974.

McClelland, D. C. *Human Motivation.* Glenview, Ill.: Scott, Foresman, 1985.

McKeachie, W. J. "Research on College Teaching." Memo to the Faculty, no. 44. Ann Arbor: Center for Research on Learning and Teaching, University of Michigan, 1971.

McKeachie, W. J. (ed.). *Learning, Cognition, and College Teaching.* New Directions for Teaching and Learning, no. 2. San Francisco: Jossey-Bass, 1980.

McKeachie, W. J. *Teaching Tips: A Guidebook for the Beginning College Teacher.* (8th ed.) Lexington, Mass.: D. C. Heath, 1986.

McKowen, C. *Thinking About Thinking.* Los Altos, Calif.: William Kaufmann, 1986.

Maddison, J. *Education in the Microelectronics Era.* Milton Keynes, England: Open University Press, 1983.

Maeroff, G. I. *School and College: Partnerships in Education.* Princeton, N.J.: The Carnegie Foundation for the Advancement of Teaching, 1983.

Magarrell, J. "Computer Teaching Systems: Little Impact on

Achievement." *Chronicle of Higher Education,* Oct. 30, 1978,
p. 5.

Mann, R. D., and others. *The College Classroom: Conflict,
Change, and Learning.* New York: Wiley, 1970.

Marques, T. E., Lane, D. M., and Dorfman, P. W. "Toward the
Development of a System for Instructional Evaluation: Is
There Consensus Regarding What Constitutes Effective Teaching?" *Journal of Educational Psychology,* 1979, *71,* 840-
849.

Marton, F., Hounsell, D., and Entwistle, N. (eds.). *The Experience of Learning.* Edinburgh: Scottish Academic Press,
1984.

Masat, F. E. *Computer Literacy in Higher Education.* Washington, D.C.: American Association for Higher Education, 1981.

Maslow, A. H. *Motivation and Personality.* (2nd ed.) New York:
Harper & Row, 1970.

Meier, R. S., and Feldhusen, J. F. "Another Look at Dr. Fox."
Journal of Educational Psychology, 1979, *71,* 339-345.

Merrill, P. F., and others. *Computers in Education.* Englewood
Cliffs, N.J.: Prentice-Hall, 1986.

Meyers, C. *Teaching Students to Think Critically: A Guide for
Faculty in All Disciplines.* San Francisco: Jossey-Bass, 1986.

Milton, O. "Accent on Learning: PSI or the Keller Plan."
Teaching-Learning Issues, no. 25. Knoxville: Learning Research Center, University of Tennessee, 1974.

Milton, O. "Research vs. Teaching?" *Teaching-Learning Issues,*
no. 32. Knoxville: Learning Research Center, University of
Tennessee, 1976.

Milton, O. *Will That Be on the Final?* Springfield, Ill.: Thomas,
1982.

Milton, O., and Edgerly, J. W. *Testing and Grading of Students.*
New Rochelle, N.Y.: *Change* Magazine and Educational
Change, 1976.

Milton, O., Pollio, H. R., and Eison, J. A. *Making Sense of College Grades: Why the Grading System Does Not Work and
What Can Be Done About It.* San Francisco: Jossey-Bass,
1986.

Myers, I. B. *Introduction to Type.* Palo Alto, Calif.: Consulting
Psychologists Press, 1980.

Myers, I. B., and Myers, P. B. *Gifts Differing*. Palo Alto, Calif.: Consulting Psychologists Press, 1980.

Naftulin, D. H., Ware, J. E., Jr., and Donnelly, F. A. "The Dr. Fox Lecture: A Paradigm of Educational Seduction." *Journal of Medical Education*, 1973, *48*, 630–635.

Neider, C. (ed.). *The Autobiography of Mark Twain*. New York: Harper & Row, 1959.

Nelsen, W. C., and Siegel, M. E. *Effective Approaches to Faculty Development*. Washington, D.C.: Association of American Colleges, 1980.

Oakeshott, M. *Rationalism in Politics*. New York: Basic Books, 1962.

Perkins, D. N. *The Mind's Best Work*. Cambridge, Mass.: Harvard University Press, 1981.

Perry, R. P., Abrami, P. C., and Leventhal, L. "Educational Seduction: The Effect of Instructor Expressiveness and Lecture Content on Student Ratings and Achievement." *Journal of Educational Psychology*, 1979, *71*, 107–116.

Perry, W. G., Jr. *Forms of Intellectual and Ethical Development in the College Years*. New York: Holt, Rinehart & Winston, 1970.

Pierson, G. W. *Yale College: An Educational History, 1871–1921*. New Haven: Yale University Press, 1952.

Pollio, H. R. "Everything You Always Wanted to Know About Humor in the Classroom But Were Afraid to Ask (with Apologies to Woody Allen *et al.*)." *Teaching-Learning Issues*, no. 57. Knoxville: Learning Research Center, University of Tennessee, Fall 1985/Winter 1986.

Rabelais, F. *The Portable Rabelais*. Translated by S. Putnam. New York: Viking Press, 1946. (Originally published 1534.)

Raser, J. *Simulation and Society: An Exploration of Scientific Gaming*. Boston: Allyn & Bacon, 1969.

Rogers, C. *Freedom to Learn*. Columbus, Ohio: C. E. Merrill, 1969.

Ronan, C. A. *Galileo*. New York: Putnam, 1974.

Rubinstein, M. F., and Firstenberg, I. R. "Tools for Thinking." In J. E. Stice (ed.), *Developing Critical Thinking and Problem-Solving Abilities*. New Directions for Teaching and Learning, no. 30. San Francisco: Jossey-Bass, 1987.

Runkel, P., Harrison, R., and Runkel, M. (eds.). *The Changing College Classroom.* San Francisco: Jossey-Bass, 1969.

Rushton, J., and Reid, I. *Teachers, Computers and the Classroom.* Manchester, England: Manchester University Press, 1985.

Ryan, B. A. *PSI—Keller's Personalized System of Instruction: An Appraisal.* Washington, D.C.: American Psychological Association, 1974.

Ryans, D. G. *Characteristics of Teachers.* Washington, D.C.: American Council on Education, 1960.

Sarason, I. G. (ed.). *Test Anxiety: Theory, Research, and Application.* Hillsdale, N.J.: Erlbaum, 1980.

Seldin, P. *Changing Practices in Faculty Evaluation: A Critical Assessment and Recommendations for Improvement.* San Francisco: Jossey-Bass, 1984.

Seldin, P. (ed.). *Coping with Faculty Stress.* New Directions for Teaching and Learning, no. 29. San Francisco: Jossey-Bass, 1987.

Skinner, B. F. *Science and Human Behavior.* New York: Macmillan, 1953.

Skinner, B. F. *The Technology of Teaching.* New York: Appleton-Century-Crofts, 1968.

Sloan, D. (ed.). *The Computer in Education: A Critical Perspective.* New York: Teachers College Press, 1985.

Smith, P. "To Communicate Truth: How Research Corrupts Teaching." *Whole Earth Review,* Summer 1987, pp. 52–57.

Sternberg. *Intelligence Applied.* San Diego, Calif.: Harcourt Brace Jovanovich, 1986.

Stice, J. E. (ed.). *Developing Critical Thinking and Problem-Solving Abilities.* New Directions for Teaching and Learning, no. 30. San Francisco: Jossey-Bass, 1987.

Sullivan, A. M., Andrews, E. A., Hollinghurst, F., Maddigan, R., and Noseworthy, C. M. "The Relative Effectiveness of Instructional Television." *Interchange,* 1976, 7, 46–51.

Tashner, H., Jr. (ed.). *Computer Literacy for Teachers: Issues, Questions, and Concerns.* Phoenix, Ariz.: Oryx Press, 1984.

Thomson, R. *The Psychology of Thinking.* New York: Penguin, 1959.

Thoreau, H. D. *A Week on the Concord and Merrimack Rivers.* Edited by C. F. Hovde. Princeton, N.J.: Princeton University Press, 1980. (Originally published 1849.)

Tickton, S. (ed.). *To Improve Learning: An Evaluation of Instructional Technology.* 2 vols. New York: Bowker, 1970.

Travers, R.M.W. *Essentials of Learning.* (5th ed.) New York: Macmillan, 1982.

Tucker, M. S. (ed.). *Computers on Campus: Working Papers.* Current Issues in Higher Education, no. 2. Washington, D.C.: American Association for Higher Education, 1983-84.

Wales, C. E. *Center for Guided Design Newsletter.* Morgantown: Center for Guided Design, West Virginia University, 1980-.

Wales, C. E., and Stager, R. A. *Guided Design.* Morgantown: Center for Guided Design, West Virginia University, 1977.

Walsh, W. B. *Tests and Assessment.* Englewood Cliffs, N.J.: Prentice-Hall, 1985.

Warren, J. R. *College Grading Practices: An Overview.* Washington, D.C.: ERIC Clearinghouse on Higher Education, 1971.

Watt, I. "The Seminar." *Universities Quarterly,* Sept. 1964, *18,* 369-389.

Weimer, M. G. (ed.). *Teaching Large Classes Well.* New Directions for Teaching and Learning, no. 32. San Francisco: Jossey-Bass, 1987.

White, E. M. *Teaching and Assessing Writing: Recent Advances in Understanding, Evaluating, and Improving Student Performance.* San Francisco: Jossey-Bass, 1985.

Whitehead, A. N. *The Aims of Education.* New York: Mentor, 1949.

Whitman, N. A., and Schwenk, T. L. *A Handbook for Group Discussion Leaders: Alternatives to Lecturing Medical Students to Death.* Salt Lake City: University of Utah School of Medicine, 1983.

Williams, R. G., and Ware, J. E. "An Extended Visit with Dr. Fox: Validity of Student Satisfaction with Instruction Ratings After Repeated Exposures to a Lecturer." *American Educational Research Journal,* 1977, *14,* 449-457.

Wilson, R. C. "Improving Faculty Teaching: Effective Use of

Student Evaluations and Consultants." *Journal of Higher Education,* 1986, *57,* 197–211.

Wlodkowski, R. J. *Motivation and Teaching: A Practical Guide.* Washington, D.C.: National Education Association, 1984.

Wlodkowski, R. J. *Enhancing Adult Motivation to Learn: A Guide to Improving Instruction and Increasing Learner Achievement.* San Francisco: Jossey-Bass, 1985.

Wood, L. E. "An 'Intelligent' Program to Teach Logical Thinking Skills." *Behavior Research Methods and Instrumentation,* 1980, *12,* 256–258.

Index

Index

Mark Twain, 72, 77
Marton, F., 203
Masat, F. E., 121
Meier, R. S., 20
Melville, H., 33
Menges, R. J., 21, 217, 218
Mentor, 109, 111
Mentoring, 216; definition of, 109; difficulties of, 109-111, 113-114; supporting and challenging in, 112-113
Mentors, faculty, descriptions of, 112-113
Merrill, P. F., 121
Meyers, C., 19
Miller, P., 53
Milton, O., 22, 117, 146, 153, 155
Montaigne, M., 226
Morton, M. S., 118, 121
Motivating faculty, 189-194; administrative responsibility for, 193-194; by extrinsic and intrinsic means, 192-193; forces against, 193; relation to scholarship, 192-193; relation to tenure, 192
Motivating students: extrinsic forces in, 182-186; fear as a means of, 187; grades and tests as sources of, 185; importance of respect in, 186-187; intrinsic forces in, 186-187; research into, 189; rewards and punishments in, 188-189; suggestions for ways of, 184-185, 188-189
Motivation: extrinsic, 181-185; intrinsic, 185-187; positive or negative reinforcement, 182; systems of, identified by McClelland, 186
Myers, I. B., 65
Myers, P. B., 65
Myers-Briggs Type Inventory, 64-65
Myths about teaching: list, 11-12; discussion, 12-27

N

Naftulin, D. H., 19
Neider, C., 72, 77

Nelsen, W. C., 219
Noseworthy, C. M., 119

O

Oakeshott, M., 84
One-minute quiz, 35
Open University, 116

P

Performance-based education, 150-151
Perkins, D. N., 30
Perry, R. P., 20
Perry, W. G., Jr., 65-67, 82, 96, 154
Personal development, of students, 110-111
Pierson, G. W., 176
Personalized system of instruction (PSI), 117. *See also* Keller Plan
Plagiarism: as a form of cheating, 166-167, 168-171; dealing with, 170. *See also* Cheating
Pleasure in learning, 3
Pollio, H. R., 60, 153
Preparing college teachers: effectiveness of "practice teaching" in, 205; in graduate school, 197-202; by offsetting effects of graduate study, 206; with respect to learning theory, 202-203; through teaching seminars, 204-205; use of film and video tape in, 205, 207
Programmed instruction, varieties of, 115-116. *See also* Self-paced learning
"Publish or perish," 217, 218

Q

Questioning: samples of, 33; techniques of, 88-91

R

Rabelais, F., 49
Reading, encouraging students in, 130